TICEHURST,
STONEGATE AND FLIMWELL

TICEHURST,
STONEGATE AND FLIMWELL

Francis Drewe

Phillimore

First published in 1991 by
PHILLIMORE & CO. LTD
Shopwyke Manor Barn, Chichester, West Sussex

Reprinted in paperback 2002

ISBN 1 86077 214 5

Printed and bound in Great Britain by
BOOKCRAFT LTD
Midsomer Norton, Bath

To my wife
Joan
who encouraged me to write
this book

Contents

List of Illustrations ix
Preface xi

1. A Parish in the Making 1
2. The Middle Years 9
3. The Parish Records 16
4. The Parish Church 19
5. Vicars, Vicarage and Churchyard 33
6. Stonegate and Flimwell Churches 38
7. Schools and Charities 43
8. Modern Ticehurst Evolves 49
9. Local Organisations 61
10. Around the Parish 69
11. Some Houses and Families 89
12. Agriculture 113
13. Bewl Water 118
14. Ticehurst House and the Newingtons 123
15. Ticehurst in Wartime 131

    Appendix 135
    Notes 141
    Index 143

List of Illustrations

1.	The Haeselersc Charter of 1018	4
2.	Domesday entry	6
3.	Ordnance map of 1813	8
4.	Lower Toll Gate	11
5.	Ticehurst church tower	20
6.	Ticehurst church, south aspect	21
7.	Ticehurst church, north-east aspect	22
8.	Plan of St Mary's church	28
9.	The Wybarne Brass	24
10.	Ticehurst church, 1785	26
11.	The Rev. Arthur Eden	31
12.	Ticehurst vicarage, *c.*1792	35
13.	Stonegate church	39
14.	Flimwell church, *c.*1906	41
15.	Ticehurst school, *c.*1880	43
16.	Hop picking, 1908	45
17.	Hop picking	45
18.	Aerial view of Ticehurst, 1952	50
19.	Graph showing population and dwellings	52
20.	The village pump	53
21.	Fire brigade in 1911	58
22.	Fire brigade in 1939	58
23.	Ticehurst football team, 1891-2	62
24.	Baptist chapel, Flimwell, *c.*1890	67
25.	Cooper's Stores and Church Street, *c.*1900	69
26.	Church Street, *c.*1920	71
27.	High Street, *c.*1920	72
28.	The square and *Bell Hotel*	72
29.	Entrance to St Mary's Lane, *c.*1900	74
30.	Balcombe's saddler's shop, St Mary's Lane	75
31.	St Mary's Lane	75
32.	Church Street, 1938	76
33.	Wallcrouch	78
34.	Threeleg Cross	80
35.	The Lodge	80
36.	Lower Platts, *c.*1920	81
37.	Ticehurst Union Workhouse	82
38.	*The Welcome Stranger,* 1904	82
39.	Flimwell, 1920	84
40.	Flimwell crossroads, 1931	84
41.	Reconstruction of Flimwell crossroads, 1931	84
42.	Flimwell High Street, 1931	85
43.	Windmill at Mount Farm, Flimwell	86

44. Ticehurst from Myskyns, *c.*1900 86
45. Bakers Farm 91
46. Old Boarzell, *c.*1783 91
47. Dunsters Mill, pre-1930 94
48. East Lymden 95
49. The Gravel Pit, *c.*1900 96
50. Hazelhurst, *c.*1948 98
51. Oakover 100
52. Charter of Free Warren to Edmund de Passeley 103
53. North front of Pashley Manor pre-1950 105
54. North front after restoration 105
56. Whiligh, *c.*1900 110
57. Witherenden Mill 111
58. Map of Bewl Bridge Reservoir 118
59. River Medway scheme 120
60. Ticehurst House and the Highlands, *c.*1820 125
61. The museum at Ticehurst House 126

Preface and Acknowledgements

This work started as an attempt to revise and update the excellent *History of Ticehurst* by Hodson and Odell (1925), now out of print, from which I have quoted freely with due gratitude. It soon became clear, however, that a completely new approach was required, and this I have tried to achieve. Acknowledgement must also be made to the *Victoria County History of Sussex* which has been quoted in places.

I am grateful, too, to all those who have helped me with suggestions and the loan of photographs and other material, who are too numerous to mention individually, but especially to Dr. Henry Cleere for permission to refer to his book *The Iron Industry of the Weald*, and to David Martin for putting me right on the structural details and dating of many of the old buildings in the parish.

I am also indebted to F. J. Reeves for his help in writing most of the article on agriculture, and for his suggestions on many other items in the book. A few of the illustrations are the same as those in Brian Harwood's excellent book *Old Photographs of the High Weald*; this is inevitable as archive material, suitable for publication, is in short supply and we have both had to use the same sources.

The volumes of the the *Sussex Archaeological Collections* and the Ruth Collingridge Collection, both at the East Sussex Record Office in Lewes, have been used frequently, and I am grateful to the staff there for the unstinting help that they have so willingly given, and the permission to use this material.

Mention must also be made of the Southern Water Authority, to whom I am indebted for permission to use sections of their excellent little brochure describing Bewl Water.

Until 1752 the new year started on 25 March and the date which we would call 16 February 1602 is often written 16 February 1601-2. This is an untidy arrangement and in this book it will be written 16 January 1602 as if the year had started, as now, on 1 January.

Francis Drewe
Oakover
Ticehurst
November 1991

Chapter One

A Parish in the Making

Ticehurst is a village in East Sussex, in the Rape of Hastings and Hundred of Shoyswell, bordering on to Kent, 10 miles south- east of Tunbridge Wells and 15 miles north of Hastings, and lies on an east-to-west ridge which carries an old Roman road, with outlying farms and hamlets on each side. It was once part of that vast, impenetrable, primeval forest known as Anderida or Andredesweald, which extended over the whole of Sussex and a large part of Kent. Camden, in his great work *Britannia*, says of this area: 'The hithermost and northern side [of Sussex] is shaded most pleasantly with woods, as anciently the whole country was, which made it impassable. For the wood Andradswald took up in this quarter 120 miles in length and 30 in breadth'.

In Ticehurst the soils are mostly deep clay overlying sandstone rock to the south of the Wadhurst-Hawkhurst ridge and lighter sandy soils to the north. The former grow huge oak and ash to perfection, the latter beech and birch, and everywhere there would have been hornbeam, alder, hazel, willow and many other species.

At first this great forest was only penetrated on the edges and on drier ground by small groups of people to fatten their swine on acorns and other mast, and to cut wood, and gradually small clearings developed with some form of habitation. These became known as 'Hursts' or 'Hersts' and 'dens' and the process was known as 'assarting'. Travelling was a problem as much of the ground was completely waterlogged and was only passable in summer on the high drier ridges, and it was not until the late Iron Age that any attempt was made to construct all-weather tracks or roads.

The Ancient Britons had long been trading tin from Cornwall and iron from Sussex with the Roman Empire, and a British iron-making site has been excavated at Saxonbury near Frant, later taken over by the Romans.[51] Iron-making started seriously here, in southern Britain, with the advent of the Belgae about 100 B.C. They learnt how to smelt iron from the Wadhurst Clay by the 'bloomery' process, whereby alternate layers of ore and charcoal were packed into mounds and fired and made white-hot by bellows worked by foot.[30] There was plenty of wood to produce the charcoal and they very soon learnt where to find the iron-ore and to dig it up. The 'bloom', fairly soft iron, collected at the bottom and was removed when it was cool. They may have worked it up by hammering on site, but more probably carted it off to central depots for that purpose, or to one of the ports for export along tracks which even then were being developed. It may have been to gain control of this trade that Caesar decided to invade Britain in 55 B.C. This expedition was a total failure, and after three weeks, with heavy casualties on both sides, he was obliged to retreat back to Gaul.[37]

The next year he tried again, better prepared and equipped, and this time he took with him five legions and 2,000 cavalry, in all amounting to about thirty thousand men, carried in a fleet of nearly 700 vessels, and landed at Kingston in Kent. He met an army under the command of Cassivellaunus who, according to Caesar, had a large force including 4,000 chariots. These and the other weapons of the British army must have needed a great deal of iron in their construction — confirmation that iron was being worked in Britain long before the Romans settled here. This time Caesar was in Britain for a month, mostly in Kent, and was finally defeated and forced to withdraw, again with heavy casualties on both sides. He reported that there was iron-making activity in the maritime district, and Strabo, writing about A.D. 0, reports exports from Britain including iron.

It was nearly 100 years before the Romans tried again, and this time they were successful. In A.D. 43 the Emperor Claudius landed on the south coast with an army of 40,000 men, but soon after he was recalled to Rome and handed over command to a distinguished general, named Aulus Plautius, who was the real conqueror of Britain. The Romans subdued the country up to the Scottish border and their occupation lasted for 300 years. During that time they developed and 'nationalised' the old British and Celtic ironworks and developed many new ones, all run by the government, but keeping the old methods of bloomery production.

In Ticehurst there are no known British sites, but several Roman 'bloomeries' are known, and two have been excavated.[30] The first, at Bardown in Stonegate, was discovered in 1909 and excavated in the 1960s.[1] The settlement covered about 7½ acres on the south bank of the River Limden. The western half is devoted to iron-working activities, and the eastern half is residential. A dump of slag, domestic refuse and other waste extends for about a hundred yards along the southern bank of the stream and there is evidence of ore-digging on the north bank and in innumerable pits within a two-mile radius of the settlement, as well as a house for 40 men.

It appears to have been started in the first half of the second century and to have continued for about a hundred years. The buildings excavated, which include a standard military-style barracks block, were timber-framed and seem to have fallen into disuse after about A.D. 200. Later iron-making continued at various satellite sites up to two miles from the main settlement. Seven of these have been identified, of which one, Holbeamwood, was excavated in about 1970. No smelting furnaces were located, but two pit-type ore-roasting furnaces and a possible charcoal burning oven were discovered.

Holbeamwood was an outlier or satellite of Bardown, probably just a working place visited daily by iron-workers who lived in the main settlement. They were connected by tracks covered with stone or slag and there was also a contour track leading down the Limden valley to Hurst Green. This settlement would have produced 40-45 tons of iron per year, consuming about six thousand tons of wood for charcoal in the process. The Romans did not use water power and the charcoal was made white-hot with hand- or foot-operated bellows in 'bloomeries'; although the sites were often located on the banks of streams, this was for a variety of other reasons. By A.D. 300 iron production had ceased here, and between then and about 1400 there is little indication of iron-making in Britain and none at all in this part of the Weald.

There was almost certainly an old Celtic road, improved by the Romans, running from Wadhurst to Hawkhurst and then on to the coast, probably at Newenden.[31] This, even in its present form, is an unusually straight road for most of the way; it follows the ridge of the hill and it has a number of names clearly indicating Roman origins. Many of the tiles excavated at the Roman iron-working sites bear the stamp CLBR, *Classis Britannica*, the Roman fleet in British waters, and it is known that the fleet then had a station at Newenden, which at that time was a port.

The first written evidence we have of part of Ticehurst, although the parish is not mentioned by name, is in the Haeselersc Charter of 1018.[3] This is a remarkable document in many ways: its authenticity is beyond question, it is well preserved, beautifully written by two scribes in Latin and Anglo-Saxon, easy to read, and it contains a number of unusual technical points commented on by Gordon Ward. The charter is between King Cnut and his Queen Ælfgyfu who gave to Archbishop Ælfstan 'a certain little woodland pasture in the famous wood Andredeswealde, which is commonly called Haeselersc'. We may perhaps translate this name as 'the wealden settlement in the hazel woods' or 'where the hazel trees have been cut down' since the terminal *-erse* in Anglo-Saxon implies cutting down and one could hardly make a settlement until this had been done.

The charter goes on to say that the land is to be held 'absque omni servitute terrena' (free from all earthly service) which is most unusual since nearly all land was granted subject to service, military or domestic and/or a rent payable in kind or in money. The document then continues with a different scribe, writing in Anglo-Saxon instead of Latin, and carefully delineates the boundaries of the land (translated):

> First along the Fearnlege burne as far as Runanlege [Rowley] boundary. From Runanlege boundary by Holanbeam boundary; from Holanbeam boundary so straight on to Wiglege [Whiligh], before [or above] the smithy to the gate and from the gate to the ditch and along the ditch into the broad burne and along the broad burne by the archbishop's boundary [i.e. his great manor of South Malling] and again into Fearnlege burne.

This land can be traced with some degree of accuracy on a modern O.S. map and extends to about one square mile or 640 acres. It includes the present Bryants' Farm, Beaumans, Birchetts Green and Lower Hazelhurst, but not Upper or Great Hazelhurst which has been identified with the Haslesse of Domesday Book (see below).

The charter is witnessed by King Cnut, Archbishop Wulfstan of York, Queen Ælfgyfu and the Bishops of Rochester, London, Sherbourne or Selsey, Winchester, Ramsbury and Wells, the three abbots of St Augustine's, Westminster and St Albans, 'Thurkil dux', i.e. Thurkil the Viking, Earl of East Anglia, and finally 'Godwin dux', i.e. Earl Godwin — altogether a most imposing list.

This is a very important charter covering the north-western corner of Ticehurst parish, described in Latin as a woodland pasture and the farm recently known as Lower Hazelhurst, now submerged by the reservoir, was probably that which gave it its name. Three properties which exist today are mentioned by name, *viz.* Rowley, Holbeamwood and Whiligh. It clearly shows that there was a settlement here with cultivated land and a smithy, approached almost certainly by a good road along the ridge.

Archbishop Ælfstan of Canterbury was also known as Lyfing.[10] He was consecrated Bishop of Wells in 999 and was appointed by Æthelred the Unready to the See of Canterbury in 1013, a year marked by fresh invasions by the Danes who devastated the country over a wide area. He took part in forming the ecclesiastical laws which were enacted by the Witenagemot held in 1014, and began the restoration of Canterbury Cathedral which had been partially destroyed by the Danes. He crowned Edmund Ironside in 1016, King Cnut in 1017 and he died in 1020.

Next we come to the entry in Domesday Book in 1086, which is much less informative. The translation reads:

> Walter Fitz Lambert holds HASLESSE of the Count (of Eu). Bishop Alric held it in fee of King Edward. Then, and now, 4 hides and a half. There is land for 9 ploughs. There are in demesne 2 ploughs and 6 villeins and 1 cottar with 7 ploughs. There is a church and wood for 10 hogs. Of this land Walo holds 1 hide, and has there 4 villeins with 2 ploughs and 1 cottar. The whole manor was worth in the time of King Edward 114 shillings. Now £7. It was laid waste.[1]

Immediately above this entry in capital letters is written: 'IN ESSESWELLE HUNDRED. THIS HUNDRED HAS NEVER PAID GELD'.

In the past there was difficulty in identifying the whereabouts of this manor and W. D. Parish, editor of the official 1886 edition of the Sussex Domesday Book, could not identify ESSESWELLE hundred, but says it contained Haslesse, Caveltone, Alsitone,

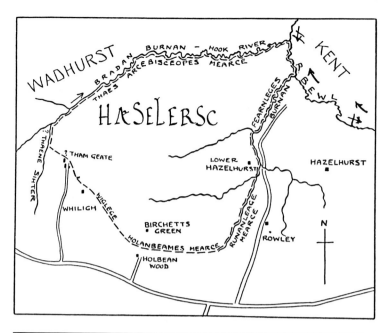

1. The Haeselersc Charter of 1018.

Raditone, etc. which are names of manors which immediately follow in Domesday. Of Haslesse he says it is Haselholte in Washington or Hazelhurst near Ore.

Esseswelle has now been identified with Shoyswell,[11] and the *V.C.H.* says that in 1086 this hundred contained the single estate of Haslesse, whose manorial hall was situated within the bounds of the hundred and, as in Henhurst hundred, a much larger group of estates which in King Edward's time had been attached to manors in the rape of Pevensey, namely Chalvington, Sherrington, Alciston, Ratton, Winton Street, Willingdon, Ripe, West Firle, Jevington, Eckington, Laughton, Burgelstaltone (probably in Ratton) and West Dean. This, combined with the fact that the hundred is said never to have paid geld, points to the hundred having been constituted, and probably deliberately colonised, at a comparatively late date.

Shoyswell itself is in Etchingham, the northern part of which parish is in this hundred, as is a small part of Burwash. This hundred still contains the single parish of Ticehurst. The above estates belonged to the lands of the Count of Eu in 1086 and the hundred subsequently descended with the honour of Hastings.

Walter Fitz Lambert was apparently one of the ancestors of the family of Scotney, from which place they took their name, who later held considerable possessions in Sussex and Kent, where their memory is still recalled by the remains of Scotney Castle at Lamberhurst, probably named after the family.[1] He also held the manors of Crowhurst, Ripe and Sedlescombe; the last in chief and the others of Earl Herald. He also held part of Alciston, which included Witherenden in Ticehurst.[8]

The Count, tenant in chief of Haslesse, was William de Oue or Eu, second son of Robert Earl of Eu in Normandy, second cousin of the Conqueror and one of his favourite commanders.[5] He was given 108 manors in nine southern and western counties, but mostly in Sussex in the rape of Hastings. He took part in the rebellions of 1088 and 1094, was imprisoned, blinded, castrated and executed in 1096.[7] His manors would certainly have been seized and it seems that Haslesse passed to the Scotneys in right of Walter Fitz Lambert, representing practically the whole of the parish of Ticehurst.[1]

Bishop Alric, whose name is variously spelt Agelric, Ethelric and Æthelric, was the last but one Bishop of Selsey (1057-1070) before the See was moved to Chichester in 1075, during the episcopate of Stigand, by a decision of the Synod of London under Archbishop Lanfranc.[6] Alric was a man eminent for his knowledge of the Saxon laws and at the conquest William received him into favour and consulted him on all matters relating to the ancient national jurisprudence. In particular he summoned him to the memorable conference between Lanfranc, Archbishop of Canterbury, and Odo, Bishop of Bayeux at the County Court at Penenden Heath in Kent, in which each party pleaded his own cause. He either died or was deposed in 1070 and was succeeded on the nomination of William by Stigand his chaplain. Presumably Alric held Haslesse before 1066 in his official capacity as Bishop of Selsey, and it would be interesting to know how long that manor had belonged to the See.

The rest of the entry tells us that the manor was of 4½ hides and had an annual value of £7. Both of these figures are large for this part of the country and, apart from the large estates of the king, archbishop and a few of the bishops and great nobles, it is as large as any in the county. A hide was supposed to be the area that a team of eight oxen could plough in a season and, although this varies widely from place to place, the most recent translation of Domesday (ed. J. Morris, Phillimore) suggests 120 acres as an average. In Ticehurst this would represent the cultivable area and the total area of the manor would have been very much more — allowing for woodlands, waste and steep gills which could not have been ploughed.

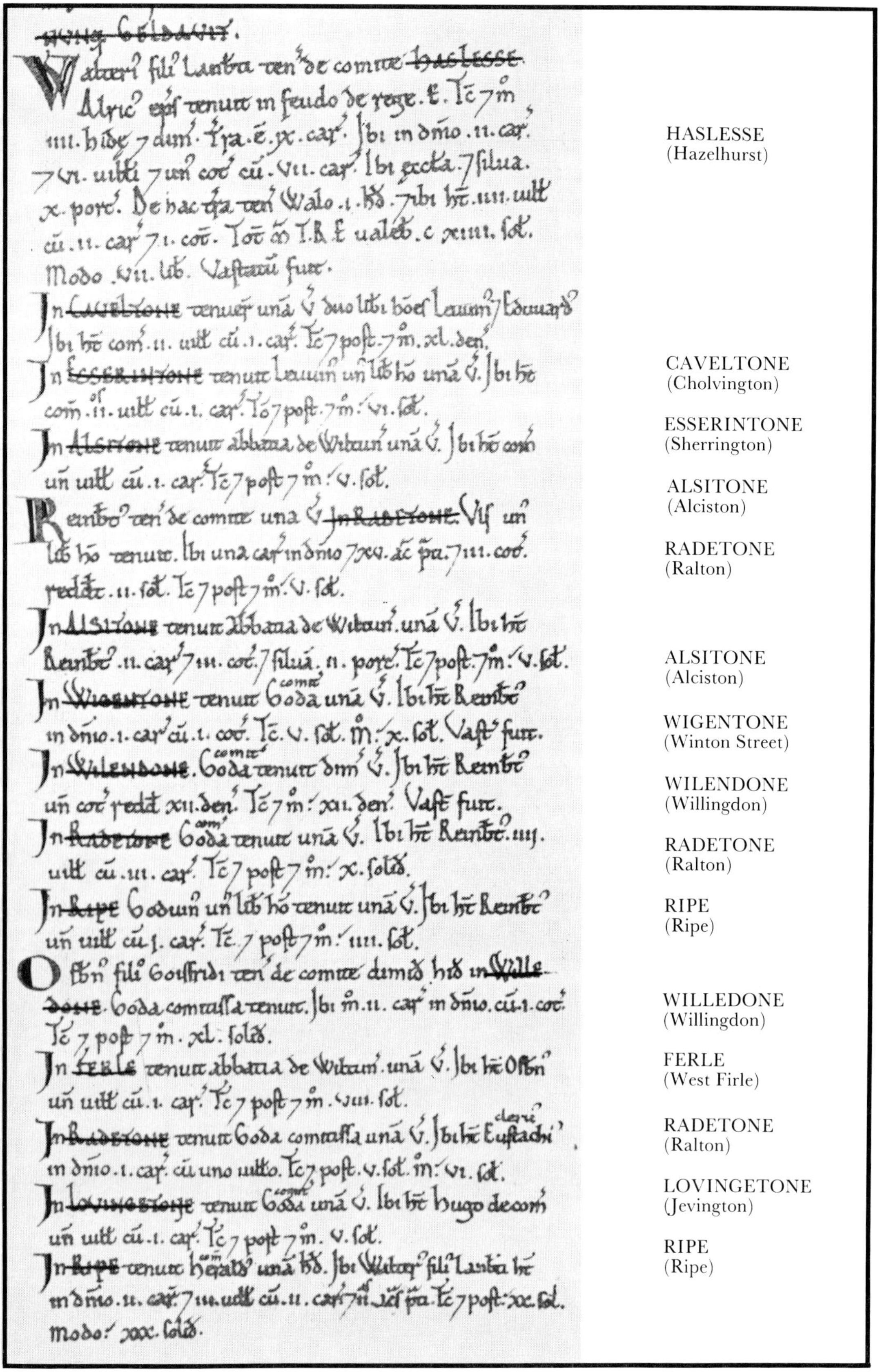

HASLESSE
(Hazelhurst)

CAVELTONE
(Cholvington)

ESSERINTONE
(Sherrington)

ALSITONE
(Alciston)

RADETONE
(Ralton)

ALSITONE
(Alciston)

WIGENTONE
(Winton Street)

WILENDONE
(Willingdon)

RADETONE
(Ralton)

RIPE
(Ripe)

WILLEDONE
(Willingdon)

FERLE
(West Firle)

RADETONE
(Ralton)

LOVINGETONE
(Jevington)

RIPE
(Ripe)

2. Domesday Book entry.

We have already seen that Haeselersc was about 640 acres in 1018. Haslesse must have been much larger, but whether it incorporated the other we do not know. It had a church, almost certainly on the site of the present church, on high ground beside what must then have been one of the main roads through the weald. 'It was laid waste'; probably by the Normans after the battle, often a punishment for non-cooperation, but it is interesting to note that the stated value in 1086 was greater than before, which is unusual when devastation had taken place.

This is all we know of what we assume to be Ticehurst until another 100 years had passed. The manor with the Anglo-Saxon name would have been pronounced 'Hazel-erse', the cutting of the hazel wood to make a settlement for men, and 'Haslesse' would have been pronounced thus and was as close as the Domesday scribe could get with his Latin script. The 1018 charter describes a clearly delineated area in the north-west of the parish; Domesday does not. Since Ælfstan died in 1020 and had power to dispose of his 'den' it may have been amalgamated with Alric's manor to form the Domesday holding and given its name. This is only conjecture but is very probable. Within living memory there have been large areas of hazel woodland in the parish. This Domesday manor is not mentioned again after the deed of 1215 mentioned below, and it is probably represented by the manors of Hammerden, Bricklehurst, Pashley and Whiligh, although the farm of Upper Hazelhurst still exists (see later) but Lower Hazelhurst of the 1018 charter is now submerged by the reservoir.[11]

Ticehurst is mentioned for the first time[1] in a deed of Combwell Priory in 1180 when Adam the priest of Ticehurst is mentioned, and in 1197 Walter de Scotney gives the church to the priory of the Holy Trinity, Hastings. In 1215 another deed by Peter de Scotney, son of Walter, confirms this.[12]

Lambarde, the Kentish historian says: '...the barne Beaul (which nameth Beaulbridge) and with the Theise which breaketh out of the ground at Tyseherst, named of it'.[9] On the other hand *The Place Names of Sussex* ascribes the name to the old English *Ticcenes-hyrst*, the clearing in the wood with the young goat, or kid's wood; such has been the motif on the village sign since about 1947.[54] The name Flimwell, spelt Flimenwelle in 1210, Flemenewell in 1288, Flemyngwell in 1309, and Flimwell in 1409, means 'fugitives' spring' and derives from the fact that it is just within the county boundary and fugitives from one county to another could first get refreshment there.

From the 13th century onwards the hundred of Shoyswell was divided into the vills or tithings of Ticehurst, Pashley and Hoadley or Hothly, of which the last named seems to have comprised the western portion, as it included Witherenden and Bricklehurst. In 1275 it was said that the hundred used to give 2s. of common fine at 'Lawday' and its brewers to be quit; but the bailiffs at Hastings had taken to extorting 10s. and yet the brewers were amerced.[11]

The name was spelt Tycheherst (11th-14th cent.), Thichesherst, Tychesherst (13th-14th cent.), Tysseherst, Tycehurst (15th cent.), and Tysehurst (15th-16th cent.). There was an unusually large number of manors in the parish in the two or three centuries following the Conquest.

The manor of Boarzell was apparently that part of the lands held in 1086 by Reinbert the sheriff, recorded as in Alciston, as a charter of 1123 records that seven hides in Boarzell and other places had been separated from the 50 hides in the Abbot of Battle's manor of Alciston, and in 1253 and 1295 Reinbert's descendants, the lords of Etchingham, received grants of free warren here.

A knight's fee in Bricklehurst and Sedlescombe, once held by Peter de Scotney, was held in 1320 and 1342 by William de Ore. The manor descended with Ore to Henry Halle, but by 1469 it was held of the manor of Hammerden by John Wybarne, who died

3. Ordnance map of 1813 showing the parish boundary.

in February 1490. The manor of Hammerden belonged to the honour of Hastings in 1280; in 1320 it was stated that the knight's fee here was one of nine fees formerly held by Peter de Scotney (see under Hammerden). Two fees in Pashley and La Forde, of which Pashley apparently held one, formed part of nine fees held in the early 13th century by Peter de Scotney; the overlordship descended with the rape. In 1366 Robert Passeley made a settlement of the manor of Whiligh with that of Pashley. At the dissolution Barehurst was a manor belonging to Battle Abbey and in the tenure of John Gascoyn. Later it is only referred to as a farm. Tenements here passed with the site of the abbey to Sir Anthony Browne in 1539.

Hazelhurst, as we have seen, was the original Domesday manor and just about a century later Walter de Scotney confirmed to Robertsbridge Abbey three virgates in Hothley 'which belong to my military fee (*feudo mee lorice*) of Haselerse'. Beyond the repetition of this phrase by Peter de Scotney *c.*1215, no more is heard manorially of Hazelhurst. All these manors will be discussed in more detail in a later chapter.

Several religious houses had property in Ticehurst, notably Combwell Priory and Bayham Abbey in Kent, while from the 12th century onwards Robertsbridge Abbey had lands at Hoadley and, by grant of Alvred de St Martin, at Holbeamwood.

Chapter Two

The Middle Years

The first reference to the bounds or the extent of the parish is in a document (now destroyed) dated 1451 and quoted by the Rev. A. Kersteman, curate of Ticehurst 1787-98 in his manuscript record *Some Account of Ticehurst, Sussex compiled from the Parish Registers and other papers*. In this he mentions[14] a statement of the 'limitationes parochiarum de Ticehurst et Eatchingham' dated 1451 as having been registered in the first parchment Book, after the erection of the Dean and Chapter, commonly called the 'Red Book', now called 'tertius'. This Red Book was supposed to have been burnt several years since with other records of the church. He gives the following as the text of this record of the boundary between the two parishes:

> The departing of them both beginneth at Gelards well, and so as the water leadeth to Wards Brigge unto Aple Dorys brigge and so to Wallrigge gate and then cross over the Long down to Hartwell as the stream leadeth to little Citchinham and so forth as the Park leadeth unto Crabden.

There are similar records of 'beating the bounds' of the parish in 1566, 1683, 1712, 1720, 1752 and 1779 where Ticehurst adjoins Etchingham, Wadhurst and Hawkhurst, and all follow almost exactly the same lines as those shown on modern maps, although of course many of the old boundary marks have vanished.[1] Apart from a very few minor alterations in the county boundary in 1974, it is probable that the parish of Ticehurst has remained unchanged for 800 years or more.

The *V.C.H.* gives the area of the parish in 1930 as 8,250 acres plus 15 acres of water, and Mrs. Odell in 1925 agrees, but the *Gazetteer of England and Wales*, published in 1842 gives the total area as 7,280 and the *History of Sussex* (Horsfield, 1834) concurs.[5] Is this a misprint which one of these usually reliable works has copied from the other? It is hard to see how 1,000 acres could have been 'acquired' and unremarked. The Ordnance Survey of 1873 also gives the area of the parish as 8,265 acres.

On the question of population we are on firmer ground: a 'census', being a 'Trew Retorne', made by the constables of the hundred of Shoyswell in 1635 suggests about 365 people in the whole parish.[69] All the reference books take the figures from the official 10-year census returns starting in 1801, and there are no reliable figures before that. The numbers are:

1801	1436[58]	1901	2931
1811	1593	1911	2853
1821	1966	1921	2611
1831	2314	1931	2650
1841	2465	1941	not taken
1851	2850 (includes 100 working on the railway)	1951	2766
1861	2758	1961	2840
1871	2939	1971	3135
1881	3007	1981	2889[59]
1891	2931		

There is a document dated 1769[15] wherein the parish is divided into three 'boroughs', given below in their original spellings:

Town Borough: Dale Harbour, Noorwoods, Singehurst, Bryants, Vineyard, part Gibsreed, Steel Land, The Chequers, Rowly, Rosemary Lane, Welches, Pitford, Borders, Three Leg Cross, Whiligh, Holbeam Wood, Birchett Green, Greenwoods, East Lymden, Wardsbrook, Burnt Lodge, Parsonage, Broomden, Claphatch.

Pashley Borough: The Hazeldens and Mompomps, Borzell, Pashley, No Mans Wood, Lower part of Bearhurst, Mill Lands, part of Maplesden, Quedley, Little Quedley, Teagues.

Hoadley Borough: Little Hammerden, upper part of Bearhurst, The Hams, Crowhurst Bridge, Biggs, Hammerden, Collington, Bardowne, High Street (Wallcrouch), Tutts, Bines, Bolsters Gate.

The principal occupation in the parish then, as now, was agriculture in one form or another; farming, hops and fruit or working the coppice in the woodlands: chestnut for hop poles or fencing on a 15-20 year rotation, hazel for hurdles and thatching spars every seven years and hornbeam for fuel and charcoal. In all the various census returns and parish records, most of the men would be described as 'husbandman' or 'labourer'. There was literally nothing else for most of the men to do and, before the advent of machines, all work was done by hand and a large number of labourers, carters, ploughmen and others highly skilled in the work of mowing, reaping, hedging, ditching and other tasks was employed. In 1835, 504 acres were devoted to the cultivation of hops.

All local government was in the hands of the church; the local representatives were the vestry under the direction of the two churchwardens elected annually. They were responsible for the welfare of the parish, and in particular, apart from ecclesiastical matters, for education, the relief of the poor and for roads. They had power to levy rates for these and other purposes. Education will be discussed in another chapter, but the poor and roads will be mentioned here.

The Overseers of the Poor were appointed each year by the vestry and it was their responsibility to ensure that paupers were given a minimum subsistence from money collected through a 'poor rate' levied on the inhabitants of the parish. They were also responsible for seeing that any pauper who strayed into the parish was returned at once to his native place to avoid expenditure by them. Paupers were forbidden to move from one parish to another without permission. In 1663 it cost 2s. per week to keep a pauper, whilst a coat, a pair of shoes and a pair of stockings cost respectively 1s. 10d., 8d. and 6d. and in that year the total expenditure on the poor was £5 10s. 2¼d. They were housed if necessary in the almshouses which stood at the rear of the present *Chequers*, facing east.[1]

In 1740 and 1760 proposals were put forward to build a Poor House incorporating a school for children, and in 1761 such a building was erected by public subscription (about £200) on Newark's Platt belonging to the parish, in the High Street on the site later occupied by Waterhouse's shop, and now empty. On 20 April 1801 it was 'agreed to hire Steward Hammell from Ashford to be governor of our workhouse, and his wife to be governess (the parish to give them £50 per annum and their board, they with one child to find themselves in clothes)'.

A return dated 5 December 1820 to the House of Commons said: 'This Parish is very much Burdened with Poor, upwards of 800 Paupers, and frequently from 30 to 50 Families out of Employ. The Farmers from the distrest state of the times being incapable of paying for their labour and Many of them not able to pay the Poor Rate and other Taxes'. A vicious system was in force in the parish of letting out the unemployed paupers to local farmers at cut-price rates for very long hours. The governor of the poor house was responsible for taking all the inmates to church, twice on Sundays and also on the usual prayer days. He was also required to hold an assembly every morning and evening and to read prayers.

In 1834 a return sent to the Poor Law Commissioners said that there was no local act for the management of the poor and that the parish was not incorporated with any other parish for purposes of relief. There was an elected Select Vestry under Sturges Bourne's Act which met fortnightly, except during harvest and hop-picking time, to consider applications for relief. Any able-bodied man with no employment was found work in digging stones for the roads. Under the Poor Law Amendment Act of 1834 Ticehurst was combined with Wadhurst, Frant, Lamberhurst, Salehurst, Bodiam, Burwash, Etchingham and Broadwater Down from 11 September 1835 into the Ticehurst Union, and a Union Workhouse was erected at Flimwell. The average annual expenditure on the poor of this parish in the three years before the formation of the Union was £1,168 and for the first three years of the new system £662 10s. 2½d. — a large

4. Lower Toll Gate.

saving. Generally speaking it would seem that the Ticehurst parish officers were more efficient and humane in carrying out their duties than were many of their fellows in other parishes.

In olden times in Ticehurst the roads, like the poor, were always a problem. Prior to the present century the only means of getting from one place to another was by walking, riding or taking a pony and trap or a larger horse-drawn vehicle, and at one time the only road reasonably passable was the old Roman main road along the ridge to Wadhurst and Frant and, to a lesser extent, its continuation eastwards to join the London-Hastings road at Swiftsden. This was the turnpike road set up under one of the various Turnpike Acts, consolidated by the General Turnpike Act of 1773, and managed by the Mayfield and Wadhurst Turnpike Trustees, but it is clear that they did not always keep parts of it in proper repair. There were two tollgates, with side-gates, one at each end of the village, and toll bars at Burnt Lodge and the Vineyard. A normal toll would be a farthing for a head of cattle and 6d. for a carriage horse. Local cart traffic and that to church or to a funeral was exempt from toll. The other roads or lanes were little better than glorified cart-tracks, dug out from time to time and the mud piled up on top of the banks, so that the roads gradually became deeper and deeper, and wetter and wetter. When stone was available, and money, they were roughly surfaced, but there were constant and justified complaints about their condition.

It is clear that travel in Ticehurst must have been, like matrimony, 'not by any to be enterprised nor taken in hand lightly or unadvisedly'! In 1542 Thomas Standen left a legacy for the repair of 'the most noysum and fowle ways within the parishe of Tisherst where as most need shalbe by the discrecyon of the honesty of the parishe'. In 1578 Barnard Randolph made a deed of agreement to pay £4 per year 'for the amendment of the horse-ways of Ticehurst to Withernden Bridge and to Hook Bridge and to Flimwell and also to the parish boundary towards Wadhurst'.

It was stated in chapter one that after the Romans left Britain no iron-making took place here until about 1400. In the Middle Ages water power started to be used for blowing the furnaces and hammering the iron — hence the name hammer pond where the streams were dammed up to work the water wheels which drove the hammer mills. The first of these in Ticehurst appears in 1433, when there is mention of a forge with a pond at Croucheland, which however has not been identified. There is mention of a mill at Pashley in the 1266 deed, but this is likely to have been a corn mill. However in about 1520 a water-powered iron mill was erected about half a mile north of Pashley near Mumpumps. This was the property of Sir John Boleyn of Pashley until 1543 when it was sold to Thomas May. The following year he was employing alien workers there; the last reference was to Anthony May who owned it in 1614.

Another iron mill in Ticehurst has been called the East Lymden mill and it was in fact on the River Limden, just south-east of Wedds Farm. Chingley forge was on the Bewl river just over the parish boundary in Goudhurst and the site is now submerged by the reservoir. It was built between 1574 and 1589; John Legas was tenant in 1726 and it was still in use 10 years later; in its time it was an important mill. Robertsbridge Abbey furnace was still operational in 1787. There may have been other mills and furnaces in Ticehurst which have not been recorded or located, and a possibility is a very much earlier mill at Hammerden, q.v. Kersteman in his diaries written in about 1796 tells us that:

> not more than half a century back many forges and furnaces were worked in this and the adjoining parishes; but upon the increased plantation of hops in this county and Kent, together with the cheapness of labour and fuel for the furnaces in the north of England, this valuable branch of trade was soon dropped.

There are several other mills in the parish which were probably built as flour mills and were certainly used as such latterly; these include the mill at Pashley, mentioned in 1266, Witherenden mill, Dunsters mill, Wardsbrook mill (for which see under those respective properties). There was a windmill, demolished in 1904, in Windmill Field above Broomden Wood, and another at Flimwell on the opposite side of the road to the reservoir, and it is clear that milling corn was an activity carried on in this parish for several centuries.

Ticehurst has never been the scene of any stirring event of national importance, and its parochial history centres mainly round the church and the 'big houses' of the neighbourhood which will be dealt with at length in a later chapter. There are however a number of things which affected the lives of the inhabitants and which might be of general interest.

The first of these was a tragic affair which took place in 1264 when Henry III was travelling through the parish on his way to meet the rebellious barons who ultimately defeated him at the Battle of Lewes. As the King's troops were passing Combwell Priory one 'Master Thomas' the King's cook

> going incautiously in advance of the army, was slain by a certain countryman. When the king heard of this he caused many of the people of the country who were assembled above Flemenewell [Flimwell] whither they had been ordered by the Lord John de la Haye, an adherent of the barons, to be surrounded, like so many innocent lambs in a fold, and beheaded. Thence he proceeded to Robertsbridge and after to Battel abbey ... where the king demanded of the abbot 100 marks, while Edward his son exacted an additional 40. For, seeking occasion on every hand to inflict burdens, they alledged that certain persons had been killed at Flimwell by the abbot's men, who had been sent thither for that purpose.

Another account of this incident puts the time at 'about the sixth hour on the vigil of the Invention of the Holy Cross' and says that the victims were 315 archers. No record exists of the actual site of this outrage, but it has been suggested that Yellow Coat Wood (600 yards south of Flimwell crossroads on the west side of the road) may be the scene of this mass execution, as archers at that period were clad in yellow 'jacks' or coats.

In 1330 a commission was issued to hear a complaint by John de Passele that 41 named defendants had

> broke his close and houses at Pesemarsh and elsewhere, hunted in his free warren, cut down his trees at Tychesherst, and other places, fished in his vivaries at Tychesherst and other places and carried away fish therefrom, timber from his houses, and other goods with rabbits, hares, partridges and pheasants and assaulted Stephen Adam, his servant.

Again in 1352, Tycheshurst is mentioned as being included among the 111 towns and villages in Sussex in which 'some evildoers have broken the parks and chases' of Queen Philippa, the consort of Edward III. These two examples are given to show the general lawlessness prevailing at that time.

In the rising of the 'Commons of Kent' in 1450, commonly known as Jack Cade's rising, many Sussex men were involved and most were ultimately pardoned, among them 'Gabriel Berward of Tysherst, yeoman and John Holbeme of the same, yeoman, constables of the Hundred of Shoyswell'. It would appear from the variety of names and places involved that public opinion in this part of East Sussex was largely in sympathy with what ultimately proved to be an abortive attempt at revolution. We have no record of how other religious and political upheavals affected Ticehurst in the 15th and 16th centuries or of any participation in the Wars of the Roses. Probably the local population knew little and cared less about events of the outside world.

One of the vicars of Ticehurst, Thomas Cowley (1535-43) got himself into serious trouble with his ecclesiastical superiors for his caustic comments on the royal policy in matters of religion, though we know not how far his views reflected those of his congregation. No Ticehurst names occur in the lists of those who suffered death for their religion in the reign of Mary, but one can imagine the impression which must have been created by the news of that horrible scene enacted in Lewes High Street on a June day in 1557, when Richard Woodman of Warbleton and nine other Protestants were burnt to ashes at the stake, for four at least of them came from places as near as Heathfield and Mayfield.

On 24 October 1639 there was a disastrous fire in the village, destroying seven houses and the smith's forge and all their contents; the distraught people appealed to the Justices at Quarter Sessions for financial assistance, but with what result we do not know. There is no record of any Ticehurst people taking part in the Civil War on either side, although it must have affected the parish deeply. Such fighting as took place in Sussex was mainly in the western part of the county, although the Commonwealth took over all the churches, and there is an ominous gap in the otherwise complete parish registers between about 1641-50. The Courthope of the time, although an adherent of the king, dextrously contrived to retain his post as a Commissioner of the Alienation Office during this period, but he had a very narrow escape from being imprisoned and deprived of his office on account of his 'malignant sympathies'.

On 25 July 1685 the church bells were rung on account of 'Munmuth being taken'. News travelled slowly in those days for the ill-fated rebellion of James Duke of Monmouth was crushed at Sedgemoor on 8 July and he himself was executed 10 days before his downfall was celebrated by the Ticehurst ringers. The bells were rung again for 'ye birth of ye Prince of Wales' who went down to posterity as James Francis Edward, the Old Pretender. A few months later they were rung again on a Thanksgiving Day for the accession of William III, and again on 19 May 1692 for the destruction of the French navy by Admiral Russell near Barfleur, and on 10 July 1713 at the signing of the Treaty of Utrecht. On each occasion the ringers were supplied with generous 'beer money' at the parish expense.

The Napoleonic wars did not greatly affect the people here, but the economic depression at the end of the 18th century and the first quarter of the 19th pressed grievously on the poorer portion of the population, as discussed earlier, and culminated in the riots of agricultural labourers which were fairly general all over Sussex in 1830.

In 1887 Ticehurst, like every other parish 'let itself go' in its anxiety to celebrate adequately the Golden Jubilee of Queen Victoria with something for everyone going on all day, ending with an enormous bonfire and a magnificent display of fireworks at 11 p.m. An equally comprehensive programme was carried out to mark the Diamond Jubilee in 1897; this included a Grand Cycle Parade with a one-mile ladies bicycle race. Again at the coronation of Edward VII Ticehurst celebrated in suitable fashion and, needless to say, similar festivities marked the coronations of George V and VI and Elizabeth our present Queen. Ticehurst during wartime will be dealt with in another chapter.

Smuggling, as might be expected from the proximity of Hawkhurst, which gave its name to the infamous 'Hawkhurst Gang', was not unknown in Ticehurst. The smugglers would ride through the parish at night on their way to or from Rye. The small pond — now filled in — which used to be on the site of the present St Mary's Close, is said to have been used for dumping kegs of spirits 'in transit', as was the old house on the opposite side of the lane where there used to be a large oak chest with a false bottom leading to a cellar below where barrels were stored; although the house was often searched nothing was ever found owing to the ingenuity of the construction of the chest. The house was demolished in 1969. There was formerly an inn called *The Unicorn* in Ticehurst on the site of the present Warwick House next to Coopers Stores, and another in Stonegate called *The Cock* (now Cock Farm near Bardown), both of which are said to have been much patronised by the smuggling community, but neither exists today.

In the 15th century there seems to have been a period of building or rebuilding and a lot of the older houses in the village and surrounding farms date from this time. They were originally typical medieval dwellings with a single hall, a fire in the middle and a hole in the roof to let the smoke escape and of half timber construction filled in with wattle and daub. Then about 1600 there was more activity and most of the buildings were 'converted' by having a floor put in to make a second storey, and a massive fireplace and chimney added, either in the centre or on one side. These chimneys can be seen clearly on estate maps of 1610-25 which include small outline sketches of each house. This subject will be dealt with more fully in a later chapter describing individual properties.

Chapter Three

The Parish Records[23]

There is no doubt that it is to the ecclesiastical records of this country — the monastic and Bishop's registers, but above all to the parish registers — that our detailed knowledge of bygone customs, families and individuals is due. We owe a great debt to Thomas Cromwell, who had been Visitor General of the monasteries and later Vicar General to Henry VIII, who issued on the king's behalf an injunction dated 5 September 1538 requiring parish clergy to enter in books, kept for that purpose, every wedding, christening and burial taking place in their parish. Orders to this effect were repeated in 1552 and 1558, but were only very partially observed.

The Ticehurst registers commence in 1559 and, apart from a gap of about ten years during the Commonwealth, run continuously until the present day. The original registers, which are in good condition and well preserved, are in the custody of the county archivist at Lewes, but remain the legal property of the vicar and churchwardens. They were completely transcribed in 1968 by the author of the present volume from 1559 to about 1850. The original transcripts are at Oakover while there are copies at Lewes and at the Society of Genealogists in London, and they can be inspected at any of these places.

From 1835, when the Ticehurst Union was formed with eight other parishes (see chapter two), all the poor from the workhouse seem to have been buried here until Flimwell was formed as a separate ecclesiastical parish in 1839 when most of them were interred there. Acts of 1666 and 1678 required everyone to be buried in a woollen shroud to encourage the wool trade and those — mostly gentry — who wished to be interred in linen, had to swear an affidavit before a Justice of the Peace and pay a fine, and a certificate had to be brought to the officiating minister and the fact entered in the register; this Act was repealed in 1814 after falling into abeyance.

From the commencement of the registers in 1559 until September 1563, the handwriting is the same, presumably that of Bartholomew Inkpen, the vicar. In November 1563 a new hand begins and continues until February 1584 and is probably that of John Wharton who was vicar for this period. In April 1584 a new scribe takes over, possibly John Leaver, and from 1602-13 the writing is in a bold, well-formed, educated hand and resumes again from 1627-36, but by then it has lost its character and the writer makes extensive use of old Latin abbreviations. There then follows a variety of hands and between 1642-53, during the Commonwealth, very few entries have been made and those that there are are hopelessly jumbled up in no consecutive order and written by a number of different people.

From 1654 the registers are written in the hand of John Callowe and he continues until shortly before his death in November 1680. William Swayne announces his own induction on 26 March 1681 in Latin and the register continues in his large flowing hand in English until 27 December 1717, and he was buried here a month later. Thomas Lord takes over in 1718 and from 1721 he writes entirely in Latin and takes a little more trouble over his penmanship than before. He continues until 1728 and then the following year the register continues in Latin, headed 'per me Davidem Allen', but after two years he continues in English.

In 1740 commences Mr. Medlicott's untidy scrawl which goes on until 1769 when his writing has become very shaky, and he was buried the year following. Mr. Evans Rice, the curate, takes over and then we have the fine and beautifully written hand of Christopher Gawthrop, the vicar, until 1787 when the registers are kept by the curate Andrew Kersteman in a bold and clear copper-plate style (see chapter two for reference to his diaries). He continues until 1798 and for the next 40 years there are a number of different curates and very little evidence that any of the incumbents took their duties seriously. The last of these curates was B. W. Dudley from 1838 and his writing develops into a carefully written copper-plate hand which in places is very beautiful. The first entry by Arthur Eden, the new vicar, and the first for about eighty years to devote his whole time to his flock, is in September 1851 and for the rest of the century the registers are largely kept by him.

In the baptismal registers there is the usual high number of illegitimate children, always mentioned as such, with the name of the putative father, if known. As elsewhere there was a great increase in illegitimate births in the latter part of the 18th century. The registers are full of human life, love and suffering; tragedy, comedy and pathos jostle with each other in these pages just as they do in real life. To quote only a few:

1585	Thomas Alye the Kitchine boye of my Lady Hendleye buried
1587	Gregory my Lady Hendlys man was buried
1587	A poor wayfaring man dyeyd in a barne at Quedlaye buried
1589	A soldier a Scottish man dyiyd at Flimwell buried

In 1593 and 1594 there seems to have been some sort of epidemic: in 1593 there were 31 burials and one John Baker lost three sons and one daughter. The next year two sons of Francis Smith were buried within two days, followed by both their parents before the end of the month.

1596	A Mayd yt was drowned at Withernden buried
1598	A grossesr that was a stranger
1603	James Lurker killed with a tree
1603	On Michaelmas Day the three daughters of Bartholomew Martindale, scholemaster, were christened Marye, Elizabeth and Myrabilis! and in the margin is written 'borne at a burthen'
1605	Jarvis Keene the elder and Jarvis Keene his son buried the same day
1656	Old Primer buried
1680	Bartholomew Thorpe who hanged himself
1696	William Irons a poor ancient man was buried
1729	Elizabeth wife of John Ollive of Horsmonden co Kent, gent, buried in woollen
1729	'lunatica quae sese suffocavit aquis' [a mad woman who drowned herself]
1777	Hannah & John, children of Isaac Tuppeny were drowned
1797	This Person died at Burwash from excessive drinking and was buried here by virtue of the Coroner's Warrant

The years 1633 and 1634 were marked by more burials than usual and in 1790 there was an epidemic of 'ye small pox'.

There are several references in the 16th century to Chrystofer Foull (variously spelt) the Rypear, Repeare or Rippier. This was very puzzling until a dictionary of old Sussex words gave the definition as 'travelling fishmonger', and it seems that he was a man who regularly delivered fish to the London market and locally.

What must surely be an almost unique case was in 1729 when Jarvase Cooper was baptised at the ripe old age of 81! There was here, as in most parishes, the usual high incidence of infant mortality and still births. The unusual spectacle of a coffin being carried to church in a waggon drawn by four pairs of oxen was witnessed at Ticehurst in

1837, when the funeral took place of Mr. Robert Reynolds, aged about sixty years, formerly of Tunbridge Wells. *The Sussex Weekly Advertiser*, in recording the event, mentions that he was of great bulk and that it was 'conformably to his own request' that this strange mode of transport was adopted.

An interesting feature of the Ticehurst registers is the long list of 'briefs' between 1653 and 1769 in the first three volumes of the registers. These were royal letters issued to bishops and through them to the parochial clergy authorising and desiring the collection of alms during Divine Service on behalf of some specified charitable or public cause. Individuals or localities suffering from some natural disaster beyond their means to meet would petition the government of the day for assistance, there being no insurance, as we understand it, at that time. Subjects that were covered include loss of churches and buildings from fire, flood and storm; 'towards the Redemption of our country men that are taken captives and made slaves by the Turks' (in 1670); for ye Captives in Algiers (1682); for the relief of Irish Protestants (1689); loss caused by the French firing and plundering the town of Teignmouth (1691). There were many cases of briefs for churches destroyed or damaged by fire.

On 10 September 1704 the sum of £2 16s. 6d. was collected 'for the relief of Seamen's widows that were lost in the late storm'. This would refer to the famous storm of 26/27 November 1703 which destroyed the Eddystone lighthouse and was 'ye greatest hurricane and storme that ever was known in England; many churches and houses were extremely shattered and thousands of trees blown down; thirteen of her Majestyes men of war were cast away and above two thousand seamen perished in them. N.B. the Storme came no farther north than Yarmouth'.[25] Many parishes in Kent and Sussex benefited from these briefs; the total number of briefs between the years given was over 600 and the average amount collected about 4s., though in some cases very much more and occasionally nil.

The surviving churchwardens' accounts[26] commence in 1685 and run continuously up to 1894, when the Vestry in its old form was abolished and the churchwardens lost all their responsibility in civil matters and became, as they are today, custodians of the church in quite a wide sense. Many of the items contained therein have already been mentioned; they have not been transcribed, but the originals can be seen in the record office at Lewes.

Anyone interested in learning more of the fascinating human and historical details which these old records reveal would do well to visit the County Record Office and browse through them. The original registers are of course best, but those not familiar with old hands might be advised to start on the transcripts which are legible, accurate, translate the Latin and put all the entries in correct sequence, which is not always so in the originals. Stonegate and Flimwell registers commence in 1839 and they will be discussed in the chapter on those two churches.

Another set of records which are worth consulting are the back numbers of the Parish Magazine; a set of these can be found in the Collingridge collection at Lewes, running from 1890 to 1939, but unfortunately they are not complete. Several people in the village have collections of these, and it might be worth trying to get them all together in the hope of making a complete set.

Copies of the *Courier* and other local newspapers are available for perusal in the Tunbridge Wells reference library; it is a somewhat lengthy procedure unless one is looking for a particular item and knows more or less the exact date, but there is a wealth of information there for the local historian.

Chapter Four

The Parish Church[62]

As we have seen in chapter one there was undoubtedly an Anglo-Saxon church in Ticehurst in pre-Conquest times, in the manor of Haslesse, probably on the same site as the present church, but of that we cannot be sure, and there are certainly no remains of it in the existing building, or anywhere else in the parish.

Until the late seventh century A.D. the people of Sussex — the south Saxons — were pagans. A small group of monks under one Dicul, who came from the far north, set up a little monastery at Bosham in the early part of the century, but the people refused to listen to them, and it was not until about 686 that Christianity came to Sussex under Wilfrid. King Æthelwald and his wife had been baptised and were full of missionary zeal, and they selected Wilfrid, who had been Bishop of York but compelled to leave there because of dissension among the clergy, and gave him land for a church at Selsey which became the episcopal see and remained so until 1075. How long it was before Christianity reached Ticehurst is not known, but it is interesting to note that the Saxon holder of the manor in 1066 was Alric, Bishop of Selsey (chapter one). The history of the patrons of the church will be given in chapter five under Advowson, but now for a description of the building.

The Church Building

The village of Ticehurst stands on a high ridge and the church occupies a prominent situation; surrounded by its broad open churchyard, overlooking the pastures and wooded slopes of the Sussex countryside, its lofty tower capped by a dumpy shingled spire proudly visible from afar. From the village square and main road from Tunbridge Wells to Hawkhurst and Hurst Green the church is barely seen; but a few steps between shops and weather-boarded cottages brings us to the wrought-iron gate and flagged pathway leading to the north porch now used as the regular entrance to the church. Before us stands the sturdy symmetrical whole of the parish church of St Mary the Virgin, 'lofty nave, with steep pitched roof and clerestory, battlemented aisles and north porch, with chamber above, long chancel with parallel gabled north and south chapels, and western tower crowned with shingled broach spire and having a stair turret at the north-eastern angle'. All roofs are now slated but the nave and chancel were formerly shingled. The masonry is mainly of local sandstone, the older parts of which have weathered to a fine mellow tone.

It is something of a miracle that the building retains so much of its ancient character and charm, for it has undergone many changes in the 700 years since its earliest still visible stones were laid. In the absence of other records we have only the styles of architecture as a guide to the age of the various parts of the building; and even this is not always reliable evidence as, for example, many of the windows which possess clear features of specific eras of style can be seen to have been reconstructed at a much later date (it is known in fact that some of the window traceries are copies of the originals).

It is from the middle period of the original Hastings Priory patronage (*c.*1275-1400) that the greater part of the present building dates. However, this can only be assumed from the styles of architecture, since no record of any of the work, apart from relatively recent restorations, has been traced. The appearance of the arms of the Etchinghams in the stonework of the porch roof and in the stained glass of one of the windows suggests that a major rebuilding of the church in the late 14th century may be attributed to the munificence of that once important family; they are known to have been responsible for the rebuilding of Etchingham church which was completed in 1363.

5. Ticehurst church tower.

The Tower

A good starting-point is the tower which seems to be the oldest and least altered part of the building as it stands today, most of it being clearly of 13th-century origin. A notable feature of the tower is the fine west window of four lights in the Decorated style which dates it to the early 14th century; the tracery is mainly original, although some of it was renewed in 1854. The arch of the west door is probably of the same date as the window above; it has a hood mould with the heads of a king and a bishop as 'stops', these being rather weathered but recognisable. On all four faces of the tower near the top are the openings in the bell chamber; these are of simple design, having a sort of elementary trefoil head in the upper curves of the masonry. That they are contemporary with the 13th-century building is shown by their similarity to the windows in the west walls of the north and south aisles, in the masonry of which can be clearly seen the line of the original much narrower aisles and steep-pitched roof. At the north-east angle of the tower is the stair turret, its wall pierced at intervals with small slit windows. The tower is crowned with a shingle broach spire characteristic of many Sussex churches and known as 'the Sussex cap', but here of rather less height than is usual.

On the north face of the tower is the handsome clock which dates from 1835; there would seem to have been at least two earlier clocks, one installed in 1692 and another some time before 1688. In this context there is to be seen scratched in one of the stones of the buttress at the south-west corner of the tower the faint markings of a very old sundial; such dials were in common use before the reformation.

The Buttresses

The tower has a pair of three-stage buttresses at each of its north-west and south-west corners and there are others where the tower joins the nave and aisles; there are also a number of single buttresses supporting the aisle and chapel walls on both sides. These all contribute to the sturdy appearance of the building as a whole.

South Aspect
Proceeding to view the church from the south we come to the walls of the south aisle as extended and raised early in the 14th century, with four windows in the style of that period, known architecturally as late Decorated. An embattled parapet, embellished with gargoyles, extends for the whole length of this aisle; this was added as late as 1901, at the expense of the late Mrs. Campbell Newington, when the battlement was also erected on the tower turret. By standing back one can see, above the aisle, the three clerestory windows which, like those on the north side, were reconstructed from rough sketches of the old designs in the British Museum. Continuing eastwards we come to the south or Pashley chapel which has two windows and a plain doorway on this aspect and an east window, all of 14th-century Perpendicular style, thus providing evidence of the original date of this chapel.

6. Ticehurst church, south aspect.

The Chancel
Due to years of neglect and dilapidation the whole of the chancel had to be practically rebuilt in 1856, but the tracery of the great east window and of the small north and south windows is a faithful reproduction of the original late 14th-century Perpendicular style.

7. Ticehurst church, north-east aspect.

North Aspect

We come now to the north or Courthope chapel, which is almost identical with the south chapel but had to be largely rebuilt, together with the chancel in 1856. In consequence the windows, one on the east and two on the north, have tracery which is a reproduction of the original late 14th-century Perpendicular style.

Finally, on our circuit, we come to the north aisle which closely matches that on the south, having been similarly widened and raised in the 14th century. This alteration can be traced in the masonry at its western end where it joins the tower. Projecting from this aisle is the attractive and interesting porch. The aisle itself has two windows to the east of the porch and one to the west, all in 14th-century late Decorated style, the former being reproductions and copied from the latter in the 1856 restoration. The three clerestory windows above, like those on the south, were re-modelled at the same time. The embattled parapet above this aisle, and the gargoyles, although similar to those on the south, were probably added very much earlier when the porch was built in the 14th century.

The Porch

The entrance to the porch has a well-proportioned arch, only very slightly pointed, as was the style in the latter part of the 14th century, and is flanked by two angle buttresses. Above the entrance is a canopied niche framing a beautiful modern carved stone figure of the Virgin Mary; this figure was placed there in 1970 and was given by Commander Hugh Mulleneux in memory of his mother, the niche having been long vacant, probably since Puritan agitation in the 17th century led to the removal of an earlier figure of the Virgin Mary, to whom the church is dedicated.

Above the niche is a window of two lights divided by a mullion and under a square label; this window lights a chamber entered from within the church. The top of the porch is battlemented and shows evidence of having been adorned with three coats of arms, now indecipherable.

Entering the porch we find it has a quadripartite vault, the ribs of which spring from corbels representing demi-angels with shields and converging on a central boss charged with the arms of the Etchinghams. On the east wall of the porch hangs a Roll of Honour to the 331 men and women of Ticehurst who served in H.M. Forces in the war of 1914-18.

The Porch Chamber

On entering the church we can see slightly to the west of the north door a short flight of stone steps, now enclosed by a vestry partition, giving access to an early doorway, with modern door, high up in the north wall. This opens onto an ancient and much worn stone newel stairway leading to the chamber above the porch. At the top of the stair is a massive door thought to be contemporary with the porch itself (late 14th-century); the door is constructed of three great slabs of oak and the original cumbrous lock and key are still in working order.

The chamber has a low-pitched domed roof with beams thought to have been taken from a wrecked ship. The chamber was used at various times as a prison, as a repository for old bones from the churchyard, as a clergy vestry, and as a robing room for the choir and for members of the Sunday School. It is known as a 'priest's room' and in ancient times visiting clergy would have slept there.

The Interior

The building, as we have seen from the outside, comprises in almost perfect symmetrical form the conventional arrangement of chancel and sanctuary at the east end, flanked by north and south chapels; nave with equal and parallel north and south aisles, and at the west end, tower arch and chamber with great west door and window.

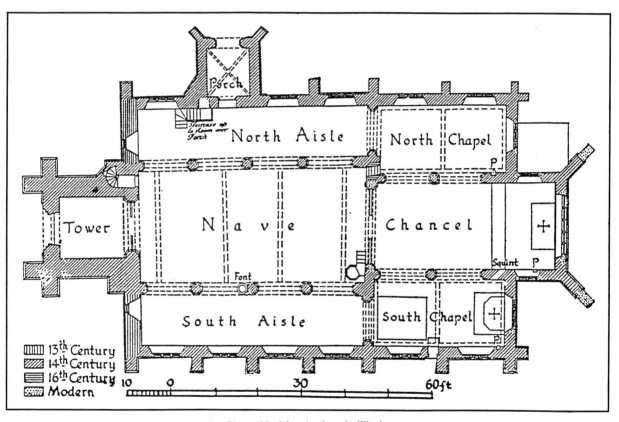

8.   Plan of St Mary's church, Ticehurst.

The Chancel

The chancel arch was rebuilt and raised by several feet in 1879; in the wall on the north side of the arch can be seen part of the 16th-century stone stairway which gave access to the rood loft. This was a gallery across the entrance to the chancel of a church, carried on a 'rood-beam' and supporting the 'rood' (a crucifix), sometimes flanked by statues of

saints. In 1561 all roods and rood-lofts in England were ordered to be demolished as 'superstitious'. The rood screen which originally separated chancel from nave was removed long ago; it is now replaced by a fine oak screen erected in 1914 by his widow to the memory of Dr. Alexander Newington, as recorded by a carved inscription. This screen was carved by a local craftsman, Frank Rosier of Frant.

The chancel has a modern hammer-beam roof of indifferent design supported on arcades of two bays of octagonal columns with moulded caps and arches of two orders, separating it from the side chapels. The beautiful oak choir stalls were installed in 1961 as a gift to the memory of Campbell Newington (1851-1929) and his wife Margaret Holgate (1857-1939) of Oakover, and were constructed by Thompson, the well-known wood carver who signed all his work with a carved mouse. When the floor was removed to fit these stalls there was found underneath the perfect skeleton of a man over six feet tall. The (presumably lead) coffin had been stolen, but on his chest rested a small brass plate inscribed 'John Roberts'. He was then covered up and left in peace![23]

9. The Wybarne Brass.

On the chancel floor on the north side and close to the Communion rail is the Wybarne Brass which was discovered during repairs in 1856. This memorial to John Wybarne who died in 1490 and his two wives consists of three separate figures placed side by side; the middle figure shows a knight in armour of a style used nearly a century earlier whilst the two side pieces depict ladies in costume contemporary with the deceased! It seems probable that the executors appropriated the brass of another man, removed the escutcheon, and juxtaposed on each side newly made brasses showing the two wives. The inscription in Latin may be translated thus:

> Pray for the souls of John Wybarne, Esquire, Edith and Agnes his true wives, who the said John died on the 16th day of February in the fifth year of the reign of King Henry VII (1490), on whose souls may God have mercy. Amen.

Unfortunately one of the three brass panels was recently prized out of the floor and stolen.

The Sanctuary

Beyond the Communion rail is the Sanctuary — the 'Holy Place'; here, above the high altar, is the great east window. This was rebuilt in its original Perpendicular style at the restoration of 1856 and filled with the present stained glass in 1879 as the gift of Miss

Margaret Holgate Foster, later Mrs. Campbell Newington, in memory of her parents, as recorded by a small brass tablet. The central light of this window, as originally painted, gained first prize at the Paris Exhibition of 1878; it represents the adoration of the lamb by the Church Triumphant and the Church Militant. The subjects illustrated in the other lights of the window are the Agony in the Garden, the Last Supper, the Crucifixion, the Resurrection, the Appearance to Mary Magdalene and the Descent of the Holy Spirit.

In the north wall of the sanctuary is a window of particular interest, being filled with fragments of old glass removed from the east window in 1879; the upper left-hand light depicts Salome with her two sons, St John and St James; the upper right-hand light shows the Virgin and Child and the lower right-hand light represents St Christopher. The remaining portion is a remarkable 'Doom' picture, dating from the late 14th century and illustrating the Day of Judgement: it incorporates the arms of the Etchinghams, also to be seen in the stonework of the porch roof belonging to the same period.

The window in the south wall of the sanctuary has glass depicting the Virgin Mary and St John; it was presented in 1875 as a memorial to Colonel Travers who lived in the house now called Apsley Court, which was at one time known as 'The Colonels'. Below this window there is a piscina with a triangular head, similar to those in the two side chapels.

The reredos above the altar was designed by the late Martin Travers, well known as stained glass artist, painter and architect and installed as part of a restoration of the sanctuary which he carried out in 1947. The reredos, candlesticks and a set of altar frontals were given by Mrs. Margaret Terry in memory of her father and brother, Francis Fitzgerald Hort (1868-1942) and his son Anthony Gilbert Hort (1916-44), as recorded by a modern benefaction board on the south wall of the sanctuary. In this wall there is also a squint giving a view of the altar from the south chapel. The chancel is separated from the chapels on each side by arcades of two bays in the Early English style, consisting of octagonal piers and responds with octagonal moulded capitals.

North or Courthope Chapel

This chapel is so named for having been, for many generations, the burial place of the Courthopes of Whiligh, a family known for over 400 years as distinguished members of this parish. It seems that in the 17th century this chapel was appropriated as a burial place, one half to the Courthopes and the other half to the families of Apsley and Newington. There are a number of memorials in the chapel to the Courthopes whose family vault, now sealed, lies below. These include a mural to George Courthope who was knighted in 1641 and died the following year; also a plaque to George Loyd Courthope, P.C., M.C., T.D., First Baron Courthope of Whiligh (1877-1955), patron of this church from 1930 until his death. He was in fact cremated and his ashes scattered at the foot of the 1,000-year-old oak at Whiligh.[60]

The Newington family is commemorated by a floor slab to Samuel Newington, Surgeon (d.1754), and the chapel at one time contained a memorial to Henry Apsley (d.1692); this is now to be seen as a floor slab in the middle aisle. Details of all these families may be found in a later chapter. There is a 17th-century Communion table here. The windows of this chapel have modern glass of undistinguished pattern; the roof is of the type known as 'king-post' with supports below the rafters. In the south-east corner is a piscina similar to that in the sanctuary.

In the course of the 1971 restoration it was thought that the foundations of the north wall and piers of the arcade had become insecure; this was thoroughly investigated and the architect was satisfied, but on his advice the vault was sealed up and the flooring, which was defective, was renewed with York stone.

The chapel is separated from the north aisle by an arch dating probably from the latter part of the 14th century. Beneath this arch is a handsome Sussex oak cabinet containing the Book of Remembrance in which are recorded the names of those whose ashes are interred in the Garden of Remembrance in the churchyard. The book is beautifully bound and hand-tooled in gold; the cabinet was made by Frank Young. They were given to the church in 1970 in memory of the late Maud Mary Wallis.

10.   Ticehurst church from the south-east in 1785, from a watercolour by Samuel Hieronymus Grimm.

South or Pashley Chapel

This chapel has always 'belonged' (at one time literally so) to the owners of Pashley Manor. The earliest memorial now to be found there is a brass floor tablet to Adrian May (d.1653) and there are ten other memorials to the May family, the most recent being dated 1819. There is also an iron slab let into the floor bearing the arms of the Mays, but without inscription. There are no memorials to the Pashleys or any of the intervening families before the Mays.

In the year 1796 the Pashley-May estate passed by the marriage of Caroline May to the Rev. Richard Wetherell, who died in 1858 and was the last person to be buried within the walls of the church. A single floor slab marks his burial place and records his wife and two of his daughters.

The chapel is separated from the south aisle by a late 14th-century arch, similar to that on the north side. The windows are filled with modern glass of no particular interest. A small 14th-century doorway in the south wall gives access to the churchyard. As in the north chapel the roof is of king-post style with supports below the rafters. In the south wall there is also a piscina, similar again to that in the sanctuary, and in the north wall close to the east end there is a squint giving a view of the high altar; this has been said to have enabled lepers, standing in the churchyard, to see the High Altar through the small doorway in the south of the chapel.

The Nave
To the south of the chancel arch is the pulpit which was erected at the 1856 restoration, replacing one of the old 'three-decker' type. On the east wall above the pulpit is a memorial to the 20 men of Ticehurst who laid down their lives in the Second World War. To the north of the arch on the east wall is a memorial to 62 men of Ticehurst who fell in the 1914-18 war. In front of this is the modern oak lectern, presented in 1964 by the late Miss Ruth Collingridge; it is also the work of Thompson, whose signature, a mouse, is carved on the foot.

Standing below the chancel arch and facing west one sees the full symmetry of the building: four graceful arches on each side separating the well-proportioned nave from the aisles; the arches are plain in style and supported by sturdy octagonal piers with octagonal moulded capitals: they probably date from the 14th century. From this position we can also see, above the arcades, the clerestory windows which, as was noted before, were copied from old drawings of the originals when their tracery was restored in 1856. They are filled with plain glass.

Perhaps the most outstanding feature of the interior to be seen from this aspect is the lofty and shapely arch at the west end, separating the nave from the base of the tower and framing the fine west window, which still contains most of its original beautiful 14th-century tracery; the glass depicting the four evangelists and the four major prophets was inserted in the 19th century in memory of Dr. Charles Newington (d.1852) and his wife Eliza.

The Font
On the south side of the nave towards the west end against the centre pier of the arcade stands the font. It has a plain stone octagonal bowl and pedestal of unknown date, and is surmounted by a fine carved oak cover which is one of the most interesting features of the church. It is of 16th-century origin and consists of eight panels, four of which open on hinges. The conical top is modern.

The panels are carved both inside and out with delicately wrought designs, characteristic of the period, consisting of intricate floral curvilinear and geometric patterns and with arched designs in the manner of church window tracery: the interior patterns include the fleur-de-lys and the emblem I.H.S. At the angles on the exterior are rounded shafts carved with scale and rope patterns. The plinth, which has been badly damaged, shows the remains of an inscription of which the only words now decipherable are 'God' and 'Elizabeth Chefe'. (N.B. On 17 September 1581 John Sheffe married Elizabeth Swattynge in this church.)

The Aisles
The south aisle has four windows all filled with modern glass, three of them in memory of members of the Newington family, all dated during the last quarter of the 19th century. The fourth, opposite the north door, is to the memory of Edward Currie

(d.1889) and his daughter Katherine (d.1883); he was closely associated with the Sunday School and appropriately the design of the glass symbolises Christ's welcome to children.

The north aisle has three windows, that nearest the chancel in memory of the Rev. Arthur Eden, much-loved and greatly- respected vicar of this parish for 57 years; the next window commemorates another member of the Newington family. The third, to the west of the north door, is of particular interest, being filled with fragments of medieval glass (probably late 15th-century) arranged in a conventional pattern, having been removed in 1879, together with other fragments now in the north window of the sanctuary, from the east window of the chancel. The figures depicted appear to represent a king, a queen, a bishop and the Coronation of the Virgin Mary.

On the walls of this aisle hang two boards painted with the creed and the Lord's prayer; there are two matching boards with the Ten Commandments which are soon to be placed alongside them.

In the west walls of the aisles are narrow slit windows with trefoil heads; these, together with the sections of the west walls nearest to the tower, like the base of the tower itself, are probably among the few remaining parts of the 13th-century building. The glass is of unknown but much later date; that in the south aisle contains the arms of the Dean and Chapter of Canterbury, patrons of the living from 1541-1930; that in the north aisle contains a representation of the Royal Arms.

The Tower Chamber

Beneath the great arch separating the nave from the chamber in the base of the tower is a panelled oak screen with ornamental glass, erected to the memory of Nathan Wetherell of Pashley (d.1887) and his wife; he was the third son of the Rev. Richard Wetherell whose memorial is in the Pashley chapel. On the walls of the chamber are the 'Benefaction Boards' regarding legacies for charitable and other purposes. The records painted in gold on black were a feature of the 18th and early 19th centuries; those to be seen here are dated 1778 (recording a legacy of 1578) and 1834. This chamber was used for many years as a vestry for the clergy and ringing chamber for the bells. This was moved higher up in 1991 by building a new floor over the tower chamber. Also hanging here are a number of framed records of special peals of bells rung on various occasions.

The Bells

Access to the present and original ringing chamber in the tower above is gained by a stone newel staircase in the turret at the north-east angle of the tower; this is entered by a doorway in the west wall of the nave immediately to the north of the tower arch. The stairs continue to the top of the tower and are lit by three very small slit windows.

Above the ringing chamber are hung six bells made in 1771 by Thomas Janaway of Chelsea, whose name is inscribed on each bell together with the date and appropriate sentences. Records show that there were bells here as early as 1542 and it is evident that the metal from the older bells was re-used in the casting of the present bells. They were re-hung on an iron frame in the restoration of 1901, and in 1950 they were taken down, sent away to Gillett and Johnstone of Croydon for re-tuning and they were re-hung on ball bearings. About this time the bell-ropes were extended and led down to the ground floor, passing through holes in the original floor with a system of pulleys, and thereafter the bells were rung from below. Unhappily, owing to the difficulty of enlisting and training ringers, these fine old bells were seldom used until recently (1987) when an enthusiastic team of ringers was formed and they are now rung every Sunday. Plans are now in hand to raise the ringing floor above the screen into the tower chamber. The inscriptions are as follows:

1.	I am she that leads the van	Thomas Janaway fecit
	Then follow me if you can	1771

1.   I am she that leads the van
      Then follow me if you can
2.   Then I speak next I can you tell
      so give me rope and ring me well
3.   Now I am third as I suppose
      Mark well now time and forth close.
4.   As I am fourth I will explain
      If youl'd keep time I'll credit gain
5.   Now I am fifth I do suppose
      Then ring me well and tennor doze
6.   This is to show to ages yet to come
      That by subscription we were cast and hung
      & Edward Lulham is his name
      That was the actor of the same.
      David Durell D.D., Vicar. Iohn Baker and David
      Hyland Ch. Wardens Iohn Noakes Gen Thomas
      May Gen Subscribers. Thomas Janaway
      made us all 1771.

The Organ

The organ stands in the south-west corner of the Pashley chapel, nearly blocking the arch communicating with the aisle of the nave. It incorporates the pipe-work of an earlier organ supplied in 1866 by J. W. Walker of Tottenham Court Road at a cost of £158 16s. 0d. This in turn was the successor of another small organ which was in the church in 1852, the first time an organ is mentioned. The present instrument was erected in 1909 by Messrs. Norman & Beard of Norwich and London. The cost was met by donations and subscriptions as recorded on a brass plate 'In affectionate Memory of the Rev. Arthur Eden, Vicar of this Parish for 56 years 1852-1908'. Curiously this inscription is inaccurate; he was vicar for over 57 years, being instituted in July 1851 and holding the living until his death in November 1908.

The organ has been cleaned and restored at various times, notably in 1957, largely owing to the generosity of Walter Spinney, and again in 1982 at a cost of £3,405, almost half of which was contributed by the new organist Robert Fuller who, with Edward Wheatcroft, organised the work which was carried out by J. Males of Polegate. The rest of the money was raised by functions and public subscription. The whole mechanism was stripped, cleaned and re-assembled, a new wind-chest made for the new reed stop and several new pipes were fitted.

The Church Plate

There are four pieces of antique silver belonging to the church which are now kept in a bank and displayed only on rare occasions. They consist of a silver Communion cup with hallmarks for 1567-8; a paten of 1713 on three feet, given by Mrs. Mary May and bearing the arms of the May family of Pashley; a very large silver flagon of 1684 given by Sir George Courthope whose memorial is also in the north chapel; and a silver alms dish of 1733 given by Mary Courthope, both the latter bearing inscriptions and the arms of Courthope.[11]

In recent years there have been demands at various times that this plate should be sold to pay for repairs to the church, but the churchwardens, in whose custody it is, and without whose permission it could not be done, have always very rightly refused to part with our heritage, given in times past to this church and to the glory of God. Incidentally one of the flagons has a Latin inscription underneath which may be translated 'Cursed shall he be who removes this from the church'.

Church Heating[23]

A full oil-fired central heating system, with pipes down the nave and aisles and in each pew, was installed in 1956 to replace the old coke boiler and hot air system which had been there for many years and was completely worn out. The Rev. Frank Law used to say 'this is the warmest church in Sussex'.

In 1963 the boiler room and crypts underneath both chapels were flooded to a depth of three feet. The worst of it was pumped out and at Sunday mattins on 17 November the vicar announced: 'as many of you will know, the boiler house is full of water. We must get to the bottom of this. Will all members of the Church Council stay behind after the service. Let us now sing the hymn For those in peril on the sea'.

A bucket party was organised to complete the job, and Captain 'Bronnie' Duckworth R.N., who was then secretary of the P.C.C., recorded in the minutes that on many occasions he had had to bail out a ship, but that this was the first time he had bailed out a church! The water, of course, did not do the boiler or its electrics much good and it was never quite the same again. It was found eventually that the water was coming into the boiler room full bore up the pipe that was supposed to let it out.

For the sake of anyone who may have to deal with this in the future the reason, which was far from obvious, will be given here. Running along the north side of the church is a large glazed drain at a depth of seven feet below ground, which collects rainwater from the roof via downpipes; it continues round the east side of the church, below the level of the boiler room and the drain in the floor discharges into it. It then continues in a south-easterly direction and empties into the ditch by the boundary wall. On this occasion some tree roots had broken and blocked the drain with the results mentioned above; this could very well happen again. The boiler was finally laid to rest in 1986, after 30 years of service, and replaced with a modern gas-fired boiler, using the old pipework, with a very significant saving in operating costs.

Floodlighting[23]

A system of three powerful floodlights was given in 1970 by Mr. Hope. They are controlled by a time switch in the church and the effect is really beautiful when viewed from the square or Church Street, bringing out the texture and colours of the stonework to perfection.

Tapestry Kneelers

A recent very beautiful addition to the church has been the tapestry covers for the kneelers, now almost complete throughout. The suggestion came from Mrs. Williams, the wife of the vicar, in 1981, and she organised the work at a series of monthly meetings. The project inspired a team of local designers and tapestry workers and the first 12 ft. length was fitted in 1983, and displayed at the Harvest Festival. Now nearly all of the kneelers are finished and reveal a remarkable degree of local talent. The subjects include flowers, crops, views of the parish, individual houses, coats of arms of Ticehurst families and various religious themes and ornamental designs. They are really magnificent and a beautiful feature of the church, and will repay a close inspection in conjunction with the special descriptive book kept at the cross-aisle.

Restorations

The fabric of the building seems to have been looked after fairly well during the 18th century as evidenced by a 1746 resolution at a vestry meeting on 2 August 1746 'that the

11. The Rev. Arthur Eden.

Churchwardens do immediately proceed to repair the Church, in such manner as shall be advised and thought proper by George Courthope Esq ...' but there is no record of the work carried out!

1856: In the early years of the following century a period of serious neglect set in, due, perhaps, to the hard times following the Peninsular War and to the fact that for some 50 years (1795-1851) the incumbents seldom visited the parish.

In 1851, with the institution of the Rev. Arthur Eden as vicar there opened a new and much happier era; not only was he by far the longest-serving vicar that Ticehurst has had, but the parish owes him an enormous debt in that he saved the whole building from virtual collapse. On taking up his appointment he found the church building in a very dilapidated condition and largely due to his efforts a public subscription was raised to carry out the necessary work. William Slater was appointed architect and his plans were carried out by a local builder, Thomas Waghorn, between March and October 1856 at a cost of £1,309. It had entailed re-building the chancel east wall from ground level and the side walls from about six feet above the ground together with their windows. The stone tracery in these windows, together with those in the aisles and the clerestory windows, was renewed as a faithful copy of the original 14th-century style. Four wooden galleries erected between 1820 and 1830 were removed, as well as the old-fashioned square box pews which were replaced by the present pews. Also a south porch of late design was removed and the doorway replaced by a window.

1879: Further work was done to improve the windows and much of the stained glass now in the church was installed; the chancel arch was also raised by several feet.

1901: Yet another extensive restoration was made to celebrate Mr. Eden's 50th year as vicar, and the pews were relaid on oak blocks set in concrete.

1949: The interior of the church was repaired and redecorated; preventive measures were taken against death-watch beetle and the oak shingles of the spire were replaced with cedar. The bells were taken down, sent away for tuning and re-hung.

1972: Urgent need was disclosed for major repairs to the exterior stonework together with the roof, as well as treatment of all timbers and redecoration of the whole of the interior. The cost was estimated at £7,000, but in the event it came to £2,000 more and took nearly two years to complete owing to structural weaknesses in the building which could not have been foreseen.

Memorials
There are numerous memorial plates, slabs and windows in the church; these were all copied out in full by Mrs. Odell — daughter of the Rev. Arthur Eden — in about 1924 and included all that could be deciphered at that date; some are no longer legible, and they are all contained in her *History of Ticehurst* which can be seen at the Record Office in Lewes. Unfortunately there is no complete record of the inscriptions in the churchyard, but many of the older ones have been recorded by Richard Dumbreck.

Conclusion
For over seven centuries the parish church has stood in the centre of the village, bearing witness to the living Christian faith. The pages above show how succeeding generations have contributed to the maintenance and beautification of the church, and have striven to be worthy of their heritage.

Chapter Five

Vicars, Vicarage and Churchyard

The vicars of Ticehurst are well documented,[1] commencing with the Combwell Priory deed of 1180 in which Adam the Presbyter is mentioned; an illuminated list hangs just to the right inside the porch but it contains a transcription error in that Thomas Cowley was instituted in 1535 and Sir John Baker became patron in 1539 and was relieved in 1541, so he would not appear to have appointed any of the incumbents.

Date	Incumbent	Patron
1180	Adam Presbyter of Tychenerste	Walter de Scotney
1266	William atte Mulle	Hastings Priory (Augustinian)
1332	Thomas	"
1358	Richard Chalkepole	"
1358	William de Cabilia	"
1365	Robert Poyntel	"
1417	William Haytoun	Warbleton Priory (transferred from Hastings)
1439	John Dygonson	"
1439	William Martyn	"
1440	William Stykeland	"
1444	John Syde	"
1479	John Ewer	"
1479	John Pensell	"
1506	John Eggerton	"
1535	Thomas Cowley	
1543	John Greye	Dean & Chapter of Canterbury (by grant of Henry VIII)
1546	John Mylls	"
1555	Bartholomew Inkpen	"
1563	John Wharton	"
1584	John Leaver	"
1612	— Hull	"
1614	Samuel Beyley, A.M.	"
1636	Thomas Westly, D.D.	"
1639	John Jefferies, S.T.P.	"
1643	John Wright —Whitby	Intruders during the Commonwealth "
1643	Gabriel Eagles	Dean & Chapter of Canterbury "
1660	John Callowe, B.A.	"
1681	William Swayne	"
1718	Thomas Lord, A.M.	"
1729	John Harris, S.T.P. also B. of Llandaff and D. of Wells	
1739	Ossory Medlicott, M.A.	"

1770	David Durell, D.D.	"
1776	Christopher Gawthrop, B.D.	"
1792	George Berkeley, D.C.L.	"
1795	William Welfitt, D.D.	"
1833	Hon. John Evelyn Boscawen, M.A.	"
1851	Arthur Eden, M.A.	"
1909	George Holmes Gray, M.A.	"
1921	Edwin Langley, M.A	"
1936	Owen Allan Sharpe Edwards, M.A.	Sir George Loyd Courthope, M.C.
1951	Frank Joseph Law, L.C.D.,R.D.	Rt. Hon. George Loyd Baron Courthope, P.C., M.C.
1967	William Gregory, L.R.A.M. }	Hon. Beryl and Daphne
1971	John Norman, M.A }	Courthope
1975	William Haigh Prudom	Hon. Daphne Courthope
1981	Benjamin Clive Williams, B.D.	John Hardcastle } Bishop of Chichester }
1990	Roy John Goodchild	-do- and Francis Drewe

Several more names of probable vicars in the early years could be added from old deeds gradually being discovered, but it is hard to be sure whether they were incumbents or assistant curates and as they do not appear in other records they have been omitted. They can be found in the Collingridge Collection at Lewes. Obituaries for most of the vicars can be found there and also in Mrs. Odell's book already referred to.

The Advowson

The Advowson or Patronage of a living is the legal right of a person to appoint a rector or vicar of a parish and such a person (who may be a corporate or ecclesiastical body) is called the Patron of the Living. In times past it used to be an absolute legal right, and when the livings were often heavily endowed the privilege could be very valuable. Today, when all the clergy's stipends are paid by the diocese, the right is only to ensure the suitability of the candidate for a particular parish, and now the bishop, churchwardens and P.C.C. can often exercise a veto.

In 1066 when the manor was held by Alric, Bishop of Selsey, the advowson was almost certainly in his hands; in 1086 at the time of the Domesday survey it would have belonged to Walter Fitz Lambert of the Scotney family, and his descendant Walter de Scotney was patron in 1180 as recalled in the Combwell Priory deed, when Adam Presbyter of Tychenherste is mentioned. In 1197 this same Walter gives the church to the Augustinian Priory of Hastings. Between 1180 and 1204 Bishop Seffrid II of Chichester confirmed the appropriation to the priory and the rectorial tithes ever since descended with the advowson. The vicar is mentioned in 1291 and the living is now a vicarage. It seems likely that this priory was founded by Walter de Scotney. The same register of Seffrid contains copies of letters by Bishop Ranolph of Chichester (1217-24) confirming the gift and in 1215 another deed by Peter de Scotney, son of Walter, also confirms it.

The patronage of Ticehurst church continued to be held by the Priory of Hastings for the succeeding 300 years. During this period in the year 1413, owing to encroachment of the sea at Hastings, the priory was transferred inland to Warbleton, whence it became known as Hasting New Priory (the site of the priory is to the east of the present Warbleton at Rushlake Green beside a stream still known as Christians River). Upon the dissolution of the priory about 1539 the patronage of Ticehurst, together with many other properties, was granted by Henry VIII to his Attorney General, Sir John Baker of Sissinghurst. His holding of the Ticehurst living was brief, for only two years later, in 1541, the king presented the patronage to the Dean and Chapter of Canterbury who continued to be patrons for most of the next 400 years except for a gap of a few years during the Commonwealth.

In 1930 the patronage was acquired by Sir George Loyd Courthope, M.C. of Whiligh in exchange for the living of Brenchley with Paddock Wood which he inherited from his father.[23] On his death in 1955 it passed to his two daughters, the Hon. Beryl and Daphne Courthope, and on the death of the last-named in 1980 it passed to her second cousin, John Hardcastle. In 1979 the ecclesiastical parish of Flimwell was re-amalgamated with Ticehurst and the Bishop of Chichester, patron of Flimwell, became joint patron. In 1990, at the request of John Hardcastle, Francis Drewe of Oakover became a (third) joint patron.

12. Ticehurst vicarage, c.1792.

The Vicarage

The present vicarage was completed early in 1967 to the plans of Mr. Beauchamp, architect of Tunbridge Wells, and won an award at Church House, Westminster as one of the best designs submitted that year. The land was formerly used as allotment gardens and belonged to the Hon. Beryl and Daphne Courthope who generously donated it for that purpose. The first occupant was the Rev. W. Gregory who moved in shortly after his arrival in the parish.[23]

The earliest vicarage of which we have records was an Elizabethan house close to the present Old Vicarage. Kersteman, the curate, writing about 1796,[22] says that it is:

delightfully situated upon a side hill, a short distance from ye church, and is, taken altogether, a commodious cheerful dwelling. The house was put into thoro' repair by the late vicar (Gawthrop), who constantly resided there during his incumbency, and has been greatly altered and much improved by the present one (Berkeley). Besides a good Barn, Stable & Lodge, there are about 14 acres of Glebe land which is thus divided viz — a large and excellent garden with a parterre (flower beds) in the front of the house, a long avenue leading up to the village, planted on either side, with a sand walk up the middle — a small copse and plantation of ashes & the rest in meadows, being in five separate fields.

This and the next entry are schedules of the vicarial glebe, the income from which was due to the vicar. Parsonage Farm to the south was entirely separate with 24¼ acres; this was rectorial glebe from which the income belonged to the patron, in this case the Dean and Chapter of Canterbury.

The following description of the old vicarage and its glebe land is taken from a terrier dated 21 April 1636:[1]

Imprimis a House and eight or nine sevrale rooms with an entry therein. A Barn with A stall, A Forestall, A Courte, A garden inclosed with Pales & a Backside by Estimation half an Acre of land. Six severall Pieces or Parcells of Land whereof one piece is Meadow Land by estimation 1 acre & a half. One other piece called the Stumblet divided into Two parts with a Gill by estimation two Acres. One Piece called the Slidinge field by estimation two acres and a half. One Piece of Land adjoining to the orchard & backside of the house by Estimation Fower acres and one other piece of Land by estimation four Acres, All of which several parcells of Land are belonging unto the said Vicaredge & do Abutt to the King's high way leading from the Street of Tyseherst aforesaid to Wardsbrook towards the West, to a Tentre & Land called Thorntons towards the North.

In 1852, a year after he had been instituted to the parish, the Rev. Arthur Eden demolished this house and erected the present building, standing in extensive grounds, a little to the north of the old vicarage. On his desk he installed a beer pump connected to a barrel in the cellar below 'as it helped him with the preparation of his sermons'![23]

When the Rev. O. A. S. Edwards arrived in 1936 he found the house to be too large and unmanageable for him, so in 1939 the vicarage was sold and Hillbury, opposite the Lane to Threeleg Cross, was purchased. This in turn became uneconomic after the 1939 war and in about 1960 it was exchanged for Lamerton near the former Wesleyan chapel and this served until the present vicarage was built.

Mr. Eden's house has had a chequered career with a number of owners and has successively been known as The Old Vicarage, White Lodge and Wybarnes and has now reverted to the Old Vicarage. The house which John Wybarne was building for a priest on his death in 1490 (see under Bricklehurst) has been thought to be the original, or predecessor of, the old vicarage described above; this is discussed at length by the Rev. Charles Gaunt in *S.A.C.* Vol VIII and the conclusion is that it cannot have been.

The Churchyard

Ticehurst has, for a village, a very large churchyard which has been added to over the years to make room for burials. Up to the beginning of the 1939 war it was kept neat and tidy by hand — the only way to clear amongst all the headstones and kerbs. In about 1950 it was decided to move all the stones[23] from the old northern part up to the road so that this could be kept mown. A few people objected — hence the stones which remain standing; there were so many objections to clearing the rest of the churchyard that this was left untouched. Unfortunately no proper record was kept of the inscriptions and some of the stones were used for repairing the paths, but the bulk of them were piled up beyond the east window where they are completely inaccessible and a large number have been broken. Richard Dumbreck has made a painstaking record and plan of the older stones still standing to the east and south of the church.

In 1965 the wall against Church Street, which used to be on the line of the present kerb, started to fall down.[23] The County Council were eventually persuaded to rebuild it in its present position in return for the gift of the piece of land now grassed over so that they could remedy a very dangerous corner. At the same time the steps at the lower end of the wall were rebuilt and an excellent job of real craftsmanship was completed using the original materials, and the mason carved the date on one of the stones. Maintenance continued to be a problem with the churchyard and in 1978 the original part all round the church was found to be completely full and so by order of the Privy Council that part of it was declared 'closed', which means that no more burials can take place there, and it is the legal responsibility of the Rother District Council to maintain it. At about the same time a new burial ground to the east of the vicarage, given by the Hon. Daphne Courthope, was consecrated by the Bishop of Lewes. The oldest inscription still visible on a stone to the east of the church is dated 1524 but no other writing is discernible. With the exception of the Wybarne Brass, this is the oldest surviving memorial, although there are many of the 17th century to the east and south of the church.

Garden of Remembrance
In the north-east corner of the churchyard, and screened by a neat hedge, is a part of God's Acre consecrated in 1962 for the interment of cremated ashes with space for memorial plaques. The names of those who are interred here are recorded in the Book of Remembrance kept in the north chapel of the church. This part of the churchyard is not closed.

Chapter Six

Stonegate and Flimwell Churches

Until about one hundred and fifty years ago the civil parish of Ticehurst was also the ecclesiastical parish but in 1836 and 1839 respectively Stonegate and Flimwell were constituted as Chapelry Districts, and subsequently they acquired the full status of ecclesiastical parishes, although still remaining within the civil parish of Ticehurst for other purposes.[1]

Stonegate

A manuscript in the custody of a late vicar of Stonegate gives the following 'Description of the Chapelry of St. Peter's Stonegate in the Parish of Ticehurst in the County of Sussex and Diocese of Chichester':

> The boundary of the District begins at Shover Green at a point marked A on the Map on the north side of the Turnpike road leading from Swiftsden to Tunbridge Wells and from such point follows the boundary of the Parish of Ticehurst to Witherenden River and from thence proceeds down the River by Witherenden Bridge to Crowhurst Bridge. From thence it follows the boundary of the Parish of Ticehurst Northward leaving Myskin's farm, which is in the Parish of Etchingham, a little to the East and crosses the road leading from Burwash to Ticehurst entering Limden Wood at a point where a Wood Post is put up with the letters T and E inscribed thereon. From such Wood Post the Boundary of the Chapelry District proceeds nearly in a straight line crossing Limden Lane near Store's farm which is within the Chapel district to a stone on the North side of the Turnpike road aforesaid having the letters C D inscribed thereon and leaving Bugsey's Farm within the Chapel district and from such Stone as marked with the letters C D to the point marked A aforesaid.

In addition to the district thus defined the earlier incumbents of Stonegate were responsible (by arrangement with the rector of Burwash) for the spiritual oversight of the district which, in 1877, became the separate ecclesiastical parish of Burwash Weald.

Stonegate church is a modern building of brick with facings of Bath Stone. The foundations came from stone removed from the mill in Windmill Field above Broomden Wood, which was demolished in 1904,[23] and the church was erected in the same year at the expense of Mr. G. J. Courthope to replace an earlier building (consecrated and dedicated to St Peter on 22 June 1838) built by his father George Campion Courthope with proceeds from the sale of some houses in London to make room for Liverpool Street station; it stood on what is now the northern part of the churchyard, near the road. This earlier building had to be demolished on account of grave structural defects.[1] The *London Gazette* for 30 December 1904 contains a copy of the official notice of the substitution of the new church of St Peter, as the parish church, in lieu of the old church of the same name. The notice is dated 15 December 1904 and is signed on behalf of the Ecclesiastical Commissioners, the Bishop of Chichester, the vicar and Mr. G. J. Courthope, the patron. George John Courthope was the eldest son of George Campion Courthope, and he was succeeded by his son George Loyd Courthope, later Sir George, and afterwards Baron Courthope of Whiligh.

The roof is tiled and there is a squat tower, containing a clock and one bell, faced with weather-boarding and surmounted by a shingled spire. The church is approached

13. The original Stonegate church.

through a lych-gate with massive curved oak beams and a tiled roof. The interior of the church is spotless. There is a nave and north aisle, separated by stone arches on stone pillars; also a fine stone chancel arch on the side of which is a memorial to the men of Stonegate who fell in the 1914-18 war, and a similar plaque for the 1939-45 war hangs on the west wall behind a handsome stone font.

There are two stained glass windows: that in the chancel represents the Nativity, Crucifixion and Resurrection and is in memory of members of the Luck family, long and honourably connected with the parish; the window at the west end depicts incidents in the life of David and is in memory of 'George John Courthope of Whiligh who built this Church'. The pews, choirstalls, wood-block flooring and all the furnishings are constructed entirely of Sussex oak and some beautiful craftsmanship is displayed. On the west wall of the church are hung portraits of some of the former incumbents, and obituaries of these up to 1921 are contained in Mrs. Odell's *History of Ticehurst*. The vicarage was formerly situated a little to the south of the church, but this has now been sold and the present vicarage is to the north of the crossroads on the road to Shovers Green.

Vicars of Stonegate:
1839	Rev. G. D. Johnston
1852	Rev. J. Dawson
1869	Rev. J. D. W. Preston
1871	Rev. W. de Vear
1879	Rev. W. May

1888	Rev. A. D. C. Clarke
1896	Rev. J. A. Kelly
1903	Rev. S. M. Wade
1914	Rev. A. A. Gray
1921	Rev. J. E. Gardiner
1929	Rev. A. V. Grant[23]
1935	Canon K. Clarke
1938	Rev. C. F. T. Field
1941	Canon A. Young
1960	Rev. F. S. Hopkirk
1965	Rev. E. A. Bailey
1979	Rev. M. Hill Tout
1983	Rev. I. Paton Hunter
1985	Dr. P. Hamilton
1989	Canon D. Maundrell

The registers, which are in the custody of the incumbent, are well kept, clearly legible and in good condition. The baptismal and burial registers begin in 1839 and are still in use. The marriage register commences in 1869, and there is a note at the beginning of the register of baptisms: 'The Ecclesiastical Commissioners issued an order dated 18th Feb. 1869 authorising Banns of Marriage to be read and marriages to be consummated in the church of St Peter, and this now becomes a full parish and the benefice is now a vicarage'. The advowson has descended with the owners of Whiligh, and in 1988 Michael Reid joined John Hardcastle and they are now the two joint patrons.

There are two charities relating solely to Stonegate church. The first of these is the George Campion Courthope Charity for the repair of the church of St Peter; it was founded by an indenture dated 19 June 1838 and produces about £17 per annum. The second is the Henry Kettel Charity set up under the latter's will proved in London on 18 December 1885. It is in two parts: the first produces about £16 per annum for Stonegate church, and the second about £9 per annum for the poor. The two charities are now regulated by the Charity Commissioners under a scheme dated 8 April 1930; those in favour of the church appoint the vicar and three persons nominated by the P.C.C. to be trustees, whilst that for the poor appoints the vicar and the two churchwardens.[1]

Flimwell

St Augustines's church at Flimwell, designed by Decimus Burton,[63] was erected on what was then known as the Furzy Field and was completed in 1839. The project was made possible by the generosity of four people who also contributed largely to the original endowment of the benefice: Richard Bury Palliser, then owner of Seacox Heath, the Rev. Richard Wetherell of Pashley, George Campion Courthope of Whiligh, and James Lambert of Hawkhurst.[1] The building as originally erected was much smaller than it is today, and consisted only of what now constitutes the nave; the tower was only a squat flat-roofed appendage without a spire (from which Sir J. F. W. Herschel, the famous astronomer who lived at Hawkhurst, made many of his observations). The shingled spire was added in 1872 at about the same time that the present chancel was built. The tower contains four bells: three were given in 1873 by Mrs. Creed and the fourth, the treble, was added a year later at a cost of £40 subscribed by the ringers.

In the north-east corner of the nave stood the capacious curtained pew of Mr. Palliser, squire of Seacox, and underneath was constructed a vault for the interment of members of his family. It is, in fact, still empty as although a young son of Mr. R. B. Palliser was

14. Flimwell church, c.1906.

buried in it his remains were subsequently removed to the churchyard where other members of the family lie at rest.

The chancel was restored and beautified in 1916 by Viscount Goschen, then of Seacox, as a memorial to his only son Lieut. the Hon. G. J. Goschen, 5th Buffs Regt. who was killed that year in Mesopotamia, whilst on active service, aged 22. The work included a mosaic wall, the erection of a beautiful carved chancel screen, filling the east window with stained glass and the construction of a commodious vestry. Other stained glass in the church commemorates his parents, the first Viscount Goschen and his wife Lucy; the latter window was destroyed during the last war and was replaced with plain glass. On the north wall of the nave is a memorial to the men of the parish who gave their lives in the Great War; a similar but less elaborate plaque on the same wall commemorates those who fell in the 1939-45 war.

The church is built of stone with a slate roof and is approached through a lych-gate from the main road. Inside there is the nave without side aisles, and the chancel with a small pipe organ in an alcove on the north side. The pews are mostly of pine and the floor is partly of York stone and partly tiled. The roof inside is of timber beams and plaster. At the back of the church is a font cased in modern oak, and about sixty individual kneelers have been covered with tapestry, each with a different hand-worked floral design.

Vicars of Flimwell:[1]
| 1840 | Rev. G. Greaves |
| 1842 | Rev. H. P. Haughton |

1844	Rev. W. Adamson
1856	Rev. F. Howlett
1867	Rev. C. J. Eagleton
1914	Rev. A. N. Johnson
1932	Rev. K. G. Packard[23]
1941	Rev. J. H. Maxwell-Staniforth
1943	Rev. S. W. A. Collins
1947	Rev. L. Richardson
1953	Rev. R. E. Scott
1956	Rev. J. Victor
1961	Rev. G. A. Armistead
1963	Rev. A. W. Parfitt
1964	Interregnum
1967	Rev. F. O. Taylor (priest in charge)
1979	Rev. W. H. Prudom (jointly with Ticehurst)

Thereafter the incumbents are the same as Ticehurst. The registers,[23] which are in the custody of the incumbent, begin with the baptism on 9 August 1839 of Henry St Leger, son of Richard Bury Palliser and Jane his wife. They are well kept, clearly legible and in good condition, although some of the bindings need attention. The baptismal register in the early years contains a quite extraordinary number of illegitimate births — in some periods well over 50 per cent — most of which are from the inmates of Union House, or the Workhouse, while most of the entries in the burial register for the same period are for people from the same place, Flimwell having presumably taken over this onerous task from Ticehurst, where the same is evident before 1839. It is interesting that the early registers have the title embossed in gold 'Church of St Augustine Sea Coxheath'. The original baptismal register was full in 1916, but the others are still in use. The vicarage used to be just to the west of the church, but was sold in 1965 when it was no longer required. The advowson belonged to the Bishop of Chichester until the amalgamation of the parish with Ticehurst; now it is a joint patronage (see under Ticehurst).

Chapter Seven

Schools and Charities

The first, indirect, reference we have to a school is in the register for baptisms for 1603 when, as we have already seen, triplets were born to one 'Bartholomew Martindale Scholemaster'.[23] Where that school was we do not know, and the next and more definite reference is in 1761 when a poor house was built in the High Street incorporating a school for children. This was still only for paupers, but in 1830 a school with two rooms, apart from the poor house, was built on part of what is now St Mary's Close, at the back of nos. 10 and 11 against the wall of the churchyard; in the following year the Rev. Richard Wetherell of Pashley acknowledges that he holds 'the land whereupon a National & Sunday Schoolroom hath been lately erected, being part of Singhurst Farm, abutting on the churchyard of Ticehurst, being 77 feet in length'. In 1834 Mrs. Elizabeth Underdown bequeathed £200 to the Minister and Churchwardens to pay the interest towards the education of poor children in whatever manner they thought fit.[1]

15.   Ticehurst school, *c.*1880.

There are two more references in the registers to schoolmasters: the first is in 1756 when Grace, daughter of John Adams schoolmaster, was buried, and the second in 1779 when Sarah Tandy, daughter of the schoolmaster, was baptised.

In 1835 there were five daily schools in the parish of which one, a National School, contained 183 children and was supported by voluntary contribution;[28] this is presumably the one mentioned above. Another would have been the school in the poor house, but where the others were we do not know. In 1844 the number of children on the books was 75 boys and 85 girls, with an average attendance of 45 and 40 respectively.

The present school dates from 1846[23] and this is marked by a carved inscription on the front of the building, and was the result of a bequest made by Joseph Petitt, draper and grocer of Ticehurst. In this he gives in trust to the Minister and Churchwardens and their successors, in return for £200 paid by them, about one acre of land 'and all buildings erected thereon or to be erected, to be forever ... used for a school ... for the poorer classes in the Parish of Ticehurst and for no other purpose'. The Minister shall have the superintendence of the religious instruction of the scholars, but in all other respects the management shall be in the hands of a committee consisting of the Minister, Churchwardens and six other persons to be elected annually with power to co-opt six ladies to assist them. The land is left in trust as above for ever and is dated 15 June 1846. The first stone of the present building was laid the following day by Mr. George Campion Courthope.

Such old records of the school as survive are at the County Record Office in Lewes under reference ESC 152 and they start with the headmaster's log book for 1863 and the minutes of the school managers' meetings of 1902. Both continue up to date and there is a great deal of fascinating day-to-day detail in them. Until 1946 the school was largely financed by private subscriptions, but under various Education Acts the Local Education Authority — which was in effect the County Council — helped more and more with grants. In 1880 the school was considerably enlarged.

In 1870 the average attendance was about seventy, and the headmaster's salary was £80 p.a.; in 1893 there were 117 pupils on the books with a muster of about ninety-three attending. In the early years there were frequent closures of the school on medical advice due to epidemics of diphtheria, scarlet fever, mumps, whooping cough etc., and in very hard weather during the winter, especially after a heavy fall of snow few, if any, of the children could get to school, and those that did were sent home. At first there was only a well on the premises, but in 1905 mains water arrived in the village and was laid on to the basins and lavatories of the school. The building was lit by candles and later by gas. Until fairly recently the summer holidays were always extended into October to include the hop-picking season, much to the annoyance of the authorities who complained that the school was out of line with most of those in East Sussex.

By 1913 the headmaster's salary had risen to £180 p.a., and the next year, following a complaint, the managers issued an instruction that boys were not to be caned in the presence of girls! One of the most outstanding headmasters was Mr. Bowers (1926-49) and he will be remembered with affection and respect by a lot of people still in the parish. The reports on him from the various Inspectors of Schools were always full of the highest praise. Two of his great delights were gardening and cricket; in the former he started a gardening class and Ticehurst won the Championship Spade several years running. The cricket team also flourished under his direction; in 1933 Ticehurst won the Skipwith Trophy for schools and Len Waghorne is singled out as the star of his side, on one occasion taking seven wickets for no runs! We held the shield again in 1947, having won all of the nine matches played. In 1939 electric light was put in throughout the school, and this was renewed when the first heating system was installed in 1955.

16. Hop picking at Walters Farm, *c*.1908.

17. Hop picking.

In 1940, when the bombs started falling, Morden Terrace Infants' School was evacuated here from London, but left soon after for Wales. In 1944 the flying bombs started to come over in large numbers and, on 18 July, 43 of our children were sent to Llanelli in South Wales, and on 4 August Mr. Bowers writes 'Flying bombs passing overhead continuously all day'. The next day 23 more children were evacuated to Cheddar. They all came back in December when the threat from these missiles had passed.

Following the 1944 Education Act changes were inevitable and in 1945 Ticehurst was scheduled as a primary school and the estimated cost of bringing it up to the required standard was £10,000. Not surprisingly the managers said that they could not afford this, so they were given the option of becoming a Controlled Church of England School which meant that the L.E.A. would take over all financial responsibility for running the school, but not the school house, and the church would still retain the ownership of all property as in the original Trust Deed. The parents could also ask that their children receive religious instruction on two days a week. This was accepted and this is still the position. The new Wadhurst Modern school opened in 1949 and all our children over 11 have since attended there.

In 1958 the school was fortunate in having Bill Jones from Wales appointed as headmaster and under his wise counsel and firm discipline the school flourished for nearly 21 years. His kind care and consideration for pupils and parents alike made him an outstanding headmaster, the numbers reaching a record total of over 260. Under his guidance many changes were made to the buildings, badly in need of modernisation; strict discipline was maintained, and the children were well-mannered, polite, neat and tidy. At the same time for nearly 40 years we were lucky enough to have on the staff Mrs. Jan Hemsley who was a gifted teacher of young people and had the priceless knack of being every child's best friend. Her contribution to the life of the school, particularly of the infants, was incalculable. Both these teachers' patience with and understanding of children has been an inspiration to all who came into contact with them, and to them we will always be eternally grateful.

Stonegate

Stonegate school was built by George Campion Courthope and was opened on 17 June 1839, according to an entry in the log book exactly 100 years later when the school celebrated its centenary; in 1844 it had 96 pupils on its books and the average attendance was 63. The earliest record, still at the school, is the log book for 1907-72, which shows that for most of that time there was a series of headmistresses, some very good and some not so good, most of whom stayed only for a short time.

There were the usual closures for minor epidemics and for severe weather, and it is interesting to note that a number of girls walked to Ticehurst school once or twice a week for cookery classes. In 1907 there were 76 children on the books, but after that the numbers gradually declined and by 1920 the number was 47, which continued to be about the average for the next 50 years. Main water was laid on in 1922, electricity in 1940 and main drainage in 1949. In 1952 the school was extended by the addition of some extra rooms and facilities. As in Ticehurst some of the children were evacuated to Llanelli in South Wales in 1944 when the flying bombs were coming over in large numbers.

Flimwell

The early records of Flimwell school are at the County Record Office in Lewes under reference ESC 72, but are incomplete. The school was just to the west of the church and was built in 1847; there is a plan of the building and a conveyance bearing this date at Lewes. The only old surviving records seem to be the headmaster's log book for 1863-92, the others not having been deposited and were presumably lost when the school was bombed. There were a series of headmasters and headmistresses during the period covered by the log book — eight in all. The school was demolished by a flying bomb in 1944, but luckily there were no casualties; the pupils had temporary accommodation at Seacox Heath, which was empty at the time, and in 1946 they moved to Ticehurst and have attended the school there ever since.

Charities

The earliest of the parochial charities is that made by Barnard Randolph Esq. on 27 September 1578 for the Fishmongers' Company in London to pay to the church-wardens of Ticehurst the sum of £4 p.a. for the upkeep of the roads from Ticehurst church to Witherenden Bridge, Flimwell and to the boundary with Wadhurst. By a codicil to his will dated 20 March 1582 he left to the poor of Ticehurst £25 p.a.; considerable litigation followed his will bequest, but the latter was upheld and is now administered by trustees appointed by the Parish Council. These sums seem small today, but at the time the income from this charity would have represented the wage of an agricultural labourer for about two years! Barnard Randolph was a native of Ticehurst and a man of some importance both here and in London and was a noted judge and Common Serjeant of the City of London. He was also a very wealthy and generous man. Much genealogical data concerning this family will be found in *Genealogical Gleanings in England* by Henry F. Waters pp. 917-25 and in Mrs. Odell's book on Ticehurst.

The next in chronological order is the Elizabeth Underdown Educational Charity of 1834, which has already been mentioned, and is now administered by the Charity Commissioners. Beresford's Charity is also vested in the Commissioners and arises from the will of William Carr, Viscount Beresford, dated 25 April 1851, in which he leaves £100 to each of seven parishes, including Ticehurst, the income to be used for the benefit of the poor. The War Memorial Maintenance Fund was founded by declaration of trust dated 22 November 1923 under which Alexander Startin and George Gillham gave £100, the interest to be applied for the maintenance of the war memorial in Ticehurst. All the above trusts are administered by trustees appointed by the Parish Council.

There is also a little-known charity set up by Deed of Trust by Mrs. Campbell Newington on 8 May 1935[23] with the National Institute for the Blind, wherein she gives them the sum of £3,000 on trust for the income to be applied for the relief of blind persons in Ticehurst and elsewhere, priority to be given to people in this parish. It is known as the 'John Rea Campbell Endowment Fund' (he was her uncle and guardian), and the original deed is at Oakover; it is administered by the R.N.I.B. Church Field was in the possession of the churchwardens in 1750 and the rent received by them has always been applied towards the maintenance of the church. The endowment consists of the Church or Park Field near Ridgeway containing 4.9 acres. It is now administered by the Parochial Church Council. There are two charities relating solely to Stonegate and they are described in chapter six.

The Village Club, or the Institute as it was originally called, is another charity.[23] This was built by Campbell Newington of Oakover to designs prepared by the architect Sir Aston Webb on land owned by the founder and was opened on 10 January 1900. It fronts on to the old turnpike road at its junction with the road to Flimwell, and is backed by a large recreation ground, containing a cricket pitch, tennis court and a children's playground. At one time there was a bowling green but this is no longer used.

The building is very substantial, constructed of brick faced with local stone and a tiled roof. It originally contained a large main hall with committee room leading off, having the public parish library, a reading room, billiards room and W.C.s; at the west end was the caretaker's cottage, and the whole building was centrally heated. It was open for men only at a nominal annual subscription and no drinking or gambling was permitted. There was a resident caretaker and his wife, Mr. and Mrs. West, and they remained, much loved and respected, until about 1945. They cleaned and looked after the premises, tended the boiler and fires and saw to the members' wants. Mr. West also mowed the grass and looked after the lawns and greens. Mr. Newington, until his death in 1929, paid out of his own pocket the caretaker's wages and the fuel bill. When he died the property descended to his daughter, Beatrice Drewe who, in 1932, conveyed it on trust to the Charity Commissioners together with an endowment fund providing an income of about £100 p.a., sufficient at that time to meet the expenses, mentioned above, previously paid by the founder.

The trustees were four foundation governors and four co-opted governors and they delegated the management to a Representative Council of 12 members appointed annually by the various local organisations in the parish. After the last war the premises fell into virtual disuse and the endowment income would not cover the cost of fuel, quite apart from the caretaker's wages. In spite of intensive efforts by all concerned, sufficient support was not forthcoming; in 1960 the governors altered the rules to allow women members to be admitted and the provision of a bar and fruit machine, and at the same time the name was changed to 'The Village Club'. There was a great improvement but still it did not pay and consent was obtained to meet some of the deficit from a small levy on the parish rate.

In about 1957 the youth club premises were added at the east end of the building, financed by a County Council grant and local donations and a separate charitable trust was formed for this, which still continues. At the same time the facilities of the club were considerably improved. The governors then decided that the present system of responsibility and management was outdated and that this should be shared more evenly over the parish as a whole, for whose benefit it was then being used. So in 1974, after consultation with the Parish Council, the governors resigned en bloc as trustees in favour of the Parish Council who agreed to act as corporate trustees of the original endowment in conjunction with the Charity Commissioners. A sub-committee was formed to manage the club, and since then things have gone from strength to strength, and the premises have been further extended, providing a much larger bar and lounge area, and a second billiards table has been installed.

Chapter Eight

Modern Ticehurst Evolves

If any of the old-time inhabitants of Ticehurst, whom we have been discussing in earlier chapters, could visit the village today, they would immediately be struck by four things: the vast number of strange vehicles on the roads, the excellent and dust-free state of the roads themselves, the large increase in the number of houses and the beautiful expanse of Bewl Water. Later they would find piped water, sewerage, electricity and television in most homes. We who live here today take all these things for granted, but it is really only since the end of the last war that most of this revolution has taken place. The previous chapters took us up to the middle of the 19th century; let us see what has happened since then. In 1836 Stonegate became a separate ecclesiastical parish, and in 1839 Flimwell did the same, although in 1979 it was reunited with Ticehurst; the whole civil parish remained intact with Stonegate and Flimwell as 'wards'.

Local Government

We have seen how the Church, through the vestry, controlled virtually all aspects of parish life, but this was now to change. The Local Government Act of 1888 established County Councils who took over the roads and at the same time the various Turnpike Acts were abolished. Under the Education Act of 1902 these councils also took increasing control of the schools, but it was not until after the 1944 Education Act that this was complete. The Local Government Act of 1894 set up parish and district councils and took away most of the powers of the vestry. Since 1921 the Parochial Church Council (P.C.C.) has assumed most of the remainder. The first chairman of the Parish Council was Dr. Herbert Hayes Newington, and the first clerk, unpaid, was George Gillham. Broadwater Down was still within the Union and Ticehurst as 'Head of the Union' became the local rural district council in 1894 until 1934 when it was absorbed by Battle and remained so until the 1974 reorganisation, violently opposed locally, when Battle and Rye were amalgamated with Bexhill to form the Rother District Council with offices at Bexhill. At the same time Sussex was divided into two counties, East and West, and our office is now in Lewes.

The powers of the Parish Council are virtually restricted to street lighting, with power to levy a small rate for that purpose, and to commenting on planning applications and similar matters. The District Council is the delegated planning authority under the County Council and is responsible for building and public health regulations; formerly also for sewerage, but this now comes under the Southern Water Authority. The County Council has overall responsibility for planning, roads, education, police, fire brigade and, of course, levying a general rate to pay for all these things.

Roads

The roads in the parish have shown a gradual but marked improvement over the last 100 years since the County Council took responsibility for them. First the abolition of the turnpike road through the village, then the construction of properly designed stone and gravel roads consolidated by steam rollers and then the advent of tarmacadam to provide a smooth, hardwearing, weatherproof and dust-free surface. The A21 was realigned in 1931[23] with a concrete structure, and the system of dual carriageway put in

18.   Aerial view of Ticehurst in 1952.

at Pillory Corner in 1964. The Flimwell crossroads were improved, and ever since the end of the last war the Parish Council pressed the County Council to install traffic lights there, but it took about fifteen years of continual effort before this was done, and then only after a fatal accident had occurred. They were finally erected in 1959 on a temporary basis, operating at peak periods only, and it was not until 1971 that they became permanent.

Another innovation, which we take for granted today but which was unknown before about 1955, is the salting and gritting of roads in cold weather; it plays havoc with unprotected cars but, except in abnormal conditions, all the roads are now kept passable and generally free from treacherous patches — far removed from the state that people complained about with good cause in the 17th century.

A new problem is the increasing number and weight of heavy lorries that use even our smallest lanes, mainly to collect milk from farms or to deliver animal food, fertilisers and machinery. The lanes were not designed for these giants and in many cases the foundations are not strong enough, but the most common cause of damage is when they are passing other vehicles and break away the edge of the road and the verge so that next time there is a hard frost the road starts to disintegrate. There is no apparent answer to this, for farms must be serviced and economics dictate the use of large vehicles. As early as 1909 the Parish Council protested to the R.D.C. about heavy steam locomotives being used to haul stone for the roads and so damaging them.

Apart from this the other problem in Ticehurst is the sheer number of cars, not so much on the roads as parked on the sides of streets reducing them to a single line of moving vehicles and sometimes blocking them altogether. This is common to a lot of villages and, short of having yellow lines, traffic wardens and parking tickets, which would be unpopular, there is nothing much that can be done. We are fortunate in this parish that we do not have a great volume of through, as opposed to local, traffic in any of the three villages.

Building

In 1835 there were 357 houses in the whole parish,[28] and the 1851 census gives 470, there having been gradual development in the 17th and 18th centuries. In the latter part of the 19th century quite a lot of building took place, mainly 'Gentlemen's Residences' and cottages for agricultural workers. This trend continued at the beginning of the present century, but up until the First World War Ticehurst was still very much a small to medium-sized village, and its two wards little more than hamlets. Between the two wars a small amount of development took place,[23] mainly at Upper and Lower Platts and the houses opposite Hillbury in Ticehurst, and along the road out of Flimwell towards Ticehurst, but probably not more than about fifty houses altogether. It was after 1950 that the development of Ticehurst really began, starting with extensions to Lower Platts and the building of Acres Rise and Horsegrove Avenue and some new houses at Dalehill. The planners were determined to keep Ticehurst and Flimwell separate, and there was, and still is, a policy not to permit any building between Dalehill and Union Street in Flimwell.

Development followed at Threeleg Cross and along the lane from there to Hillbury, at Cross Lane House, at the Gables and 'infilling' at a number of other places. There were not so many private houses built at Stonegate or Flimwell, but quite a number of 'conversions' of oast houses and barns throughout the parish. In all a total of about five hundred new dwellings have been created since 1920, the vast majority since the last war. Alongside this there has been a massive programme of council house building, listed below:[64]

1937	Coronation Cottages (Tinkers Lane)	13	dwellings
1947	Red Oast Cottages, Flimwell	6	"
1948	Hillbury Gardens	16	"
1948	Owls Gardens, Stonegate	6	"
1950	Tinkers Lane	2	"
1952	Forgefields, Stonegate	12	"
1954	Springfields, 1-24, 76-9	46	"
1966	Woodroffe Lode, O.P.	18	"
1966	Springfields second stage, 25-75	51	"
1986	Newington Court, O.P.	18	"
		188	"

The new houses built in the parish in the last 60 years catered not for an increased population, but to provide a higher standard of living and to alleviate the overcrowding which undoubtedly was prevalent before. It must be noted, too, that the council houses are available for anyone living in the rural district and are by no means confined to residents of the parish. Also, many of the new privately built houses have been offered for sale on a national basis and the majority of them have been bought by newcomers to the parish. The price that developers are prepared to pay for building plots is such that if anyone can get planning permission there will be a house or houses there within a very short time, regardless as to whether they are needed or not.

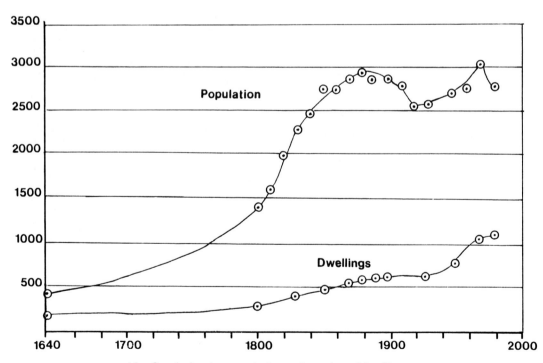

19. Graph showing population and number of dwellings.

A recent departure has been the quite phenomenal rise in the price of houses in the last few years, and this combined with the present very high interest rates puts almost insuperable barriers in the way of some first-time buyers. The figures given by the District Council for the present number of dwellings are as follows:

Ticehurst	688
Stonegate	160
Flimwell	199
	1047

This differs slightly from the figures given in the official census returns due to small discrepancies in boundaries. The graph (fig. 19) shows the population since 1635 and the number of dwelling houses. The tied farm cottage, of which previously there were many, has now virtually disappeared, and most have been sold to commuters and a wide range of other people for their own occupation after modernisation.

20.   The village pump in 1897.

Water and Sewerage

Prior to this century there was no main water in the parish, and people relied on collecting rainwater from the roofs and storing it in large butts or underground tanks to be pumped up as needed, supplemented where possible by springs and wells. There was a village pump on the site of the present bus shelter in the square, erected in 1888 with a glass roof and recovered with tiles in 1897 to mark Queen Victoria's Diamond Jubilee.[1] Apparently this well would run dry sometimes during the summer and the pump below Springfields would have to be used. There were also many other wells and springs in the parish as can be seen from the 1875 O.S. maps. It is interesting to note that on the 1612 map a hexagonal structure is shown on the exact site, which surely must have been the village well.

The general water supply to the area developed following the setting up of two or three small private limited water companies in 1904.[65] There were wells at Crowhurst Bridge, at Robertsbridge and Etchingham near the stations and at Flimwell with reservoirs at Robertsbridge and at Flimwell near the present site. Pipes were laid from Flimwell to Ticehurst House and down Church Street as far as the school which was connected in 1905. Soon after this the source and treatment works at Crowhurst Bridge were constructed, by sinking wells and installing slow-sand filtration and a pumping plant.[23] These works were established by the Heathfield and District Gas & Water Company and they sold water to the Ticehurst Water Company and to the Robertsbridge Water Company, both of which collapsed in about 1912. The Heathfield and District Water Company was established by Act of Parliament in 1913, and thereafter supplied water direct to consumers in their area.

By 1922 the mains had reached Stonegate and in that year the school was connected, but it was not until about 1930 that a large main was laid from Crowhurst Bridge, through Cottenden to Ticehurst, giving an improved supply and a much wider coverage, including Threeleg Cross. At the same time the pumping station and treatment works were improved and a new reservoir was constructed at Flimwell on the present site, on land purchased from Lord Goschen of Seacox Heath, and a second one alongside is now (1990) being constructed to afford additional storage. In 1959 The Heathfield and District Water Company was taken over by the Eastbourne Water Company who are now the supplier for this area.

A sewerage system, in the form of modern main drainage, came to Stonegate in 1949 and to Ticehurst and Flimwell in 1954 and to Threeleg Cross in 1959;[23] before that all the properties drained into the nearest stream or gill and, apart from being very insanitary and polluting the rivers, with the advent of main water and the universal use of water closets and the proposed post-war development, something had to be done before more houses were built. At that time the Battle R.D.C. were responsible for sewerage and their engineers designed and installed the two schemes. Stonegate has a treatment works half a mile south-east of the church; Ticehurst had works in Tinkers Lane, but they were replaced by a pumping station when the reservoir was proposed and the works moved to below the Dale Hill golf course and pumping stations adjacent to the school and one in Flimwell near Wardsdown Nurseries were added. Apart from a number of outlying houses and farms, most of Ticehurst and Flimwell are now connected. Ticehurst House has its own disposal works above Broomden Wood and a few of the larger houses still have their own septic tanks. The Southern Water Authority has now taken over the responsibility for sewerage from the District Council.

Gas

The Ticehurst Gas Consumers' Company Ltd. was formed in 1867 by local subscribers and in October of the same year construction of the gas works commenced on a site to the left of the road as one drops down to Lower Platts.[1] The first gas lamp was publicly lighted by Mrs. Eden, wife of the vicar, on 29 January 1868 and a great many houses were connected. Before that the only source of light was either a candle or oil lamp. The undertaking flourished for a while and then began to wane, and it became a struggle to keep the plant going. Between the wars the plant was closed down and gas was piped out from Wadhurst from their works just below the railway bridge near Dewhurst. That company met with the same fate and was closed in about 1950, gas then being brought out from Tunbridge Wells. Not long afterwards North Sea gas was being developed over the whole country with a nation-wide network of large pipes and Ticehurst was connected in 1972. One of the consequences of this operation is that local coke is no longer available, nor clinker nor ash for farm roads, nor creosote nor tar which, although important in the country, is not a high price to pay for the efficiency, cleanliness and non-toxicity of modern gas.[23]

Electricity

A supply of electricity first came to Ticehurst in the 1920s, to Flimwell in 1931, and to Stonegate in 1939. The first electric street lamps were installed in Ticehurst in 1926, in Flimwell about 1932 and in Stonegate in 1939.[66] At first there was not a lot of power available and outlying properties could only be connected at exorbitant cost and with restrictions on the amount they could use. Some of the larger houses, such as Ticehurst House, Oakover and East Lymden, continued to use their own plants, which had been installed at the beginning of the century, until well after the last war. These consisted of single-cylinder paraffin engines with an enormous fly-wheel driving a 100 volt D.C. generator and charging a room-full of batteries.

In 1950 a new high voltage line was brought in over the hill by Myskins, up the Sheepwash valley to a new transformer station just below Warren's Coaches. Service cables were led from this, mostly underground, and only then was there a really adequate supply in the parish.[23]

G.P.O. and Telephone

The 'penny post' was introduced in 1840, and before that the mail was carried by stage coaches and charged for by distance and weight. It seems that Ticehurst and the villages around had a service of sorts in 1820, but it was not until about 1860 that post offices began to appear in rural areas. The first one here was in a very small room tacked onto the side of Woodbine House, almost opposite Whatmans, and was kept by a Mr. Harris. It probably started in 1863 and the pigeon-holes for the letters were still there when the house was sold in 1980; the post office moved to its present site about ten years later and is thus shown on the 1873 O.S. map. Mr. George Gillham later lived at Woodbine House and kept the Central Stores, and his son Henry had a horse-drawn waggonette and collected beer from Wadhurst station for all the public houses in the neighbourhood.[56] The first telegram to Ticehurst was received by the Rev. A. Eden on 28 November 1870, and exactly six years later he received a letter from the G.P.O. headquarters in London saying that authority had been given for the establishment of a daily mail service to Ticehurst.[47]

George Gillham was the prime mover in getting the telephone laid on to Ticehurst; he was told that he would have to find ten subscribers, and this he succeeded in doing. The original ones were Oakover, Myskins, the doctor, Dr. Alec Newington at Woodlands, Dr. Herbert Newington at The Gables, The Vicarage, Whiligh, Ticehurst House, and Mr. Gillham at Woodbine House. A local telephone call then cost 1d. for five minutes and anywhere else in the country cost 6d.

The first telephone exchange was in Woodbine House in 1902 and three years later it moved to a small building behind Northgate House where it remained until about 1938, when the dialling system began to be introduced into rural areas and specially designed exchanges were built. In Ticehurst this was in St Mary's Lane, and there is a small one in Flimwell in the High Street. Stonegate has never had a telephone exchange; part came under Ticehurst, and part under West Burwash. A much more modern building to cater for present-day electronic S.T.D. equipment (Standard Trunk Dialling throughout the country and, now, throughout the world) was erected in about 1962 in Ticehurst, close to the previous one.

Originally the mails were sorted here in the post office, starting at about 4 a.m. and the postman would make two deliveries a day on his bicycle. In 1900 an ordinary letter posted in the morning would usually reach London the same evening, in time to receive a reply the next day!

Railways

It was in September 1851 that the railway line from Tunbridge Wells to Robertsbridge was first opened to traffic, at a cost of £202,000, but not until the following New Year's Day could the early traveller get to Battle and still later before he could reach Hastings.[1] The only station in this parish was originally called Withernden, changed to Ticehurst Road after the line had been open for some months and re-named Stonegate in 1947. When the service first began there were but two trains daily in each direction for third class passengers, although another train was provided each day for first and second class.[23]

It took about three years to complete this 15½-mile section and up to 500 men were employed at various times, all the work of course being done by hand with picks and shovels and horses and carts. All the stations from Frant to Robertsbridge were designed by William Tress and built by Edward Carter. It soon became apparent, however, that the contractors, Messrs. Warton & Warden, had not done their job properly. Certain parts of the track had to be re-laid, but more seriously it was found that all the tunnels were below specification, having only one layer of cemented bricks instead of four, and were quite unsafe. Eventually it was decided to re-line them with additional brick arches, thus making them narrower than standard. At first this was not very important, but as traffic increased and rolling-stock became larger it posed a serious problem. In 1924 the special 'Schools' class 4-4-0 steam engines were designed with the top of the cab and tender curved slightly inwards and the carriages and wagons were also made narrower to clear the tunnels and no other rolling-stock could operate between Tonbridge and Hastings. These magnificent locomotives remained in service until 1957-8 when they were replaced with special diesel units making up trains of six or twelve coaches. The bogey design was not all that it should have been with the consequent uncomfortable ride that passengers had to endure.

The line was electrified with a third rail from Tonbridge to Hastings and the defective tunnels altered to single line working at a cost of £20m. so that standard stock could be used; the new electric service from London to Hastings was opened to the public on 27 April 1986. Access to Stonegate station is difficult for people living in Ticehurst or Flimwell, and even from Stonegate it is a good walk if no car is available, so Wadhurst station has always been much more widely used and for many years it has had a connecting bus service. The result was that Stonegate became little used and in the days of steam very few trains stopped there; it also meant that the 'up' trains had to start on a fairly steep gradient from Etchingham to Wadhurst. With the growth in the number of commuters and the advent of diesel and electric trains things have changed and now most trains stop. The car park has had to be greatly enlarged and so has Wadhurst, which can now accommodate the several hundred cars which are left there every day.

In 1946 there were two people who commuted from Ticehurst to London on a daily basis, of whom the author was one.[23] It was unheard of then for a family to have more than one car, so they had to be taken to the station and fetched again in the evening. It was unusual for more than six cars to be parked at Wadhurst and for more than two or three wives to arrive to meet any evening train! Before 1945 it would have been unthinkable to travel daily to London from Ticehurst and the inhabitants all worked locally, most on or in connection with the land. How different it is today with comparatively few earning their daily bread in the parish.

Bus Service

Until 1910 there was no bus service in the village but a conveyance drawn by two horses and known as the Red Car Bus made the journey to Wadhurst station twice daily, leaving at 9 a.m. and returning at 11.20 and again in the evening. The driver was Albert Pierce who later drove for the Maidstone and District, and the 'bus' was kept in a garage between the *Duke of York* and what is now Ticehurst Motors. In 1910 they were bought up by the Autocar Co., starting from *The Bell* and run by the Elliot brothers, who in turn were bought by the Maidstone and District, who ever since have run a frequent and extensive service.[56,61]

Mention must be made here of Warren's Coaches, run by the late Derek Warren and built up by him to become one of the largest and best known luxury European travel firms in the south-east of England. Started by his father Philip in the 1920s with a single Model T Ford lorry with detachable seats, the business developed into a bus and taxi service which, among other things, had the contract for taking children to and from many of the local schools. Derek came back from the war in 1946 and joined his father, who died in the early 1960s, and the firm then went through a period of rapid and sustained expansion.[23]

The Police

Under the County Police Acts of 1839 and 1840 police forces were set up in most counties, and in East Sussex this was so in 1840. In 1841 there were constables in Wadhurst and Robertsbridge, and it is likely that Ticehurst had one soon after. In 1840 the Chief Constable reported that 'At Ticehurst there was a cage constructed of wood and moveable'.

Originally, and until the end of the last war, the local 'Bobbie' would have a bicycle and more often than not he could be seen patrolling some part of the parish. He would know everyone by name and who were the likely trouble-makers. Some of them on catching youngsters red-handed were wont to take off their leather belts and give them a good thrashing. Illegal maybe, but a very effective means of justice! Nowadays it is very different; in line with general policy our village policemen are seen less frequently 'on the beat' but have official radio-equipped cars and receive instructions from Battle or from the county H.Q. at Lewes, and are in constant touch at all times wherever they may be. There is a modern local police house in Ticehurst at Lower Platts, although our official police station is at Battle.

The Fire Service

Ticehurst had a volunteer fire brigade formed in 1910 with a primitive horsedrawn contraption with hand pumps, kept in a shed next to the *Chequers*. This was replaced in about 1930 with a more modern petrol-driven appliance, given partly by the Doctors Newington at Ticehurst House and partly financed by subscriptions raised by Mr. Dungey who had just come to the village to take over the Central Stores, previously

21.   The fire brigade in 1911.

22.   The fire brigade in 1939, with Messrs. Picknell and Dungey.

Gillhams. This machine was kept in the old Red Car Bus garage in the square and was finally disbanded after the last war;[61] there it was very well placed to deal with a disastrous fire in 1938 which destroyed the garage, fortunately without loss of life, and the local brigade was able to keep the fire from reaching the petrol pumps.[56]

There was also a private fire engine at Ticehurst House for many years,[23] but otherwise Ticehurst has always relied on Wadhurst or, if they are not available, on Heathfield or one of the other towns or villages so equipped. The service on the whole is very efficient and the appliance and a well-trained crew can be expected here within 15-20 minutes of sending out an alarm.

Medical Services

There has been a resident doctor in the parish for a very long time; the first we know of is Joseph Newington of Witherenden (1610-86) who practised in Wadhurst and Ticehurst. Another member of the same family, Samuel, was a physician of Ticehurst and was buried in the Courthope Chapel in 1754. His nephew, another Samuel, founded Ticehurst House, and he and his sons, grandson and great-grandsons were all members of the medical profession and lived in Ticehurst, and almost certainly had a practice here as well as running their asylum. The last of these were Dr. Alec (d.1914) and Dr. Herbert (d.1917); (see chapter fourteen). After them came Dr. Woodroffe, Dr. Kendrew and Dr. East; the latter retired in 1960 and was succeeded by Drs. Tudgay and Child, after whom came Dr. Collis. At Flimwell, Dr. Hitchens from the Hawkhurst practice also held a surgery in the garden room at the Vicarage. The nearest ambulance, and the one to which we are officially attached, is at Heathfield, and the nearest main emergency hospitals are the Kent & Sussex at Tunbridge Wells and Pembury Hospital.

There is a good chemist's shop opposite the post office which in about 1965 superseded the previous pharmacy which was alongside and in front of Beech House in the High Street. Until quite recently there was always a single district nurse in Ticehurst who looked after Stonegate as well, making regular inspections of the children at both schools, delivering babies and looking after the elderly and ill. For most of this century this work has been done by three much-loved and respected women: Nurse Long until the First World War, Nurse Lilly Colbourne until about 1948, and Sister Muriel Bagnall who retired in 1978. Flimwell had its own district nurse and midwife before and after the Second World War, Nurse Jarrett who lived in Hollands Row. Nowadays things are worked rather differently.

The Hurricane[23]

On the night of 15 October 1987 a severe depression was forming in the Bay of Biscay, and there were strong winds in France heading for the Channel, but the Meteorological Office had warned of nothing more than severe gales in southern England. At midnight there was a heavy gale raging in the Channel which quickly built up to storm force, and soon afterwards a hurricane came in from the south-western approaches, tore up the Channel, swerved inland and roared (quite literally) through Sussex and Kent and then turned north through East Anglia. The area round Sevenoaks probably bore the brunt of it with gusts of over 90 knots (100 m.p.h.), but the whole of East Sussex was affected nearly as badly. This was a hurricane such as we seldom get in this country — in fact the last time we had winds like this was probably in the great storm of 26/27 November 1703, as mentioned in chapter three.

The 1987 hurricane was at its height between 2 and 6 a.m. on Friday 16 October with the most violent gusts in Ticehurst at 3 a.m. The noise of the wind was horrendous, completely drowning the crashing of the trees and no-one realised the devastation that would meet their eyes at daybreak. Trees, large and small, were blown flat everywhere, or snapped off in the middle; enormous oaks which had stood for centuries were uprooted or, in some cases, literally blown to pieces with only part of the trunk left standing. Parts of the countryside will never be the same again. Tiles and slates were ripped off roofs and trees crashed into buildings. Every road in the parish was blocked by hundreds of trees and there were about two hundred trees across the railway line between Tunbridge Wells and Hastings. At the height of the storm the National Grid failed, completely blacking out London and all southern England; most overhead lines were destroyed by falling trees and nearly all telephones were dead.

Such was the daunting prospect that Friday morning: no electricity, no phones, no papers, mail or milk; no railways and the roads unusable. Incredible as it may seem, over the country as a whole, and at sea, there were hardly any casualties, and in Ticehurst none. So it was back to candles in the evenings and everyone who owned a chain-saw set to work. The various public services were magnificent: rail travel to London was restored within three days; electricity and telephones took longer to re-connect — on average about four days — but some remoter houses and farms had to wait up to a month. The County Council put all their available men and equipment to clear the roads, helped by men from the Royal Engineers, contractors, foresters and local landowners and farmers and their staff. In a surprisingly short time most of the roads were open to at least one line of traffic and then the Seeboard and Telecom engineers got to work; specialists were drafted in from all over the country and they worked all hours of daylight until the job was finished. Seeboard had the worst task because nearly all their lines were on pylons or poles and nearly every one had been broken, some in only one place while others had been completely destroyed. As one spokesman put it 'It took us 35 years to erect this network and now we have to re-erect it in 35 days!'

So in a surprisingly short time life got back to normal but we shall always grieve for the tens of thousands of trees lost for ever. If the hurricane had hit us a few hours later when the roads and railways would have been crowded, the loss of life just doesn't bear thinking about.

Chapter Nine

Local Organisations

Cricket Club

Ticehurst: The first cricket club was formed in Ticehurst at the end of June 1877 when the *Sussex Adventurer* of 25 July 1877 reported a match played here with the Lamberhurst Early Risers on 20 July in which Ticehurst lost by nine wickets. It stated that the Ticehurst club had been started barely a month before and they had not had much time for practice or to play as a team. The club continued to prosper, but unfortunately no-one seems to have the old score books which would be most interesting; although it is possible that they may turn up somewhere. Between the wars there were some very useful sides and Jack English, who ran the laundry, was the king-pin, if probably the slowest batsman ever known! It is said that he opened one innings with F. A. R. Reeves and was last out for six runs while Mr. Reeves had scored 116.

Regretfully, with the sad loss of Jack West, the caretaker of the Institute and a wonderful groundsman, in about 1945, the club dwindled due to the lack of specialist maintenance of the square. In fact without Mr. West's genius it became very dangerous when a fast bowler was in action. There were however some wonderful sides in the years since the Second World War and at least two unbeaten seasons, captained by Ian Akers-Douglas, an old Kent player, and splendidly supported by a number of very competent cricketers from the village such as Messrs. Yates, Golding, Iveymay, Ford and the Waghorn brothers, to name but a few.

Stonegate: A club was formed soon after the First World War and they played then on the field opposite Linkhurst, moving up to the present playing field in about 1930. At first there was not a great deal of support, but Basil Smith started it again in 1949 with a strong local side, all much of the same age, and it continued well until 1960 when it folded through lack of players coming on. Since then various people have got teams together at different times and cricket has been played, but there has been no regular village side. The present pavilion was erected in 1978.

Flimwell: Cricket has been played at Flimwell since at least the middle of the last century and Ray Barfoot and his father (Alf, now 83) have been stalwart supporters all their lives. The latter still cuts the ground and does 101 jobs on the playing field. A feared fast bowler, he played into his sixties and took over 100 wickets most seasons. Nowadays a vicar who throws himself into village life, and sport in particular, is a comparative rarity, but Flimwell was blessed with such a man in the 1930s; Frank Packard was a man held in high esteem who captained the side for a number of years and would sometimes arrive at a game a little bit late and peel off his robes to reveal full cricketing gear underneath!

Football Club

Ticehurst: The following account is taken from an undated newspaper cutting with the title removed in the Collingridge Collection at Lewes:

> It isn't in the towns that men get up at 6 o'clock on a winter's morning to practice by moonlight, when the ground is white with frost and hard as iron, but in the villages. And it isn't in the towns

that you necessarily find the most enthusiasm or the best players either, as I found when I investigated some of the past history of the Ticehurst Football Club.

It was way back in 1890, so Mr. R. C. Morris, one of the founders of the club, told me, that football in Ticehurst began. They had finished the cricket season and everyone was rather despondent at the thought of no more sport until next summer; and then someone suggested starting a football club. Everyone thought it was a brilliant idea, the main objection being no one knew the first thing about the game except Mr. Morris himself. However the idea germinated, with the result that Mr. Morris approached the Rev. G. G. Knox (curate of Ticehurst) who was a good footballer himself. He, too, raised the objection that nobody could play, but under the persuasion of Mr. Morris, found someone to give a ball and took a personal interest in the scheme, which resulted in football being a sort of winter relaxation for the cricket club.

23. Ticehurst football team 1891-2. Top row: Mr. Churton, F. Rogers, C. Day, R. C. Morris, W. Vidler, C. Wood, Mileman. Bottom row: P. Symes, Everett, Rev. C. G. Knox, F. Morris, W. Manwaring.

They played their first match on 21st. Feb. 1891, against Burwash, and a wonderful game it was too, Burwash proving that brains beat brawn by scoring an easy win. Then they travelled to Tunbridge Wells and played the Old Excelsiors, and lost 17-0. Apparently Ticehurst found their tactics of rushing down the field and charging their opponents directly the whistle blew were not very effective, but in their defence it must be said it was done through ignorance, not malice.

They progressed, however, and at the end of 1891 Mr. Morris' brother, Fred, who captained the Leicestershire Regimental Team, came home and played for Ticehurst for a few seasons. Later he left the village, but returned again, this time to become captain of the side. After that, declared Mr. Morris, they got along quite well, until in 1896 they were in the final of the Tunbridge Wells Charity Cup against Horsmonden School.

In 1895 a football club was formed, separate from the cricket club, and great interest in its development was taken by the Drs. Herbert and Alec Newington, who incidentally used to drive through Tunbridge Wells when the team was playing there, flying the Ticehurst colours from their carriage.

Talking of the outstanding club players of the older days, Mr. Morris mentioned Walter Vidler, Jesse Hyde, Arnott, Thompsett, Pilbeam, Frank and Fred Skerrett and J. Vincent, who was one of the originators of the Ticehurst League. All of them, he averred, were outstanding men in those days, and he recalled how in the season of 1899-1900 the team were champions of the Tunbridge Wells League, that being the first year of the League, and how ten years afterwards, they were champions again.

He told me of the heroism — I can call it nothing less — displayed by the team in their anxiety to get enough practice, for as they did not leave off work until it was dark they had no chance to keep in training after tea. So they actually used to get up at 6 o'clock in the morning and play football by moonlight before going off to work. Imagine that on a cold and frosty morning! I really begin to believe that there is something in this decadence of the modern generation business.

At first they played on the Bell Field, but when the Institute and recreation ground was opened in January 1900 they played there on and off until it was found impossible to maintain a football ground in the winter and a cricket pitch in the summer; so they arranged to use the Bell Field, and have played there since. Between the wars Ted Field was very much involved with Ticehurst football as secretary to the club and to the Ticehurst League. Since the Second World War the club has maintained continuous football in various local leagues with inconsistent results, having played for the last 24 years in the East Sussex League, now fielding two teams. Numerous individuals have been actively involved since the war, chief amongst them being Arthur 'Jonah' Jones, a member for over 50 years, Ray Prince, Alec Whiteman and 'Best' Thampsett. The present chairman and secretary are both long-standing members, Ronald Kirkby and Andrew Stanbridge respectively.

Stonegate: Stonegate had no separate team and always played with Ticehurst except for one or two seasons in about 1949.

Flimwell: Ray Barfoot's memories are worth quoting in full:

Football has been played at Flimwell for at least 100 years. My grandfather used to take players to matches in a horse and cart around the turn of the century. In those days, and certainly up to the second world war, it was often the village pub that provided changing rooms and a tin bath, full of cold water, to wash off the mud afterwards. It was also obvious that the licensing laws either did not exist or were flouted, as beer was dispensed directly after the game and revelry would often go on until closing time.

My father recounts that having won an important game at Smarden, 50 or so years ago, and duly celebrated at the local pub, it was decided that two cars full of players would visit the *Miners' Arms* at Churchsettle (now a pub no more). On the way the driver of one of the cars, a certain Bill Young, realised he had a puncture in a rear wheel. A band of inebriated helpers leapt out to render assistance, but when they were driving away afterwards the punctured tyre was still there as they had changed the wrong wheel! I suspect they drank real beer in those days.

Football was always played in the field adjoining the *Hare and Hounds* until 1974 when the new playing field was taken over. The Flimwell soccer team of the 1920s and 1930s was certainly the strongest in the area, and all the players lived within half a mile of the crossroads — truly a village team.

In a remarkable period from 1927-1932 Flimwell won the Weald of Kent league — which included towns like Rye, Battle and Tenterden — five consecutive times. They also won the Ticehurst and District league five times in this period as well as the prestigious Hawkhurst Charity cup in 1932. In two consecutive seasons in this period they were unbeaten. The side included my father Alf, a prolific goalscorer centre-forward, and his three brothers, Arthur, Frederick and Stanley.

Footpaths

In the 1950s the local authority produced a 'definitive map' of all the footpaths and bridleways in the district and the parish council formed a sub-committee under the chairmanship of Hubert Beale of Dunster's Mill to look after them. A lot of work was put in and they were all signposted, cleared and kept in order. Gradually interest waned and in 1975 John King formed a Footpath Society with the aim of keeping the paths clear and to get people interested in using them. At the moment about nineteen households belong and they meet on the second Sunday in every month. Great enthusiasm is shown and they are doing a grand job.

The Sussex Express for 20 October 1838 contains a brief paragraph about a vigorous old gentleman, 'Mr. Edwards, glover, of this place' who, in spite of being in his 94th year, 'walked last week from hence to Lewes, a distance of 24 miles, without any inconvenience to himself. Notwithstanding his vast age, Mr. Edwards can still make a glove with neatness and dispatch'. A 'John Edwards, Village Glover' appears in the rate book for 1792.

Gardeners' Association

The Ticehurst Gardeners and Allotment Holders Association, as it was formerly called, has its origins lost in the mists of antiquity; it was probably started at the beginning of this century or the end of the last. Its object has always been to promote an interest in the growing of flowers, fruit and vegetables and, latterly, in wine-making, handicrafts etc. At first there were classes for large houses with professional gardeners, for smaller houses and cottages and for holders of the hundred or so allotments in the parish. There are now 72 classes and they are open to members of the Association or to residents in Ticehurst, Stonegate or Flimwell, and the subscription is now £1 per year.

The summer show has always been the main attraction of the year and for the last few seasons a spring show has been held as well. Until about 1950 the summer show was always held on the recreation ground, with an enormous marquee for all the exhibits and a smaller one for sit-down cream teas. A full brass band was hired for the occasion and there were numerous side-shows, sports for the children and teenagers and usually one special event such as a motorcycle rodeo. Usually the local travelling fair would arrive, complete with steam engines, merry-go-rounds, dodgem cars and their own side-shows. This was the big event of the village year. Everyone would turn up and a lot of money changed hands, usually to the great advantage of the Association. With rapid post-war inflation it became impossible to cover the expenses and the outside activities were gradually terminated and the show moved inside.

The membership is now over 120 and meetings are held monthly at *The Bell*. Fourteen trophies are presented annually, and these — mostly silver — now have a value of about £4,000. A trading hut supplies fertilisers and other requisites for members and has a turnover of about £1,200 p.a. There is now an inter-society competition between Ticehurst, Hurst Green, Brightling, Etchingham and Wadhurst; one village is chosen each year as the venue and the different societies put on exhibits which are judged.

Good Companions

This organisation for the over 60s came into being largely owing to the foresight of a very caring Medical Officer of Health at Battle (Dr. Silverton). He persuaded a number of people to found a club in Ticehurst and the inaugural meeting was held at the Village

Club on 8 January 1959 with 27 members present. Joan Drewe was elected the first president and has been so ever since; the membership is now about fifty, but has been as high as 120. They meet once a month for a tea party with guest speaker or entertainment and have several coach outings during the year. The highlight is a grand Christmas lunch party, and there is no doubt that the club is very popular and fills a much felt need.

Meals on Wheels
This, like the Good Companions, was also the brainchild of Dr. Silverton and relies on a band of volunteers, working on a rota system, to distribute hot lunches sent out three times a week from Battle to old and infirm people in Ticehurst who would have difficulty in fending for themselves. The numbers vary but there are now about twelve, and there is no doubt that this too provides a much appreciated local service.

The Mothers' Union
Founded in Ticehurst in 1918, Mrs. Darby was the first to enroll, and by 1938 there were 118 members. Now known as St Mary's Fellowship, the group meets once a month at various houses.

The Red Cross
A branch of the Red Cross was formed here in 1942 to train in first aid. F.A. post was at Pickforde. Part-time nursing was instigated to help out at Furze House. The branch was disbanded in 1946, but a Cadet Unit was formed in 1951 and at the age of 15 cadets were enrolled as full members. First aid and home nursing were taught and they now help local doctors and nurses if required.

The Royal British Legion
The men's section was formed on 25 June 1921 at *The Bell* which was to become their headquarters, and the first president was Capt. E. G. Bramall. Annual parades with standards have been held at the war memorial every year since then, except during the Second World War, followed by a service of remembrance in church. Poppy day collections are held each November for the Earl Haig Fund and a special Christmas Appeal results in a large hand-out to deserving people. Regular meetings are held. One very distinguished member was Field Marshal Sir Geoffrey Baker — always known as George — Master Gunner St James Park and Governor of the Tower of London, who joined in 1971. Capt. A. C. (Bronnie) Duckworth R.N. was a very active president for many years until his death in 1987 and kept the branch very much alive during the difficult years of the '70s and '80s. He was awarded the Royal British Legion Gold Badge and started the very successful Christmas Appeal.

The Women's section was formed on 3 April 1951 because a number of women had served with the forces, and it was thought a good idea that they should have an organisation of their own to keep up their camaraderie side by side with the men's section. The first president was Joan Drewe, and in the first year there were 51 members, but support has waned considerably since then. Their standard is always paraded with the men's, and for a long time they organised the Poppy Day collection.

Scouts and Guides
Started in Ticehurst in 1922 by Admiral Harper who lived at The Yett, the group first met in a cottage opposite the church. It later moved to a small wooden building opposite the old laundry in Lower Platts which had previously been used as overnight

accommodation for laundry staff, and from there to the Drill Hall. Admiral Harper was succeeded in turn by Albert Colvin and Robert Field. The troop attended the Wembley Jamboree in 1924 and the following year went camping in France. One of the earliest members was Tom Newman who joined when he was 13, the troop at that time having four patrols: Beavers, Wolves, Kangaroos and Lions, the total number of boys being about twenty. Stonegate never had a separate troop, but Flimwell had one for a number of years until about 1960.

In 1935 the troop was sadly closed down due to a lack of a suitable scoutmaster and the equipment was given to the Flimwell troop. In about 1959 Mr. E. Wickeson restarted the troop at the invitation of the Rev. Mr. Law, and Mrs. Simms started the cub pack. Mr. Wickeson continued for six years until he moved and handed over to Walter Brown, who retired in 1976 due to poor health whenthe troop was closed again, but the cub pack continued.

In 1979, with eight boys from the pack, Peter Collins and A. Warlow restarted the troop which continues today. The present H.Q. was conceived at a meeting in 1981 when the troop was based at The Highlands in the grounds of Ticehurst House. It was clear that a permanent H.Q. was needed and the decision to raise funds was taken then and the present building was erected down Pickforde Lane. Today Margaret Poland is group leader, R. Piper is group chairman and there is a flourishing membership.

Snooker League

Billiards has been played at the Village Club, or Institute as it was originally called, since its foundation in 1900, and in 1948 a separate Billiards Club was formed: a club within a club with its own rules and finances. Very soon snooker became the main activity and billiards has not been played since 1984. They became part of the Hurst Green League and purchased a second table from their own resources. From then on Ticehurst has had two teams and in 1951 they won division two of the league. In 1988 they won the first division and there are about thirty active members in the Ticehurst Club today.

Toc H

Originally founded during the First World War by the Rev. 'Tubby' Clayton at Talbot House, a branch was established here soon after hostilities had finished and flourished for a time. It appealed largely to veterans of that war and by about 1970 the active membership was down to four. Now it has ceased, although a banner still hangs in the church.

The Women's Institute

Stonegate and Flimwell once had separate branches, but some time ago they merged with Ticehurst, whose group was founded in July 1918 with 40 members, and Lady Julian Parr, who had just come to live at the Gravel Pit, was their first president. The initial project seems to have been smocking, and they held regular classes which must have been very popular because, at their second annual meeting in 1920, their membership had grown to 200. Smocking became a flourishing industry. Monthly meetings were held in the Village Club, and also classes and lectures of all kinds, concerts and plays. Membership reached 224 and then settled down to about 150.

The Youth Club

Ticehurst: The Youth Club was formed in about 1955 by Brigadier Geoffrey Marnham with its own committee to regulate activities. A few years later he was instrumental in raising funds and obtaining grants to build the present Youth Centre which was added on to the eastern end of the Village Club. The club members elected their own management committee, but the premises were vested in a Charitable Trust, whose function has now been taken over by the Parish Council.

Stonegate: Stonegate now has a junior and senior youth club, run by the headmaster of the primary school, Henry King.

Flimwell: In about 1955 a group of youngsters founded a youth club and raised money to buy the Sunnybank Rooms; sadly through lack of numbers the club has closed down and the building is held on trust.

Chapels

Ticehurst: Ticehurst had two chapels, as already mentioned: the Wesleyan chapel opposite Marlpit Gardens, which was licensed for marriages in 1870, and a Baptist chapel behind.

Stonegate: Stonegate had no chapel except the one at Shovers Green which is in Wadhurst parish.

24. Baptist chapel in Flimwell, *c.*1890.

Flimwell: Flimwell had a Baptist chapel in the High Street in part of what was then Pankhursts Stores and a Wesleyan chapel in Union Street near the workhouse. All of these chapels are now discontinued and are used for other purposes.

Chapter Ten

Around the Parish[1 63 78 56 23]

We will now take a tour around the parish, noting any buildings of historical or architectural interest; in this respect reference is made to the schedule of listed buildings kept by the Local Authority, to the *Victoria County History of Sussex*, to previous histories of the area and to local knowledge of many people still living. There are also three maps which will be referred to constantly in the following pages: a 1612 estate map showing the lands of Anthony Apsley Esq., Lord of the Manor of Hammerden; the 1839 tithe map of Ticehurst, and the 1873 O.S. map. All these are at the Record Office in Lewes and will be called the 1612, 1839 and 1873 maps.

In the 1612 map there is a little sketch of each house, and about 35 can be identified in the village itself, mostly two-storied with pitched roofs and chimneys, and in the same places as the buildings are today. A number of properties will be listed in capital letters, e.g. HAMMERDEN, and these will be dealt with in the next chapter with a more detailed

25. Cooper's Stores and Church Street in about 1900.

description of the houses and the families who have lived there. We will start in Ticehurst and work outwards to Flimwell and Stonegate, beginning from the centre of the village.

As one comes out of the north gate of the churchyard there is, in front and to the right, the range of buildings known as Coopers Stores, and in the last century as Petitt & Sanders (Joseph Petitt, grocer, was the originator of the trust deed for the school in 1846). This is an 18th-century front to a 16th-century building with a timber-framed back range, in the remodelled roof of which are many original timbers and an enriched barge-board with the initials W.M. and the date 1605. It was formerly a large general store with a grocery department to the south and a drapery shop to the north; it now has two shop-fronts at the south end and Warwick house is part of the same building. One-hundred-and-fifty years ago this was the site of the *Unicorn Inn*, much frequented by smugglers. The posts between the road and the pavement in front have recently been replaced.

The next building is the early 18th-century pharmacy, and next to this is Holgate House, built in about 1830. Mr. Gillham once lived there and it was occupied during the 1930s by Mr. Mercer, a shoemaker. Next are the Central Stores variously called Gillhams, Dungeys and Buttons. It is an 18th-century building of painted brick with a modern shop window, and since about 1900 it was mainly owned by those three families. The *Duke of York* is part of the same building, and probably dates from Regency times; in 1851 the landlord was Thomas Winch. A framed history of the inn hangs in the bar, and says that the *Duke of York* started in 1602 with a licence to sell beer and cider, the landlord then being Caleb Farehill; that it was once a coaching inn and the mails were sorted there; that after the turnpikes were abolished it fell on lean times and part of it was used as a butcher's shop and that in the 19th century nearly all of the landlords were butchers. No authority is given for any of this and it has not been possible to confirm, but the present building is early 18th- century.

Opposite Coopers Stores is one building consisting of five cottages (21-25 Church Street), 17th-century or earlier, re-faced with stucco on the ground floor and tile-hung above. Next to that is another building of about the same size and date, formerly Old Timbers, now called Northgate House which although much altered retains some 16th-century work in the roof and has ceiling beams and exposed joists on both floors. It used to be a house and shop, kept by Field the butcher, but is now one dwelling, timber-framed and re-fronted with brick below and tile-hung above. Like the previous building, this once had an overhanging upper storey; the northern part is mid-16th century and was originally heated by a timber chimney. The southern part was added later the same century and, when built, was gabled to the street. During the 17th century the building incorporated a mercer's shop run by William Denley and Thomas Lawrence.

Next comes an L-shaped building of about 1830 now containing three shops (Cheryl, Leslie and Leach), and next to that Franklyn Villa, where Mr. Sancto the cobbler had his shop, and the post office, and beyond that, set back from the road, is a single building comprising Caxton Cottage, Old Merryams and Beech House. This is timber-framed and re-faced with red brick and grey headers with roughcast and imitation timbers above, a parapet at each end of the front and a steeply pitched hip-tiled roof. The east range incorporates a 15th-century hall, with a first floor and chimney-stack inserted in about 1600. The interior has moulded ceiling beams of 15th- and 17th-century date, and the roof retains an original cambered tie-beam with octagonal king-post, and other smoke-blackened timbers. Caxton House was the site of Beech House Press, run for many years by Jack Oliver, which later moved to where Cheryl the cleaners are now. From there up to the High Street is another very similar building of the 17th century, containing Ford the Butcher, Lloyd's Bank and, on the corner, a small part now used as an office, but at one time it was 'ye Olde Sweet Shoppe' which later moved further up High Street as mentioned below.

Going up the High Street on the left-hand side there is a small 18th-century house, painted brick below, weather-boarding above, attached to what is now the early 19th-century Plantation Tea Company, which was kept for many years by Mrs. Hodges as a sweet shop. Then, standing back from the road, is Beech House with white painted weather-board and a small shop attached, projecting nearly to the street, which used to be the pharmacy. This was kept for many years by Mr. Siggers, a little old man with gold-rimmed spectacles on the end of his nose who would surely have qualified for the title 'Apothecary'! The shelves were crammed with jars and huge glass bottles containing liquids of many colours and the whole set-up looked like something straight out of Dickens. Adjoining this is a new shop attached to Field's, having on the north side a small 19th-century shop front, formerly a draper's shop kept for a long time by Miss Field.

26. Church Street, c.1920.

After the lane comes Tile Cottage, formerly the coal office and then two similar 18th-century buildings, red brick below and tile-hung above, nos. 1-8 Hazelwood Cottages, and then North Fields Cottage. That is the end of the old village and the rest will be described under Wadhurst Road. Opposite these cottages is the early 19th-century Croft Cottage and next to that, going back down the street, is a large 19th-century shop, now empty, which was for 172 years Waterhouse's Stores, and before that on the same site was the original workhouse, built in 1761 at the expense of the parish. Then there are two cottages and what was once Marlpit Dairy. Here Mr. Bishop had his jewellers and

27. High Street, *c.*1920.

28. Ticehurst village square and *The Bell Hotel*.

watchmakers shop for many years, and the clock at the village club was supplied by him and has his name on the dial. Mr. Booker took over from him and remained there until his retirement in about 1970. After that is the footpath leading back to the Cross and then one building containing an estate agents, The Surgery and Croft Villa, formerly two cottages, all 18th-century. Then there is the bakery and the NatWest Bank, all one early 19th- century building, red brick below, tile-hung above.

After a gap comes the *Bell Hotel*, a 16th-century timber-framed building formerly with an overhanging upper storey now re-faced with red brick below and tile-hung above. There is a modern gable projection in imitation timber-work forming a porch with roof over and an 18th-century extension to the east with two window bays. The inn is almost certainly very much older than this, and would have been the original staging post for all the old coaches. There is a framed notice in the bar tracing the history back to 1296, but again no authority is given for the very doubtful statements made! Between the *Bell* and the cottages were the stables and coach-houses which were demolished when no longer required and the ground grassed over; it has now been made into a car-park for the inn. John Adams is shown as the innkeeper in 1851 and Mr. F. Skerrett was landlord there for many years until 1903. For the last 50 years or so it has been run by the late Mr. and Mrs. Reeves and their daughter Pam.

Below this are the three Bell Cottages in one 18th-century building, painted brick below and tile-hung above. Behind the inn is the Bell Field which is used by the football club and for other purposes; there, too, is the council car park. Then, after PICKFORDE Lane, APSLEY COURT stands back from the road, as does also THE YETT. There follows Duette the hairdressers, a 19th-century building, and then *The Chequers* with two cottages adjacent, and the old almshouses behind. The inn itself is 19th-century but one of the two cottages is of 16th-century origin, and the other is probably 18th-century. It is interesting that on the 1839 map the two cottages are shown and their occupants are listed separately, but the inn did not exist then, and it is not listed as such in the 1851 census. *The Chequers* used to be 'a common lodging house', obliged to put up all and sundry who asked for shelter for the night and, when the workhouse was full, they would take in men and bed them down in the barn behind! That is really the end of the old village in this direction.

On the opposite side of the road is The Long House, formerly called Laurel Lodge, an early 19th-century building of no particular merit, for a long time the home and yard of Startin, the builder, who used to employ up to 50 men. Next to it, coming back up the hill are nos. 1 and 2 Cerne Cottages, one early 19th-century building faced with weather boarding. Then there is Westbourne Villa of the same date, used as a surgery in the 1930s and, next to that, The Cottage, faced with weather-boarding, of a century before. In front of this is The Corner Shop, a single-storey building which has had rather a chequered history and is not shown on the 1873 map or any of the previous ones. Mr. Amos French kept a general store here at the beginning of the century which stocked giant cheeses out of which mice could be seen popping their heads! He pushed a cart of groceries and a barrel of paraffin round the parish and there is a story that he would tell of a night when he got lost in Bedgebury Wood and shouted out: 'Man lost, man lost'. An owl replied 'Woo-ooo-ooo', and he answered 'Mr. Amos French from Ticehurst'.

In the little road leading up to St Mary's Lane there is, on the right-hand side, Woodbine House; early 19th-century, faced with weather-boarding, tiled above, with a small ground-floor addition which used to be the original post office. On the opposite side of the lane is the L-shaped 18th-century house, Whatmans, of painted brick with a slate roof and modern porch and weather-boarded on the first floor. The south-west wing is curved to follow the line of the lane.

29. The entrance to St Mary's Lane, *c*.1900.

Going back to the High Street there is some modern development and then Ticehurst Motors which was still at the beginning of this century the principal forge in the village. The bus shelter (as mentioned in chapter eight) was once the village pump, and it is worth repeating that a hexagonal structure, which must surely have been the village well, is shown on the 1612 map in that exact place.

Going down St Mary's Lane from the Church Gate, there are two buildings on the right, each containing two cottages; nos. 1 and 2 are 16th-century and 3 and 4 are 18th-century, and opposite these is an attractive new house called Coopers Cottage. Below this the small lane leads to the High Street and then there is a cottage, then Fairview, which was once a saddler's shop, and finally 18th-century White Cottage, of two stories faced with weather-boarding, a hipped slate roof and a doorway in a moulded architrave surround, which was once a dressmaker's.

On the opposite side of the road is the modern development of St Mary's Close, with one vacant plot which was refused planning permission to preserve the view of the church from this aspect. After long discussions it was offered by the developers to the Parochial Church Council who accepted it and it is now held by the vicar and churchwardens on trust. There is more modern development on this side of the lane, including the large modern automatic telephone exchange mentioned in chapter eight.

This leaves Church Street in the village proper; starting from the Church Gate again, on the left are the two Church Gate Cottages. Originally there were four more below them, but they were purchased by Mrs. Campbell Newington at the beginning of the century and demolished to open up the church. Opposite these cottages is one building, previously two dwellings, re-built in 1758 (as the date on the chimney stack shows, with

30. Balcombe's saddler's shop in St Mary's Lane.

31. St Mary's Lane.

the initials I.N.E.) by John Noakes and his wife, timber-framed re-faced with weather-boarding below and tile-hung above, with 19th-century windows and an 18th-century doorway. It contains four cottages, the upper one of which was, for over 100 years, a tailor's shop. The last to practise this trade was Mr. Laing, who as a very old man used to sit cross-legged in the window sewing his cloth; he finally retired in about 1950. In the 18th century it seems to have been called *The Chequers* and it has been said that it was once a pub. If this is so it may be that it moved when the present inn of that name was built in about 1850.

32.   Church Street in 1938.

Adjacent to this is another rather similar building containing two cottages, and then we come to Gable End, set back from the road and built about 1830. Cinque Cottage comes next, formerly two dwellings, mainly 17th- and early 18th-century, but incorporating 16th-century remains, timber-framed with plaster infilling. The decorative panel in the north side wall is unusual locally. Romany Cottage (again previously two) of about the same date is of painted brick with a tiled roof. Two more small houses follow of a later date and then the lane to the Old Forge. This was a smithy until about 1950 and was kept latterly by Mr. Croft who owned and worked it for a great many years, and his father before him. The lane, now blocked off, used to continue on to Rosehill and Sunnyside Cottages which are now approached by the lane opposite Churchgate Cottages. There used to be a builders' yard and coal-merchant there.

Below the lane is Church House, an early 19th-century building, painted brick with weather-boarding above, opposite the lower church steps. It is believed to have been built on the site of a 17th-century building — or maybe earlier — sometime during the 1700s. It was used as the school house, having no windows at the rear and only a Jacob's ladder leading up to the first floor. The workshops were added in the early 1820s by the Young family, builders and undertakers — latterly undertakers — who lived and worked there until 1978, shortly before the death of Frank Young, the fourth generation to do so. It then reverted to a family home, only leaving the possession of the Young family in 1988. Next to that are the four Campbell Cottages, in one building of brick and tile, erected by Miss Margaret Foster — later Mrs. Campbell Newington — in about 1885 in memory of her uncle, John Rea Campbell, who built the original house at Oakover. Then there is Bardens which was built by Miss Marjory Hardcastle in about 1936 and finally Hurst Cottage, formerly nos. 1 and 2 Church Street, an 18th-century building with 19th-century gabled porch.

On the opposite side of the road is THE VICARAGE (described in chapter five), THE SCHOOL (chapter seven) and THE OLD VICARAGE (chapter five). That is really the end of the village in this direction and going on down the hill should be called Wardsbrook Road. We come then to OAKOVER set back on the left with the stable block and clock tower opposite — now made into four separate houses. Sheepwash Farm, which was originally built, about 1905, as the kennels for Oakover is approached down a steep lane. Below Oakover is PARSONAGE FARMHOUSE with its cluster of farm buildings and adjoining Sussex Fireplaces, the buildings having been constructed by the author as a saw-mill in 1950 and discontinued 10 years later.

At the bottom of the hill is the lane leading off on the right to WEDDS FARM and almost opposite is WARDSBROOK FARM. The parish ends at the bridge over the stream and starts again at the bad corner after Myskins, the latter being in Etchingham parish.

Starting again where we left off in the High Street and going towards Wadhurst, we come to Warren's Coach Station, where there was once a quarry for stone used in the restoration of the church and then Hillbury council houses, both described in chapter eight. Opposite them is some modern development, built after the old forge kept by Malpass and Gillhams coal wharf had been demolished in 1933, leading up to the lane to Threeleg Cross. At the junction with the lane is Tollgate, originally the Toll House c.1762, having one storey faced with weather-boarding painted white and a hipped tiled roof. Opposite this is Hillbury, a Victorian house, used between 1939 and 1960 as the vicarage.

After Hillbury there are several houses built within the last 30 years on the site of what was The Gables, formerly Prospect House. This was the residence of the Medical Superintendent of Ticehurst House and was pulled down in about 1950, as was THE VINEYARD in the angle between the main road and Vineyard Lane. Just before this junction, on the other side of the road, are several fairly modern houses and also the much older GRAVEL PIT. Continuing along towards Wadhurst, standing back on the right-hand side is the large building of TICEHURST HOUSE and, in the grounds, THE HIGHLANDS; both of these and the Vineyard are mentioned in chapter fourteen.

Further along on the left is Brickkiln Farm, which was the Home Farm for Ticehurst House and had a private nine-hole golf course in the fields below. After that is the long drive leading down to EAST LYMDEN, and opposite is Burnt Lodge Lane with a group of four modern cottages on the corner, built to replace The Ridgeway which was destroyed by a bomb in the last war. Then there is Limden Lane which will be covered under Stonegate, and further on, on the other side, is the lane going to Spindlewood Guest House. This was previously called Woodlands and will be discussed in chapter fourteen together with Quarry Villa, now called Stone Place, both of which belonged to Ticehurst House.

We come next to the hamlet of Wallcrouch with a cluster of houses on either side of the road. Wallcrouch Farmhouse is an 18th-century red-brick building with weather-

33. Wallcrouch.

boarding above, and The Old Farmhouse, which was at one time two cottages of about the same date or a little earlier, is also of red brick but tile-hung above. The Rosary is a listed building of red brick with grey headers with white painted weather-boarding on the west side. The Yew Tree is an attractive house, brick below and weather-boarded above. New Pond Farm is just outside the hamlet on the left and the Cattle Breeding Station on the right. Then comes the drive on the left leading down to Bugseys Farm where an attempt was made to drill for oil a few years ago without success, and further along are the Brickyard Cottages on the left, these last two being in Stonegate parish. Opposite is the drive leading down to Holbeamwood, the north wing of which is 18th-century, with red brick and grey headers, stringcourse, eaves cornice of brick cogging, and a tiled roof. The south wing of one window bay was added early in the 19th century.

The parish boundary is at Shovers Green and follows the line of Bardown Road up to the main road. The old chapel on the corner is in Wadhurst parish but WHILIGH is in Ticehurst, as is Shovers Green House on the left. This is an L-shaped building with an early 19th-century front to a probably older building which is of red brick and tile-hung above.

Taking the various lanes which lead off the main road and starting with Vineyard Lane; this leads round the back of Ticehurst House and passes Broomden, a lovely 18th-century farmhouse, red brick below and tile-hung above with a hipped tiled roof, and nearby a 17th-century barn faced with weather-boarding and with a hipped tiled roof with central wagon entrance on the east side with pentice to the north and south of this and tie beams with arched braces inside. Further down the lane is Burnt Lodge Lane and, turning right, the mid-18th century house of Burnt Lodge is on the left. Further on is the beautiful 15th-century house of ROWLEY. The road ends here, having been cut off when the reservoir was made, and Copens Farm further down is no more. Neither is Tindalls Cottage, a late 17th-century building taken down when the reservoir came and now awaiting re-erection at the Weald and Downland Open Air Museum, near Chichester.

Back up the lane to the crossroads and turning right we come to Upper and Lower Tolhurst, both listed buildings, and on to Birchetts Green, a 17th-century or earlier timber-framed building re-faced with weather-boarding. On then to Chessons Cottages, an 18th-century building with two parallel ranges re-faced with red brick below and tile-hung above. There is a fine barn there of similar or earlier date and construction. Chessons Farmhouse is to the north of the cottages and is of 16th-century date; it was fully timber-framed, but is now brick below, weather-boarded above, and has been extended at both ends. Depending on which road we take we can come to Bryants Farm, a small 17th-century or earlier timber-framed building, red brick below and tile-hung above. New Barn Farm is nearby in Ward's Lane and is a similar style of house, both having splendid views over the reservoir.

Claphatch is said to have been an old timber-framed building re-faced in the 19th century, with two oast houses and a granary adjacent. The last house before the road is cut again by the reservoir is Beaumans, an 18th-century building with two parallel ranges, red brick below and tile-hung above. The Old Farmhouse, built originally as a small 15th-century hall-type house is opposite and is a timber-framed building re-faced with red brick and grey headers and tile-hung above; it was doubled in length in the 16th century, the original part then being downgraded to a kitchen, an unusual layout. Nearby is Beaumans Oast, all grade II listed buildings. The Fuggle family farmed here for several generations and grew hops, one famous strain of which (the Fuggle Hop) was named after them. They were finally driven out because most of their land was flooded, but the family has now returned to Chessons, nearby.

Returning to Threeleg Cross and taking the lane leading thereto we come first to Cross Lane House with the Cross Lane Gardens estate behind and Landscapes Farm on the corner and then to the Cross with *THE BULL INN* at the junction and a number of cottages clustered around. April, Prospect and Ebeneezer Cottages form an L-shaped range dating from the early 19th century, and most of the others are similar. Down the lane to the left is Boarders Farmhouse, which was a 17th-century barn onto which a small cottage was added in the 18th century. The barn section was only converted into a house this century. The upper floor is tile-hung in the front and weather-boarded behind. Taking the right fork brings us to BAKERS FARM and beyond is UPPER HAZELHURST — Lower Hazelhurst is now under the water. Taking Huntley Mill Road we pass NORWOODS FARM on the left and the new Overy' Farmhouse on the right, built recently to replace the original farmhouse which had stood nearby for centuries but is now submerged. Further along we come to DUNSTERS MILL HOUSE which has been moved bodily up the hill above the water-line.

Now, going back into the village and taking the Hurst Green road, after the *Chequers*, where we left off, there is the entrance to the large council estate of Springfields, and in front of this there are the warden care flats known as Woodroffe Lodge because they were built on the site of what was once the home of Dr. Woodroffe, a much respected family doctor who practised in the parish for a great many years. Likewise, the other block of similar houses down Pickforde Lane was called Newington Court after another well-known local medical family; and then some relatively modern development before coming to the former Wesleyan chapel, erected in 1897 as a successor to two previous buildings on the same site built in 1821 and 1840; the latter also contained two

34.   Threeleg Cross.

35.   The Lodge with Mrs. Woodroffe and her daughter Violet.

schoolrooms and a cottage. It fell into disuse after the last war and is now flats. There
used to be a Calvinist chapel behind.

Next to the chapel is Clayhams, an attractive tile-hung house of indeterminate age,
and opposite is the relatively modern estate of Marlpit Gardens. THE INSTITUTE
(chapter seven) is on the right, and next to that used to be a small hut, now a garage,
where Mr. Hodgkin the cobbler sat all day mending shoes. Opposite is Park Garage,
which until about 1960 consisted of a large corrugated iron shed much nearer the road
and was kept for many years by Mr. Debley. Little Clayhams is next to the garage and is a
listed 18th-century building, once two cottages, of red brick with grey headers and tile-
hung above. Facing that, in the angle of the junction, is Lower Tollgate, which was
originally what its name implies. It is an 18th-century L-shaped listed building, once
three cottages, of painted brick and tile-hung above.

36. Lower Platts, c.1920.

SINGEHURST on the right, now two houses, is 17th-century or earlier. Gibbs Reed
Farmhouse is an L-shaped 18th-century building, mostly faced with red brick below and
tile-hung above, but with some weather-boarding. Birchenwood Farm stands on the
sharp bend and the Cottage is early 19th-century, faced with weather-boarding, a hipped
slate roof and a gabled porch. PASHLEY MANOR, the only grade I listed building in the
parish, comes next, Three Gates Farm is in Etchingham and Little Boarzell is in
Ticehurst. It is a double L-shaped building of the 17th century or earlier, with a stuccoed
ground floor, tile-hung above, two small gables over first floor windows and weather-
boarded west gable-end. London Barn Farm and Swiftsden Farm off the road at the
bottom of the hill are also in Ticehurst, but Swiftsden House is not. Neither is the
modern Boarzell, although OLD BOARZELL was.

37. Ticehurst Union Workhouse.

38. *The Welcome Stranger* in 1904.

If we go back to Lower Tollgate and take the Flimwell road we pass on the left the site of the old laundry and, behind it, the site of the gasworks and the builders' yard. After that comes the modern development of Acres Rise and Lower Platts, and opposite is the Police House and then Horsegrove Avenue. On the left is the road leading to the new house and buildings of Steellands Farm and then the *Cherry Tree Inn*, which is an 18th-century building, of painted brick and tile-hung above, shown as two cottages on the 1839 map and not listed as an inn in 1851, so the pub presumably dates from after that. The one-way system at Dalehill follows. DALEHILL FARMHOUSE is described separately. In the middle between the two roads are one or two old cottages and quite a lot of modern ones, and there used to be a laundry here. The Dalehill golf course has its club house on top of the hill, and the entrance is just over the brow on the right. It was established and constructed by Anthony Wilson in the 1970s. The sewage treatment works are below the golf course.

At the bottom of the hill Tinkers Lane goes off to the left with the group of Coronation Cottages on the corner. The lane then makes a sweep and comes out at Threeleg Cross, passing Walters Farm, which is an L-shaped 18th-century or earlier building faced with weather-board, with a tile-hung south wall and stuccoed chimney breast. After this comes Berners Hill and Rosemary Lane, which is the boundary between Ticehurst and Flimwell. Going down this lane DOWNASH is on the left, and further down we come to Ketleys, a mid-18th century farmhouse nearly identical in design to Burnt Lodge. Another 16th-century building, which was known as Ketley Cottage, was moved to Cousley Wood when the reservoir was built. Ballards Wood, once a farmhouse, is on the left near the bottom. Ticehurst Parish finishes with the causeway over the top of the reservoir.

Going east from the top of Rosemary Lane we are in Union Street, Flimwell. On the left is the site of the old Workhouse, later called Furze House, a home run by the County Council for old people and families who were unable to support themselves; it is now a small private housing estate called Bewl Close. Next to that is the site of the former nurseries and, opposite, the road down to QUEDLEY. There is scattered ribbon development, mostly modern with a few old cottages, up to the crossroads, and there used to be a Baptist chapel there. Now there is a post office and one or two small shops. There was once a pub here, called *The Welcome Stranger*, but this was closed about the beginning of this century and was incorporated into Pankhurst's Stores, now a small restaurant. It is not listed as an inn in the 1851 census.

Flimwell was originally open common land with a few scattered cottages and is shown thus on 'The Dalehill Map' of about 1630 (E.S.C.R.O. Add Ms4614) with a number of tracks or paths crossing the London to Hastings road. The crossroads were re-aligned in 1931 and on the corner is Alsford's sawmill and garden centre and shop for D.I.Y. materials. They salvaged the old signpost, restored it and re-erected it outside their premises. Down London Road there is a coach station on the left and, on the other side, *The Royal Oak* public house, kept by Joseph Walker in 1851. The landlord says he was told by Courage, the brewers, that their records show it was built in 1792, but he has found much older cellars below and thinks that there was previously an inn on the same site.

The parish and county boundary comes just before the dual carriageway starts. Back on the main road towards Hastings we pass YELLOWCOAT WOOD (chapter two). Mumpumps has two parallel ranges, the rear one probably of 17th-century date and tile-hung; Roughfields nearby is modern. The lane on the left leads to Boundary and Brookgate Farms; the former is 18th-century or earlier with one storey and attic, weather-boarded; the latter is an L-shaped house 100 years older re-faced in the 19th

39. Flimwell in 1920.

40. Flimwell crossroads in 1931.

41. The reconstruction of Flimwell crossroads in 1931.

century, with two stories and attic, red brick below and tile-hung above. At the south-west of the south wing is a massive shouldered red-brick chimney breast. There are also two attractive oast houses and a granary, kept by John Vidler in 1851. The parish boundary is at the point where this lane joins the main road.

42.   Flimwell High Street in 1931.

The remaining part of Flimwell is from the crossroads along the road to Hawkhurst. The *Hare and Hounds* public house is on the corner, an old coaching inn which was certainly well-established by 1765 when a lease of 21 years was granted to Thomas Hilder at 5s. 0d. per year. In 1792 it was occupied by John Hilder and in 1806 a new lease was granted to Samuel Vidler for 21 years at 7s. 6d. From the top of the hill onwards the area is known as Sunnybank. At the brow of the hill on the left is Mount Farm, now a fish smokery, where once stood a large windmill, demolished in 1902, this and the farm being worked for many years by the Barfoot family. There are some cottages on the right and to the north is the entrance to the youth club and into Bedgebury Forest, which suffered badly in the hurricane of 1987. Further down is Sunnybank garage and on the other side the Old Vicarage, built at the same time as the church, about 1839, similar to houses in Calverley Park, Tunbridge Wells, and probably designed by Decimus Burton. Next was the school, destroyed by a flying bomb in 1944 and then the church, described in chapter six. Mount Pleasant Farm is opposite on the left and shortly after is the drive leading to SEACOX HEATH on the right, followed almost at once by the parish and county boundary.

Now for Stonegate: we left Ticehurst at Wardsbrook Bridge; continuing over this we are in Etchingham, and Sheepstreet Lane forking left at the junction is entirely in that parish; so is the road to the right until the bad bend after Myskins, known locally as 'death corner'. Then we enter Stonegate and come to COTTENDEN which was originally a small village called Cottenden Street in the 16th/17th century (see 1612 map of the Hammerden manorial survey). There is a converted oast house on the left, and straight on there is Hoadley on the left and then two cottages known as Clayhall Cottage and Little Ale House. This was formerly a beer house called also *The Welcome*

43. Windmill at Mount Farm, Flimwell.

44. Ticehurst from Myskyns, *c.*1900.

Stranger and is marked thus on the 1873 map, but is not shown in the 1851 census. Opposite this is Bearhurst Farm, formerly Winters Farm, which was the original egg-packing station for Stonegate Eggs which started after the Second World War. Old Bearhurst was down near the river and approached through Hammerden Farm and continuing on along the lane; it was burnt down in 1952 and has not been re-built. On the corner is Clayhall, now a riding establishment, and then the large Victorian house of Battenhurst on the right. Old Battenhurst Farmhouse, which is probably a 17th-century building, comes next. Finally EATONDEN MANOR FARM on the right and then the level crossing and the waterworks already described. The parish boundary with Burwash is on the bridge over the Rother — Crowhurst Bridge.

Starting again from Cottenden and going towards Stonegate, there is New House Farm on the left and then some modern residential development and the council estate of Owls Gardens, with the playing field, pavilion and village club opposite and S.C.A.T.S. on the corner of Limden Lane, with some modern development all around and Atkins' Stores and post office on the other side. This is one of the very few villages with only one shop, albeit an extremely good one. There are some very recent buildings on the south-east corner in front of Stonegate Farmhouse which is 18th-century or earlier with an old barn of the same date. Planning permission has recently been granted for a greyhound exercising track to be constructed opposite New House Farm, in spite of violent opposition from the whole parish.

Following the road to the station, the school is on the left and then the church and the old vicarage, all described previously, and opposite are a number of relatively modern houses. Linkhurst and Bramdean are on the right and opposite them is the lane going down to Hammerden Cottages. Halfway down on the left is Little Hammerden, now two cottages, a 17th-century timber-framed building refaced with red brick and weather-boarding in the 19th century. The station has already been mentioned, and just before that is *The Bridge Inn* built when the railway came in 1851. HAMMERDEN is approached down the lane which is now the approach to the station. At the bottom of the hill is WITHERENDEN FARM and the mill-house and oasts, described separately. The parish boundary is on the bridge over the river.

Limden Lane starts on the crossroads by S.C.A.T.S. and Mabbs Hill is the first farm on the left, followed by West Lymden and then LYMDEN on the other side. Over the bridge Storrers is on the left, and nearly at the top of the lane there is the very attractive conversion of an oast house, known as Melford. Almost opposite is Twitten, a house built by Marjorie Matthews in about 1930 and roofed with some lovely old tiles taken from a barn at Wardsbrook which was re-roofed with corrugated iron.

On the road from Stonegate to Shovers Green the modern vicarage is on the left and shortly after is the lane down to Coopers Farm. This is an L-shaped building of medieval origin, much altered in the 16th to 18th centuries, refaced with red brick on the ground floor and tile-hung above, with a tiled roof and modern gabled porch. Bardown is next on the right-hand side, a much restored old house, and on the left is BRICKLEHURST, followed by the drive down to MAPLESDEN. Then, on the right, after Churchsettle Lane, is Normanswood Farm, the house being 18th century or earlier. The parish boundary with Stonegate, Ticehurst and Wadhurst is at Shovers Green.

This completes a quick look at the parish. Many houses have of necessity been omitted owing to lack of space, but it is hoped that it will give an adequate description of the type and character of the various properties, some of them very beautiful, which may be found here. It is difficult to know how much detail to give, but as there is so much to cover, a lot has had to be omitted. Suffice it to say here that most of the old buildings in the parish started as 'hall' type houses, constructed of exposed timber framing infilled with daub, usually of one room with a fire in the middle venting out through louvres in the roof. A first floor was often added about 1550 and a large chimney, either in the centre of the house or at one end, in about 1600. The red brick, tile-hanging and weather-boarding were the result of subsequent alterations or for protecting the ageing exterior from the elements, and carried out mainly in the 17th century.

Chapter Eleven

Some Houses and Families

We now look at the properties picked out in capital letters in the last chapter; they have been selected because they are of special interest or because the families who lived in them took a prominent part in the affairs of the parish. For ease of reference they will be listed in alphabetical order.

APSLEY COURT is a large house standing back from the main road opposite the *Duke of York* and it has been given various names in the past; until recently it was known as Steellands. On 25 March 1682 there was a sale from Gabriel Eagles to Henry Apsley[1] of a messuage and lands in Ticehurst commonly known as Leavers for £350, together with 17 acres, late in the tenure of Henry Rogers, held of the Manor of Hammerden.[32]

Horsfield says that the house was 'erected by Mr. Apsley and sold by his son, John Apsley of Lewes, gent, to Cole Dry, a wine cooper in London who settled it in jointure on his wife, and, after her decease, on his son Benjamin Dry of Lincoln's Inn, barrister at law, who gave it the name 'Le Voirs'.[5] If this statement is correct the house must have been built before 1697, for Henry Apsley, father of John, was buried in that year. There used to be an old beam above the kitchen fire-place bearing the date 1713 and this might be when additions or alterations were made by Cole Dry. The Benjamin Dry mentioned above was living here in 1724, as a 'Benjamin Dry Esq. of Lewes' is mentioned in Budgen's map of Sussex of that date and he is probably the same as that recorded in the Ticehurst burial registers on 17 July 1754, although there he is described as 'from Sevenoaks'. The occupier given in the 1851 census is William Noakes and the house is then called The Colonels, and Col. Travers died there in 1875. After that it returned to a branch of the Noakes family and reverted to its former name of Steellands.

From 1864-73 it was occupied by Mr. Segar and, in 1873, it was purchased by John Blake Cummins who also bought the land immediately in front of the house and enclosed it.[32] In the same year he leased it to James Innes Hopkins for seven years and it was enfranchised in 1874. In 1880 it was owned and occupied by J. B. Cummins. In 1911 the house was bought by E. C. Kingdon who sold it in 1920 to Josiah S. Cowling, who sold it to Henry Stapylton-Smith, whose family lived there for many years. They converted it into flats and changed the name once more to Apsley Court. The flats have been sold off separately and the house is now in various ownerships. It is a late 17th-century listed building, refronted in the 19th century and fitted with a doorway with curved head and semi circular fan-light.[63]

BAKERS FARM beyond Threeleg Cross is first mentioned in 1547 when John, Thomas and Peter, sons of Peter Mannser deceased, were admitted as copyhold tenants of this farm, which was held of the Manor of Hammerden.[1] In 1614 Thomas Harte was admitted to Bakers Farm and two years later he and his wife Mary sold the farm to Thomas Brook and his wife Ann. The Brook family continued in possession until 1663 when John Brook and his wife Frances sold the farm to the Rev. John Callow, Vicar of Ticehurst. He died in 1680 and left his copyholds to be divided between his two sons, Roger and John. Roger died in 1733 and left the residue of his estate, which seems to have included Bakers Farm, to his granddaughter Ann Berkeley. She married Thomas Hussey of Burwash, an ancestor of Edward Hussey of Scotney Castle, and the latter was still the owner in 1924. Various members of the local Field family were tenants for over a century: Benjamin Field was rated for it in 1792, Edward Field is listed in the 1851 census and another Benjamin Field in 1894. In that year W. Fowler became tenant, and was succeeded in 1903 by G. Griffiths.

The house is a well-preserved building erected about 1500 with central hall and service kitchen and solar; the latter, on the south, has been pulled down.[11] The plastered timber-framing has been faced with brick. The east wall has an overhang and contains a doorway with a four-centred hollow-chamfered head. In about 1600 a floor was inserted and a chimney stack built in the middle of the hall to replace some earlier form of heating. The screen, on the north of the entrance passage, has two doorways with four-centred arches in square heads and carved foliage spandrels. From the west end of the screens the original stair, with solid triangular steps, leads to the first floor of the service bay. The two main cambered tie-beams, with curved braces, are carried on heavy shaped wall-posts and the roof above the hall retains the end king-posts with curved braces and struts.[63]

BARDOWN in Stonegate on the road to Shovers Green has been referred to in chapter one as the site of Roman iron-works dating from the second half of the second century A.D., discovered in 1909 and excavated in the 1960s.[1] The property is mentioned in 1410 and again in 1562, and in 1605 Anthony Barnes was rated for Bardowne. In 1663 the family of Ollive appears from the parish registers to have been resident here. Thomas Constable owned it in 1757 and in 1820 William Catt appears as occupier and he was one of those who had a seat reserved in 'the farmers' gallery' in the church at the same date. The 1851 census names David Baldwin and in 1924 Joseph F. Potter was the owner and occupier. The house has recently been much repaired and restored, and again after considerable damage was done in the hurricane of October 1987.

BRICKLEHURST in Stonegate, on the road to Shovers Green, is an early 19th-century two-storied red-brick building. A knight's fee here was once held by Peter de Scotney, and it is mentioned in 1279 and 1288. It was held in 1320 and 1342 by William de Ore, and the manor descended with Ore to Henry Halle, but by 1469 it was held of the manor of Hammerden by John Wybarne, who died 16 February 1490, and whose brass is in the chancel of Ticehurst church. He was younger son of John Wybarne of Hawkwell in Pembury, had property at Maplesden in Ticehurst, and died while he was building a house near the church. In this house a priest was to have free lodging provided he sang a De Profundis for John's soul every night. Where this house was has never been discovered.[11]

John's son and heir removed to Bayhall in Kent and in 1591 John Wybarne of Pembury died seized of the manor of Bricklehurst, and his son William, dying in 1612, left as heir a nephew, Edward, son of his brother John, who was succeeded in 1624 by his son Benjamin. He, with Edward Wybarne, made a settlement of this manor in 1632. John Wybarne was concerned with the manor in 1682. In 1788 Thomas May of Pashley and Mary his wife conveyed the manor to George Courthope Junior and William Constable. This manor was also spelt Breycleherst, Brixleherst, and Brikelherst in ancient times. It may be of interest that the manor of Bricklehurst originally included lands in Sedlescombe, including the whole of the western side of Sedlescombe village.

THE BULL INN at Threeleg Cross is a medieval house of the usual domestic character, dating probably from about the middle of the 15th century, which has all the normal

45. Members of the Field family outside Bakers Farm, *c*.1868.

46. Old Boarzell, *c*.1783 (watercolour by S. H. Grimm).

details of construction and conversion into a two-storied house during the 16th century. It is half-timbered but the brickwork of the lower storey is apparently 18th-century work. The upper storey is covered with Victorian tiling, but behind this much heavy timber exists, a great deal of it being visible in the walls of bedrooms.

The house has three roof-bays only, the solar clearly being at the south end, and all three bays appear to be roughly equal, at about ten ft. each. The plan is the usual rectangle, and two shaped brackets in the east wall of one of the bedrooms carried the roof over the recessed 'wealden' front. The building was flush-fronted and the roof rebuilt to a more shallow pitch in the 18th century. The crown-post and its braces, and the medieval roof-trusses over the bay partitions were all taken out, no doubt in order to provide more attic space. The roof was actually wholly reframed, with the reuse of the old blackened rafters and short collars, as these still remain and are supported by heavy purlins and struts.[52]

In what is now the public bar, just in front of the bar counter, there is a large moulded beam acting as a girder to the ceiling, but which is actually a part of a hall with services to the south. Beyond this beam, on the south side, the medieval joists of this room are exposed. They are of the usual massive square section, and on one side can be seen the 'trimming' of the opening through which the original stairs ascended to the upper floor. Another medieval feature is visible in the two large braces under the central tie-beam of the hall which now form part of a partition between two bedrooms. The house was carefully restored just before the last war. It is not known when it first became an inn, but it was only a 'beer house' at first,[61] although on the 1873 map it is clearly marked P.H., a public house as opposed to a beer house, nor is it mentioned in the 1851 census. It appears to have had a spirit licence only after the last war.

COTTENDEN FARMHOUSE in Stonegate is a 16th-century building,[1] extended in 1699 and much altered in the 18th century.[63] Judging from the frequency with which the name Cothernden, with variations of spelling, appears in the early pages of the Ticehurst registers, it seems that a family of that name was well established in the parish in the 16th century, and it may well be that they were originally associated with Cottenden. In all probability the name Cruttenden, which is a common name locally, is but another variation. A Robert Crotynden of Ticehurst occurs in Budgen's Map of Sussex in 1724. The Ticehurst registers mention Richard Thomas as being 'of Cottenden' in 1656, and in 1792 we find Thomas Rabson rated for the property. Later it belonged for many years to the Buss family and, when advertised for sale in 1832, it was in the occupation and ownership of a Buss who was also the owner of Limden. He it was who planted the conspicuous clump of Scots Pine, now, alas, no more, on the sharp bend in the road near the farm. In 1851 it was occupied by Henry Tilden Smith.

In the accounts of the Rev. Ossory Medlicott,[1] vicar of Ticehurst, for 1744 we find 'forgiving the Widow Blundel her Easter Offering for Farm at Cottenden'. In 1820 Mr. Benjamin Buss of Cottenden had a seat reserved in the 'farmers' gallery' in the church.

George Bramall moved up here from Wedds after the First World War and built the first squash court by his patented method which he called 'ofrango' and which he had developed on active service to prevent tents being blown away in a gale. The system consisted of stretching a heavy canvas screen between two uprights and applying cement slurry to each side with a large brush, then placing wire netting over at intervals to give reinforcement. This was continued until the walls were thick enough. His son John took on the farm, built more courts by traditional methods and founded the Cottenden Squash Club.[23]

DALE HILL FARM is situated on the south-east side of the road where there is a one-way system at Dale Hill,[1] adjacent to the golf course. There is a Dale Hill House, formerly cottages, just below it on the same side, and another Dale Hill Farm on the other side of the road above the *Cherry Tree* with an oast converted into a house. They used to be distinguished for rating purposes as East and West Dalehill and one must be careful not to get them confused when dealing with old records. The one we are concerned with here is East Dalehill, now known as Dale Hill Farmhouse, which is the older one.

The Hunt family built this house in the 15th century. It is a wealden hall-house of the same dimensions as the *Bull Inn* and Rowley — probably by the same carpenter.[11] It was extended during the late 16th century and had the usual first floor and chimney inserted. The timber-framing, now faced externally with modern brick and tile, is exposed inside and has shaped wall-posts of unusual size. One room has 17th-century panelling and overmantel and the farmhouse contains a fine old oak staircase.[74] The Hunt family seem to have owned it for a considerable time, for their name occurs frequently in the parish registers, the first entry being in 1575. In 1627 a heriot was due from William Hunt's executors of Dale Hill to Mr. May of Pashley. In 1639 John Roberts of Boarzell was seized of Dalehill, and in the 1851 census the occupier is given as Thomas Jarvis.[46]

DOWNASH in Rosemary Lane is now a grade II listed building and is a large Tudor-style brick house built in about 1880 by George Burrow Gregory to a very high specification. It was first occupied by his son, George Gregory. The house then had a number of owners and in 1946 it was purchased by Mrs. Loxton, who ran it as a school for 10 years. In 1966 it was converted into 11 well-designed flats to provide homes and assistance for retired public servants from former British Overseas Territories, and has been run as a trust ever since.[80] In 1985 an additional 20 leasehold flats for the active elderly were built in the grounds to the east of the house. The whole complex is now owned and administered by the Sussex Housing Association for the Aged.

DUNSTER'S MILL is now submerged by Bewl Water and the very old miller's house was taken down, piece by piece, and re-erected above the water-line before the valley was flooded. It is in rather an isolated and inaccessible position — more so in days gone by — and access was mostly gained from the A21 by means of a footpath and bridle track through Chingley Farm. In the days when the miller's craft was more prosperous its output was supplemented by another small mill on the river Bewl, below the main one.[23]

Various members of the Huntley family owned and operated the mill for over a century; they are said to have been noted for their quiet and religious disposition, and to have been distinguished for their stature, there being at one time six sons in the family all over six feet in height.[1] Thomas Huntly is listed as owner in the 1851 census with many members of his family. William Orpin succeeded the Huntleys and built an engine-house with an exceptionally large boiler and worked the mill for several years by steam. He was succeeded in about 1880 by Mr. Wickham, who was still working the mill, together with Witherenden Mill, in 1924.

The house is 15th-century and of very unusual design,[34] incorporating an aisle. A perfectly proportioned arch still crosses the hall. Part of the house was rebuilt in the early 16th century and other modifications, including insertion of the massive brick stack, were carried out in the 17th century. It was largely taken down and rebuilt in 1949, and dismantled again in 1975, moved up the hill and reconstructed at the expense of the Southern Water Authority, when the reservoir was built, after a long fight by the owner, Hubert Beale.[23]

47. Pre-1930 view of Dunsters Mill.

EAST LYMDEN was built in 1907 as a summer residence for Frank C. Haselden, who had a business in Egypt, to the designs of the architect H. C. N. Farquharson.[53] Mr. Haselden had bought Wedds Farm from the Whiligh estate in 1906 with 100 acres, and chose the highest part of his land for his new house with good views over the rolling country to the south. In about 1925 his widow sold the house and Wedds Farm to Major W. H. Tolhurst who, in 1928, sold them to P. N. Kemp-Gee. The latter made a number of alterations and improvements to the house, including the enlargement of the staff quarters, the installation of full central heating, the building of a large range of stables for polo ponies and the construction of a covered swimming pool. In 1929 he also bought most of the cottages in Church Street and Rosehill which had previously belonged to Campbell Newington of Oakover. Wedds Farm was sold before the 1939 war and in 1946 Mr. Kemp-Gee's widow sold East Lymden to Capt. J. Heber-Percy. He, or his executors, retained the house and some land until 1964 when it was bought by Mr. Gilbert, whose intention it was to divide the property into flats, convert the outbuildings and cottages and sell them all off. Fortunately he did not succeed although some cottages and buildings were sold. In 1970 the estate was bought by Mr. and Mrs. P. J. Butler, who in turn sold it to the present owner Mrs. Michael Fitz-Gerald.[23]

The house is approached by a long metalled drive from the Ticehurst-Wadhurst road opposite Ridgeway Farm. This still belongs to the previous owners of the adjacent land, at one time a private golf course, but the owners of East Lymden have a right of way and the obligation to maintain it. The house has a courtyard in front surrounded by a high brick wall, and the whole effect is reminiscent of some of Lutyens' early domestic work, being mainly brick below and, in parts, tile-hung above, with a tiled roof. The tall chimneys were originally all of the same height, but when alterations to the house were made in 1929 chimney-pots were added to some which altered the appearance. The massive front door faces north and, on entering, one is really at the back of the house, all the main rooms facing out to the south over a wide terrace which runs the length of the house and steps descend to the garden. The alterations blend in well with Farquharson's original design and the house fits into its environment as if it had grown from it. The local materials used — brick, tile, oak, cast-iron and stone — are deployed in a manner typical of the Sussex Weald. Inside there is equal harmony: thick oak floors and generous quantities of panelling, mostly oak, but also other hardwoods and pine.

48.   East Lymden.

EATONDEN MANOR FARM in Stonegate stands back from the road just above Crowhurst Bridge level crossing. The name is quite modern, and was given by a previous owner, Col. Eaton;[11] it was previously known as Biggs Farm from the family of Bygge or Le Bygg found in the parish in 1296. John Barrow was living there in 1851.[54] It is an L shaped timber-framed building faced with weather-boarding and tile. The eastern range is of medieval origin, but reconstructed in the 17th century, little original work remaining except the ashlar base of the central chimney- stack and some reused smoke-blackened rafters.[63] Inside, both floors have exposed framing and ceiling beams; the wall-posts are moulded and support stop-chamfered wall-plates. In the central stack, which has a wide fireplace, is a large recess for smoking bacon. There is an 18th-century wing of red brick behind.

49.   The Gravel Pit, *c*.1920.

THE GRAVEL PIT, just off the main road almost opposite Hillbury, was for many years in the mid-18th century the home of the Eagles family; a George Eagles being rated for it in 1745. It may well have belonged to several generations of his ancestors as the name is of frequent occurrence in the parish registers in the 17th century. Then it passed to the Noakes family, and the will of John Noakes dated 1772 and proved 1774 refers to 'premises purchased by me of Rev. John Dry, clerk, known as Merriams with 130 acres'. In 1820 Henry Noakes of Gravill Pitts had a seat reserved in the 'farmers' gallery' of the church, and in 1851 it was owned by John Noakes. The last member of this old Ticehurst family was Henry John Noakes who died in 1914 and his trustees sold it to Rowland Gorringe, who leased it in 1916 to Lady Julian Parr. On her death in 1928 it was purchased by Miss Maud Wallis and Miss Ruth Collingridge who changed its name to Merriams and made some additions to the house.[32] They subsequently moved to Flimwell and sold the property to F. A. R. Reeves, whose wife was daughter of Henry John Noakes, and on his death it passed to his daughter, Diana, wife of Tom Stopford, and they restored the name to The Gravel Pit. It is an L-shaped house, probably 17th-century, red-brick below and tile-hung above, now called Baber House and owned by Philip Langford.[63]

HAMMERDEN (Homerdenn, Hammerdene) near Stonegate station: the first element of the name is probably the ordinary word for a hammer, referring to an old forge hammer. If this is correct — and it is difficult to see what other sense the first element can have — we have reference to forge hammers at a considerably earlier date than has hitherto been recorded.[54] At one time this manor, together with Pashley, owned most of the parish of Ticehurst. In 1280 it belonged to the honour of Hastings and in 1320 it was stated that the knight's fee here was one of nine fees formerly held by Peter de Scotney.[11] John of Brittany, Earl of Richmond, granted the manor to Bertram de Monboucher and Joan his wife, Edward II confirming in 1310, and it descended with Filsham in Hollington. This manor, with others, had passed to John of Brittany by grant from Edward I as part of the barony of Hastings. After the death of Bertram his son Reginald was permitted to resume the property.[1]

By the marriage of Isabella Monboucher, granddaughter of Reginald, to Robert Harbotell, the last named family first became associated with the manor and in 1418 half the estate was held by Isabella and half by her nephew Bertram Monboucher. Eventually the whole estate came to Isabella and in 1462 her grandson, Bertram Harbotell, died, leaving Ralph his son and heir. He settled the property on his son Guichard (or Wychard) on the latter's marriage with Johanna, daughter of Sir Henry Willoughby of Wollaton. By an inquisition *post mortem* taken at Robertsbridge on 30 March 1517, Guichard was found to have died the preceding September, leaving a son George, then nine years old. George Harbotell died childless in 1528, and this line ended with his sisters, one of whom, Eleanor, married Sir Thomas Percy who was executed for high treason by Henry VIII, while her sister Maria wedded Sir Edward Fitton of Gawsworth, Cheshire. Thomas Percy is said to have saved the forfeiture of much of his estates by a feoffment made before his treason and Lady Fitton eventually held the estate which passed from her to Barnard Randolph, founder of Randolph's charity.

Barnard Randolph died seized in 1583 and, his son John having died in his lifetime, was succeeded by his grandson Herbert, during whose minority the manor was leased to John Stone at £48 p.a. On 1 June 1603, by indenture, the manor was settled on the intended marriage between Herbert and Judith, daughter of Anthony Shirley. Herbert died a few months later and an inquisition *post mortem* held on 28 August 1605 found that his sister Judith, aged 26 years, wife of Anthony Apsley, was his heir. She, with her husband, conveyed the property in 1606 to John Lunsford, a relative. In 1612 the 'heirs of Barnard Randolph' held the manor, and there is in the County Record Office at Lewes a map of the lands of the estate in 1614, titled 'Hamerden' and, at the bottom, 'being the lands of Mr. Anthony Apsley' and it includes most of the area between the parish boundary with Burwash, Wadhurst and Etchingham up to the Stonegate to Cottenden road. There is a companion map, of which the original is at Lewes, dated 1612 (previously referred to as the 1612 map) with the same titles and covering the land from Wardsbrook up to the village. This will be discussed in more detail under Wardsbrook.

For some unstated reason James I granted the manor in 1614 to Robert Morley and John Baker in fee, and they conveyed it to Thomas Aynscombe. These transactions were probably for purposes of settlement as, early in the next reign, Anthony Apsley was in possession. By 1636 and 1655 the manor was in the hands of Anthony's son Henry. It then descended with the manor of Cortesley in Hollington until, on the death of John Apsley Dalrymple in 1833, it was purchased by George Campion Courthope of Whiligh, and in the 1851 census the occupier is given as John White. It was still owned by the latter's grandson, George Loyd Courthope, in 1924 and occupied by J. Luxford. Soon after the property was parted from the Whiligh estate and sold.

The old house was situated just to the north-east of the present Stonegate station and approached by a road which went through the station car park. The present house of brick with a tiled roof dates probably from the 19th century and is on the same site. The original court rolls go back a long way and most properties in the southern part of the parish commence their title with an extract from the entries in the rolls of the manor of Hammerden, but, as can be seen from the foregoing, it has had a long and complicated history. For pedigrees of these families connected with Hammerden see the Collingridge Collection File 5/1.

50. Hazelhurst, c.1948.

HAZELHURST. There used to be two farms of this name: Upper and Lower Hazelhurst. The latter can probably be identified with the Haeselersc Charter of 1018 (chapter one) and is now submerged by Bewl Water reservoir; the former has been identified with the Domesday Haslesse and ceased to exist manorially shortly afterwards. The modern Hazelhurst may or may not be on the same site — if indeed there was a manor house on the Domesday holding, which has been doubted. Very little is known about the present farm house. In 1605 Richard Droweby was rated for 'Mr. Thomas' land called Hasilherste'; in 1673 it belonged to Peter Parke and his wife Margaret, who sold it the following year to John Stead, a London haberdasher. He, like many other tradesmen who have rashly ventured their savings in agriculture, seems to have had financial problems, as he soon mortgaged the farm to Thomas Hatchet and in 1677 sold it to Roger Callow, son of the vicar of Ticehurst. Whether Hazelhurst formed part of Roger's residuary estate and so passed, together with Bakers Farm, to his granddaughter Ann

Berkeley and thence to the Husseys of Scotney, is not known, but it seems likely that it did. In 1831 the owner is given as Alf Playsted, and the occupier Thomas Newington.[1]

The house is said to be 17th-century or earlier, ground floor faced with weather-boarding, and tile-hung above with a half-hipped tiled roof.

LITTLE WHILIGH, originally a farmhouse, is down the lane below the main house, and is an L-shaped 18th-century house of red brick, tile-hung above. [63]

LYMDEN is situated at the bottom of Limden Lane in Stonegate and is an L-shaped house of medieval origin with a southern range and chimney added about 1600; at this time the southern range was gabled to the road, but this was removed in the early 18th century when the medieval part was largely rebuilt. Until 1975 an exceptionally fine 15th-century barn stood adjacent to the house. Among the signatories to the 1180 Charter of Combwell Priory (chapter one) there appears Warinus de Limundene, which probably relates to this property. Thomas Burt is described as 'of Lymden' in the parish registers for 1619, and about 1660 we find the family of Baker in possession.[1 63]

In 1831 Mrs. Ford was given as owner and occupier, and in 1832 it belonged, together with Cottenden, to the Buss family. In 1867 the farm, together with the adjoining farm of Storrers, was purchased by Maria Isabella Foster, widow, who died in 1871 and left it to her daughter, later Mrs. Campbell Newington. It is now the property of Mrs. Derek Warren.[47]

MAPLESDEN in Stonegate seems to have been part of the landed property held by the monks of Robertsbridge at the time of a confirmatory charter granted to them by Richard I in 1198. John Wybarne had property there in 1480 (see under Bricklehurst) but it is not clear whether he owned the farm. George Humphrey, as appears by an inquisition *post mortem* held at East Grinstead on 28 July 7 1610 died on the preceding 5 January seized of lands called Maplesden in Wadhurst and Ticehurst, leaving a son and heir George 'aged 14 and not more'. In 1792 Robert Roberts was rated for Maplesden, and later it belonged for many years to the Watson family; in 1831 the owner and occupier was given as Dan Watson, and in 1851 John Watson.[47] Among more recent owners have been W. O. Carter, J.P. of Hurst Green and J. P. Potter, later of Bardown.[1] He sold it to John L. Reid and the present owner is his son Michael, who keeps a fine herd of Sussex cattle there.[23] The original part of the house is a 17th-century building, timber-framed and the north front was refaced or added in the 18th century.[63]

NORWOODS FARM beyond Threeleg Cross is a very old property; it was given to a charity for the income to be applied to Horsmonden church in 1618 by William Wyke of Lamberhurst. This charity held it until 1920 when the Horsmonden Charities, acting for the executors of William Wyke, sold it.[1] It is now the property of Robin and Ann Howard. The building is 16th-century, timber-framed and refaced with red brick below and tile-hung above. There is a modern L-shaped wing to the north-west. It was originally a 'smoke-bay house'.[63]

OAKOVER, down the hill below the church, was built originally in 1870 as a small Victorian Villa by John Rea Campbell on former glebe land which he purchased, together with Parsonage Farm, from the Ecclesiastical Commissioners in 1868.[23 43] His sister was Maria Isabella Foster, widow, of the Holme, Regents Park. She died in 1871, leaving her only child, Margaret, then aged 14, in the care and guardianship of her brother and his wife, Sarah Jane Campbell. John Campbell died in 1884 and Sarah in

51. Oakover.

1886, leaving Oakover to their niece, Margaret, who had also inherited The Holme from her mother.

The 1881 census gives: 'at Oakover were living Mr. & Mrs. John Rea Campbell and their niece Miss Margaret Holgate Foster aged 23; Butler, Coachman, Footman and four maidservants. At Oakover Lodge (now North Cottage) was Riley Scott, aged 29, gardener'. In 1896 Margaret married Campbell Newington of Ridgeway, Ticehurst, and they lived here for the rest of their lives, purchasing a lot of the surrounding land and the farms of Shoyswell, Turzes, Myskins and Dalehill and most of the cottages up Church Street and at Rosehill. Campbell Newington was a breeder of champion pedigree Sussex spaniels and of Sussex cattle, with both of which he won the highest awards. He died in 1929 and she in 1939, having both been considerable benefactors to the parish, and leaving an only child Beatrice who, in 1918, married Cedric Drewe of Wadhurst Hall.

The Drewes had their own home at Broadhembury in Devon, and Oakover was to have been sold; but then the war came and it was unsaleable. In the event it was requisitioned to evacuate the boys from Brockley Park school in London, who looked after the house very well. It was handed back in 1945, and the Drewes' eldest son, Francis, came to live here with his family. His mother made the estate over to him in 1946, the outlying farms mentioned above having been sold on Campbell Newington's death.

Mr. and Mrs. Newington decided, soon after their marriage, to enlarge the house very considerably and employed an eminent architect, Sir Aston Webb, to draw up the plans and supervise the work which was carried out in 1899. At the same time the stable block with its clock tower was built, together with the Lodge, a magnificent range of farm buildings, and the garden and grounds were laid out. In 1914 further additions were made, this time by Sir Aston's son Phillip Webb, the top drive was constructed, and further additions made to the garden.

The author's mother, Beatrice Drewe née Newington, says in her memoirs:[50]

> indoors we had the large staff considered necessary for running a house of that size; the kitchen was run by 'Mrs.' Godson, a courtesy title always given to cooks; she had under her a kitchen maid and a scullery maid. There was also a young and inexperienced dogsbody who was known as the 'between maid' or 'Tweeny' and who was at the beck and call of both the cook and the head housemaid. The latter was 'Bakie' who ruled over a succession of young housemaids; my mother's 'lady's maid' and my governess; also a butler, a gloomy looking man called Mason, and two footmen.
>
> Attendance at church was compulsory for servants every Sunday, suitably clad in black, and no-one was allowed out after dark. 'Young men' were definitely frowned on; in fact they were all treated exactly like children of a very strictly brought-up Victorian family, but in spite of this they all seemed extremely happy, and as nearly all of them finally left to get married, they must have found ways of getting round some of the rules!

There were two bell-pushes in every room, the right-hand one for one of the maids from upstairs and the left for one of the men. The garden was run by a magnificently bearded old man called Parrish, and he had 11 men under him. There was also the coachman, later the chauffeur, and his assistant, and a man to run the electric light plant and look after all the services to the house.

By 1947 it was clear that this large house was much too big for one family, and so one end of the house was converted into three self-contained flats, one on each floor. The present owner is still Francis Drewe, who, with his wife Joan, lives in the rest of the building. Their son Adrian is in Parsonage Farmhouse at the bottom of the garden.

OLD BOARZELL, originally a manor (Boreselle, Borsel, Borshull, Boresell, Boorshill);[11] the name is derived from the Saxon *bar hyll*, 'wild boar's hill'.[54] It was apparently that part of the lands held in 1086 by Reinbert the sheriff and shown in Domesday as 'in Alciston' (see chapter one). A charter of 1123 records that seven hides in Boarzell and other places had been separated from the 50 hides in the Abbot of Battle's manor of Alciston, and in 1253 and 1295 Reinbert's descendants, the Lords of Etchingham received grants of free warren here.

How long the Etchinghams held Boarzell is not clear, but it seems to have passed to the family of Haremere, who held land nearby, by 1316, and William de Haremere held the manor in 1432. It was later in the possession of the Roberts family who held land in the parish in 1488 when Walter Roberts received licence to impark land in Cranbrook, Goudhurst and Ticehurst. In 1557 Thomas Roberts was concerned with a water-mill and lands in the parish, as was Walter Roberts with a windmill and lands in 1624. Walter died here in 1632 and his son John died at Boarzell in 1639 seized of this capital messuage and another here called Dalehill. His son Walter was concerned with the manor, definitely so called, in 1683, and died in 1700. John Roberts, concerned with the manor in 1710, died in 1728 and was followed by a son John who lived at Boarzell. His son John succeeded in 1732 and died in 1741. Until 1783 we find mention of Samuel Roberts of Boarzell, and then two more Johns, John Roberts of Warbleton being proprietor in 1835. The original house was a stone building, reconstructed in timber about 1600; a detailed room-by-room inventory for the house survives.

Most of this family lie buried in the chancel of Ticehurst church. The Roberts sold the property and the house was demolished in 1859, but the site of the house is still marked by the remains of a moat, situated on the left of the lane leading from the Swiftsden road to London Barn Farm.[1] A pedigree tracing the descent of this family from Thomas Roberts of Glassenbury, Cranbrook, *temp.* Henry VII, will be found in Berry's *Pedigrees of the County of Sussex.* A new house was built soon after the old one was pulled down, standing near the main road from Flimwell to Hurst Green and for many years it has been a school, but it is not in Ticehurst parish.

PARSONAGE FARM has been part of the glebe lands of Ticehurst, belonging to the church, for many centuries; in 1266 a commission was set up with a jury of 12 men to decide a dispute on the payment of tithes in Ticehurst.[1] The ownership of the glebe descended with the advowson, or gift of the living (chapter five), which was held by the Priory of Holy Trinity, Hastings, until 1413 when the Priory was transferred to Warbleton.[11] Upon the Dissolution of the Monasteries in 1538-9 Henry VIII gave the patronage of Ticehurst, together with many other properties, to his Attorney General Sir John Baker of Sissinghurst.[39]

In July 1541 the latter, with his wife Elizabeth, surrendered the advowsons of Ticehurst and Ashburnham in exchange for other properties, mainly at Frythenden in Kent, to the Dean and Chapter of Canterbury. They held it until 1868 when John Rea Campbell bought the glebe land and farmhouse, but not the advowson, from the Ecclesiastical Commissioners who had been established some years before (for the subsequent title see under Oakover). In 1973 Francis Drewe gave the farmhouse to his son Adrian.

The Parsonage Farm lands were rectorial glebe, i.e. the rents and tithes were due to the rector — in this case the Dean and Chapter of Canterbury or their lessees. The vicarage lands were vicarial glebe and rents were due to the vicar. So much for the owners; the occupiers are more difficult to trace, but there may be some undiscovered records in the library of the Dean and Chapter. The 1612 map shows a sketch of a house similar to the present one, but larger, on the same site; so also does the 1839 map which gives the land as 24¼ acres which is the same as that purchased by J. R. Campbell.[31 40]

The present house dates from about 1670, although there was an older and larger house on the same site before that, rated for the Hearth Tax of 1662 for nine flues, occupier Mr. Hartridge, gent., and this house is shown in a small sketch on the 1612 map. In 1671 a survey was made of the Sussex estates of the Dean and Chapter of Canterbury, and their tenant, still Mr. Hartridge, then lived at Parsonage, which was called 'the Rectory howse'. He had just spent £200 on reparations which at that time would have been sufficient to rebuild the house completely in its present form, and it seems that this is what he did, for there is nothing in the existing building dating back before then. It is timber- framed, but on a red brick base, now tile-hung, with a catslide hipped tiled roof.[75] The occupiers so far identified are:

1660   Mr. Hartridge, gent.[75]
1707   John Gibbs, tenant.[41]
1751   Rev. Mr. Strother, tenant.[42]
1774   John Dengate paid £12 tithing to Mr. Durell, vicar of Ticehurst, as a year's rent for the glebe land.
1792   John Dengate paid £10 poor rate for Parsonage Farm.
1840   Sarah Dengate as occupier and Rev. John Constaple of Ringmer as 'owner' holding a lease from the Dean and Chapter.[40]
1851   The census gives the occupier as John Dengate.
1867   Rev. C. Dodson surrendered his lease to the Ecclesiastical Commissioners, and

the property was put up for sale.[43]

1910   Walter Gardner, Campbell Newington's stock-man lived there until his death in 1951 He took over the farm in 1929.[23]

1951   His son Henry took over the farm until 1967.[44]

1967   G. H. Blake rented the house only.

1970   Alec Whiteman rented the house only.

1978   Adrian and Fiona Drewe came to live here; restored the roof, walls and interior, esposing and cleaning all the oak beams and original brickwork.

52.   Grant of free warren to Edmund de Passeley (1317).

PASHLEY MANOR is our only Grade I listed building, and since a great deal is known about its interesting history, it will be given more space than some other properties.[1] It is first mentioned in a deed of Robertsbridge Abbey dated about 1185, when Elias de Passeley appears as a witness. In 1272 Sir Robert de Passeley, son of Ralph de Alderstode, took the name Passeley on his marriage with the heiress Sarah, daughter of Gyles de Passeley mentioned in the same deed. In 1317 Robert's son Edmund, born *c.*1270, a prominent court official, received grant of free warren from the king in Pashley and his other Sussex demesnes. In 1307 Edmund received licence to grant 120 acres of land in this parish, Wadhurst and Lamberhurst to a chaplain to celebrate divine service daily in Pashley chapel for his soul and others. These lands were granted to William Tipper, Robert Dawe and others in 1592. In 1317 King Edward II gave him a grant of free warren here.

Edmund held, in 1320, 1½ fees in Pashley and La Forde,[67] and married Maud, daughter and heiress of John de Ketchenour of Ketchenour in Beckley. They had two — possibly three — sons and three daughters; the eldest son was William. Edmund was a noted lawyer who amassed extensive estates and was knighted in 1319. He owned 17 properties in Sussex and 17 in Kent and a town house in London. Maud died in 1318 and he then supposedly married Joan in London and probably had a son Edmund. Then he married Margaret, widow of Sir William de Basing, possibly bigamously, and by her he had three sons and a daughter. In February 1327, whilst at Margaret's manor, he made his will, leaving as heir Sir Thomas de Passeley, youngest son of Margaret, and disinheriting his son William.

There were allegations that Margaret had murdered her husband and his eldest son William, and she was certainly involved in the murder of Edmund, Sir Edmund's son by Joan, at Coulsdon in Surrey. Margaret died in 1341 and the property came to Sir Thomas, who died childless in 1359 and was succeeded by Sir Edmund, his eldest full brother who died two years later and was succeeded by another full brother, Robert. He died the next year and the property passed to his son, later Sir Robert, who was under age, and he held it until 1393 when it passed to his only son Robert Passeley Esq. The latter died in 1406 when it passed to his eldest son Sir John who held it until 1453. He married Elizabeth Woodville and the manor descended to their son John.

In 1463 John Lewkener conveyed the manor, apparently held in right of Joan his wife, to trustees who conveyed it to Geoffrey Boleyn, who died seized the same year, leaving a son and heir Thomas. The younger son, Sir William, held Pashley in 1489, and his eldest son Thomas, who held a court here in 1518, was father of Anne Boleyn and was created Earl of Wiltshire. His brother and heir, Sir James Boleyn, succeeded in 1538, and in 1543 quit-claimed the manor to Thomas May and his son Thomas of Combwell. The property then conveyed included 600 acres, a water mill and iron-furnace.

Thomas May 'of Ticehurst' died seized, presumably in 1552, leaving a son Thomas, who in 1610 was succeeded by his son Anthony, Sheriff of Sussex in 1629. Anthony was succeeded in 1635 by his son Edward, who left children Thomas, Edward and Susanna, successively owners of Pashley. Edward the younger died in 1693 and Susanna, who married Sir Richard May, died in 1718. Francis May of Pashley made a settlement in 1749 and died in 1759, his son Henry being concerned with Richard Hollist with the manor in 1789.

This line of the May family, who had held Pashley for 250 years, ended in 1796 with an heiress, Caroline, only surviving child of Thomas May. In that year she married the Rev. Richard Wetherell and the estate passed to that family. Caroline died in 1833, her husband surviving until 1858, and he was the last person to be interred within the walls of Ticehurst church. They had eight sons and six daughters, and the third son, Nathan, a barrister at law, married Susan Gould and died in 1887; they had two daughters: Susan Margaret who married Jonathan Darby, and Harriet Elizabeth.[1] Susan died in 1911 and Harriet in 1921, and the property then passed to Dr. Gerald Wetherell Capron Hollist, whose mother was Ellen Lydia Wetherell. He died in 1923 and the property was sold, being empty and badly neglected between the wars. It was purchased in 1945 by Mr. Royce who sold it shortly afterwards to Capt. Neil Forsyth with 47 acres of land.

There is mention of a mill here in one of the 13th-century deeds, probably a flour mill. There was no mains water or electricity in the house until 1944, but there is an excellent supply of fresh water from a spring in the grounds.

The original part of the present house belongs to the mid- or late 16th century and had a half-H plan, the central gable being added in 1621 as indicated by a date at the apex of one of the carved barge-boards, and at the same time the front door was moved

53.   The north front of Pashley Manor before restoration.

54.   The north front after restoration in 1950.

to the centre of the façade. It was enlarged in the 18th century, when the ends of the wings were joined to enclose a small central courtyard. Some ashlar walling and moulded ceiling-beams in the basement below the stairs appear to be remains of a 16th-century house. The original front faces north-east and is close-studded with unstained timbers, uncovered in 1950 when the house was carefully restored by the Forsyths and the heavy Victorian plastering removed. The entrance hall is lined with moulded panelling of about 1625. There is mention of a chapel there in the 1307 deed and Norden's map of 1690 shows the house marked with a cross, indicating a church or chapel.

Perhaps the most perfect room in the house today is the dining-room. The panelling is of the Carolean period with a carved frieze in bas-relief, and there are pilasters similarly carved which break up the panelling itself. The overmantel matches it with its three panels framed by a carved grapevine; the central panel bears the arms and crest of the Mays and the two outer panels a pattern of fleur-de-lys. In the past the panelling had been painted, grained and varnished; later it had been stripped and stained to resemble fumed oak. Attempts to strip this proved unsatisfactory, and eventually it was decided to distemper the whole room in a light corn colour which proved most effective, picking out the coat of arms in the correct heraldic colours.

PICKFORDE, down the lane next to *The Bell Inn*, was probably the residence of Richard de Pyggevorde in 1296 (S.R.Lay Subsidy Rolls), John de Pegeford in 1332 and Thomas Pikeford also in 1296.[32] Nothing is known of the intervening history and the present house is probably Victorian. In 1831 Mr. Glanville was given as owner and occupier, and in 1851 Charles E. H. Newington. Edward Currie lived there for 25 years and died in 1889. Col. Macpherson then lived there and sold the house in 1909 to E. E. P. Brammall, born in 1865, who lived there on his return from Egypt until his death in 1930.[47] Since then the house has had a number of owners, mostly for short periods.

QUEDLEY lies off the main road to the south between Rosemary Lane and Flimwell crossroads, approached by a long drive.[1] References to 'The Den of Quedle' and to 'Quedlye Cross' occur in the Pashley Manuscripts and 'Quedleigh' is mentioned as among the lands owned by Herbert Randolph on his death on 9 August 1605. The name is spelt in many different ways, one variant being Quedlaye which occurs in the registers for 1587. An undated manuscript of the mid-18th century refers to Quedly Lands as then being farmed, together with Philmwell Lands by Edward Winch. In 1851 James Austin was living there and in 1894 Charles Powell of Quedley was a parish councillor. Some people contend that the origin of the name is to be found in two Anglo-Saxon words signifying 'the Devil's meadow'. If this is so, the Prince of Darkness was evidently regarded as closely associated with this part of the parish, for not far from Quedley is a wood bearing the name Devilsden Wood, and also a stream known as Devil's Brook.

The house is of 15th-century origin, largely rebuilt in the mid- to late 16th century and re-roofed and much altered in the mid-18th century. It is unusual for its size in that it is heated by a massive chimney built against the rear wall, instead of rising through the roof. It is tile-hung above, with a half-hipped tiled roof.[63]

THE ROUNDELS at Witherenden were converted out of two oast houses and a granary.

ROWLEY lies at the bottom of Burnt Lodge Lane and is first mentioned in the Haeselersc charter of 1018 (chapter one) wherein it is stated to be just outside the land near Lower Hazelhurst which King Cnut conveyed to Archbishop Aelfstan. The house was fortunate to have escaped the recent inundation of the waters of the reservoir and now stands with a magnificent view over this beautiful lake. Very little is known about its past history: that there was a house — and farm — in Saxon times is beyond dispute, but the present house dates from the 15th century and is timber-framed, restored and refaced, red brick below and tile- hung above. It was originally a wealden hall-house onto which a crossing was added in about 1600, and it was badly damaged by fire earlier this century.[63]

In 1565 John Stevens the elder of Rowley was buried, and George Mills was rated for 'Rowleigh and Clabhatch' in 1605. From the parish registers it appears that the Ollive family lived here from at least 1660-1774.[47] In the early years of the 19th century the family of Springett was settled here, and one John Springett of Rowley was buried under the cross-aisle of Ticehurst church in 1826, and in 1831 Mr. Springate is given as owner and occupier. In 1894 Jacob Field of Rowley was a member of the Parish Council.

SEACOX HEATH is just beyond Flimwell crossroads on the way to Hawkhurst and is the last house in Sussex in that direction. Tradition has it that the original house was built in 1748 by Arthur Gray, one of the 'Barons' of the Hawkhurst Smugglers, often referred to as 'The Seacocks Gang'. Richard Palliser was living here in 1839 when the church was built (chapter six). William Beckwith is listed in the 1851 census, followed by the distinguished Goschen family, and they replaced the house with a tall mansion in the style of a French chateau in 1871, the architects being Messrs. Carpenter and Slater.[63] In 1946 the property was sold and bought by the Russian Embassy, who now use it as a country retreat.

SINGEHURST, situated on the Hurst Green road, almost opposite Lower Tollgate is now two dwellings, but, until recently, it was all one private house, previously a farmhouse. It is 17th- century, red brick below, and tile-hung above. It was once part of the Pashley estate and the few occupiers who have been traced are listed below:

1518   Symon Fysenden; 13 acres called Senghurst.[22]
1628   Tamison Wynch wid. rated for her farme of Sengehurst.
1820   Mr. Gilt. Jarvis of Singehurst has a seat in the 'farmers' gallery' in the church.[1]
1851   The census shows Henry Overy living here.
1859   Nathan Wetherell (of Pashley) mortgaged to James Maclaren of Ticehurst.[32]
1879   James Maclaren died.
1880   Nathan Wetherell occupier.
1887   Nathan Wetherell died. The Ford family lived here for many years and used the farm in conjunction with their butcher's shop in the village.
1923   Estate sold to George Ticehurst.

WARDSBROOK FARM lies half a mile south of the church and it may possibly take its name from William Warde and Agnes his wife, to whom Sir Robert de Passele, Knt. made a grant of 60 acres of land in 1372. Records exist of the sale of the house in 1499 from William Saunders of Ticehurst to Sabinia Brykenden, widow, and in 1534 William Broking of Ticehurst, gent. purchased the property for £80 from William Brykenden, tailor, of Cranbrook, son and heir of John Brykenden. One William Manser was then the yearly tenant of the farm. According to a manuscript relating to the Pashley estate, Anthony Apsley owned Wardsbrook in 1570.[1]

This is the same person who owned Hammerden in 1605 and the 1612 map, referred to under Hammerden, showing the lands of Anthony Apsley Esq., lord of that manor, has an enlarged sketch of Wardsbrook entitled 'View of The House'; a large gabled

55. Wardsbrook from a map of 1612.

mansion, with three wings, a courtyard and farm buildings, orchard and vegetable
garden. The stream has also been dammed on the west of the road to form two mill-
ponds, and a water wheel is also clearly shown. In May 1630 the property was sold by
Anthony Apsley to Anthony May of Pashley. In 1851 Stephen Standen was the tenant
farmer and in 1868 it still belonged to Pashley, but soon after that it passed to the Baker
family who have owned it ever since.[18]

The original house on the site is of early 16th-century date and now forms the south
range. In the mid-16th century the impressive north range was built, either by Barnard
Randolph or his grandson Herbert. In its original form it was gabled with a projecting
two-storied porch and impressive bay windows. The oasthouse, adjacent to the house,
incorporates the remains of a mid-16th-century detached kitchen and still retains its
unglazed windows, one complete with its original sliding shutter. The barns are also old,
one dating from the late 15th or early 16th century.

The north range of 16th-century date seems to have been built with two stories, an
attic floor and chimney-stack being added later. Across the centre of the wing is a ceiling-
beam, the moulding of which is carried down the carved braces. The east quarter was
screened off, the screen wall with its two doorways with moulded four-centred heads

remaining.[11] The overhanging first floor is carried on curved braces, and on the north side is closely set vertical studding and an original two-light window. A parallel south range has exposed timber-framing and a roof of queen-post construction. On the site are many medieval worked stones, including the circular newel of a vice, which suggest an earlier stone-built house. Nearby is some timber-framed 17th-century stabling with an oast house.[63]

This is an instance when the gentry owner of the manor was an 'absentee', i.e. he did not reside on the manor, even though he was a resident of Ticehurst; such an arrangement is not uncommon. The gentry mansion — not the manor house — is what counted for status at that period;the two are often one and the same, but sometimes they are not. The Old Mill, on the opposite side of the road is an 18th-century red brick building, with weather-board above and a tiled roof.

WEDDS FARM, approached by a long drive to the west of the Ticehurst to Cottenden road, opposite Wardsbrook, undoubtedly takes its name from a family of former occupants, the surname Wedd being of very frequent occurrence in the registers during the early years of the 17th century.[1] In 1792 Daniel Waghorn was rated both for this farm and for East Lymden. In 1906 Frank C. Haselden bought Wedds from the Whiligh estate and his widow sold it in about 1925, together with East Lymden to W. H. Tolhurst, who in 1928 sold the two properties to P. N. Kemp-Gee. The latter sold Wedds separately a few years later.[33] Since then there have been a number of different owners and the farm has now been largely split up. George Bramall farmed Wedds for a time between the two wars, before moving up to Cottenden.

WHILIGH is first mentioned in the Anglo-Saxon Haeselersc charter of 1018, where it is spelt Wiglege; Willee in 1246, Wylegh(e) in 1279, meaning a 'clearing where heathen rights are practised', or perhaps simply a wood or glade or spring or stream; but the Anglo-Saxon word 'Wig' (used in 1018) usually denotes 'idol or heathen temple'.[34 & 55] Nothing further is heard of it until 1366 when Robert de Passeley made a settlement of the manor of Whiligh together with that of Pashley.[11] In 1372 he granted 'all his land called Whiligh' to William Warde and Agnes his wife, and their grandson Thomas settled it in 1427 on Ralph Shoyswell and Elizabeth his wife, widow of Thomas Playsted and mother of two sons, Ralph Playsted and Roger Shoyswell; their shares were purchased in 1479 and 1501 respectively by William Saunders of Goudhurst, who bequeathed this manor in 1512 to his daughter and co-heir, Elizabeth, wife of John Courthope of Hartfield. Katherine, wife of Robert Hawkesley and granddaughter of William Saunders claimed half and started a suit that lasted until 1541; but the Courthopes won and have held the manor continuously from 1512 until 1980, when the last of the line died.

In 1539 John Courthope granted Whiligh to his younger son George, whose elder brother, John, released all right in 1541; George died in 1577 and his son John altered the manor house in 1586 and died in 1615. The latter's son, George, knighted in 1641, died the following year and was followed by six generations of Georges, always passing from father to son, until 1835. The first, knighted in 1661, wrote *Memoirs*, published by the Royal Historical Society in 1907, and died in 1685. The last George's son, George Campion Courthope, built the original church at Stonegate and was a substantial contributor to the building of Flimwell church, and was followed in 1895 by his son, George John Courthope, and he in 1910 by George Loyd Courthope, created a baronet in 1925, a Privy Councillor in 1937 and a Baron in 1945. He died in 1955 and was succeeded by his two daughters, the Hon. Beryl and Daphne, and on the death of the last-named in 1980,[29] the property passed to her second cousin, John Hardcastle.

56. Whiligh, *c*.1900.

The Courthopes were, for many years, the chief landowners in the parish, but gradually the estate was broken up. Whiligh oaks have been famous for centuries and timber from the estate was probably used for the roof-beams in Westminster Hall in about 1390, again for the restorations in 1920, and again after the Second World War. The late Lord Courthope always said that only 'heart of oak' must be used with all the sapwood cut away.

The main range of the building is of mid-16th century date, and a parlour crosswing was added in 1586, and the gable on the left is probably contemporary with it, and is certainly an addition to the main range. The central gable was added in the 17th century, in similar fashion to that at Pashley, and many alterations were made over the years, mainly in 1840, so that by the end of the last war the house had become unmanageable and one large wing was demolished.[63] Whiligh has recently been divided into two dwellings — one half retaining the original name and the other half being known as 'Courthopes'.

WITHERENDEN is a house at the bottom of the hill between Stonegate and Burwash Common near the bridge over the river Rother. The two earliest references are to John de Wydryndene, who in 1266 was one of 12 men who decided a dispute as to payments of tithe in Ticehurst, and Christina de Witherynden is mentioned in a deed of 1296. Sir Adam de Newington is mentioned in the Heralds' Visitation of 1662 as living at Withernden in the parish of Ticehurst in 1481, and this family continued to live there for several hundred years as millers of flour with water power from the river, and as farmers. The pedigree and succession of the Newington family will be found in chapter fourteen. In 1499 the heirs of one Wybarne held of the manor of Hammerden, lands called Wytherenden.

In 1831 Mr. Dyer was given as owner and occupier of the farmhouse and Joel Newington of the mill-house.[17] After the Newingtons, the mill was worked by Mr. Brissenden, at first alone, but later in partnership with Charles Martin, and he was shown as the occupier in the 1851 census. When they gave up the business it was worked successively by Mr. Stedman, Mr. Hicks and Mr. Wickham. The last named became tenant of the mill in 1887 and was still milling in 1924, as he was also at Dunsters mill. In 1851 the occupier of the farm-house was Richard Tyler. One must be careful not to confuse the mill-house with the farm-house; the latter is a medieval hall-house building to which a parlour crosswing was added in about 1620. The house was all but destroyed in the late 18th to 19th century when that part of the house was rebuilt as a range set parallel to the 17th-century crosswing.[16]

It is timber-framed but refaced in the 18th century with stucco on the ground floor in front and red brick behind, the whole of the first floor tile-hung, but the timbering exposed in the east wall. The gabled north front has an overhanging upper floor with moulded bressummer; there is an original fireplace with fluted flanking pilasters and an

57. Witherenden Mill.

ornate overmantel divided by caryatid pilasters.[63] The present owners are John and Joan Scoones.

WITHERENDEN MILL (originally the miller's house), west end 17th-century, east end 18th-century; two stories, four windows, red brick below, tile-hung above. The mill-house (illustrated) was on the river bank, but has now been demolished.

THE YETT on the north side of the High Street below *The Bell* has been developed from a 15th-century hall-house with a first floor and chimney-stack added about 1600, and refaced with brick, but retaining original timbering in the gabled east wall, which has an overhanging first floor.[11] Inside, much of the timber-framing is visible, and the roof retains two bays, each 11ft. 6in. wide, divided by a cambered tie-beam with octagonal king-post; a similar beam and plain square king-post mark the west bay. There is a tiled roof with crown-post roof inside.[63] It was apparently once known as Yew Tree House, and The Yett is a corruption of this.

Chapter Twelve

Agriculture[79]

Geology and soils

Farming in the Ticehurst area has been influenced throughout the ages by the soil types that we have. These were laid down under many different conditions millions of years ago and uplifted to form a mountain at the time of the Alpine earth movement; subsequently after many geological ages they were eroded by weather so that the only visible part of the original top layer of the weald is the chalk of the North and South Downs.

Ticehurst soils are derived from the lower deposits and form what is known as the Hastings Beds of the Tunbridge Wells Sands, which consist mainly of sandy soils and clays. The latter lie mostly to the south of the Ticehurst ridge and this is difficult farming country due to poor natural drainage. The former are somewhat better from an agricultural point of view, but, being of a very fine sandy nature, they do tend to 'cap' after a rainy period followed by rapid drying, thus forming a crust which sometimes makes it difficult for young seedlings to break through.

Roman times

When the Romans first came to Britain in 55 B.C. the whole of this part of Sussex was covered in a dense primeval forest of various hardwoods — mainly oak — and coppice of hazel and other species (see chapter one). Caesar remarked that there was some iron-working in the maritime districts, but inland it was mostly wet and impenetrable. After the conquest of A.D.43 and the subsequent occupation the iron works were developed, and two sites have been excavated in Ticehurst and several more identified, as stated earlier. It does not appear that the Romans made any serious attempt to develop agriculture here.

Saxon times

The Saxons, from soon after the Romans left until the Norman conquest, undoubtedly settled in the weald by a process known as 'assarting', or clearing patches of woodland to make settlements and farmland; they also made a number of all-weather roads and improved those that the Romans had left. The Haeselersc charter of 1018 (chapter one) is a good example of this and in it are mentioned several farms which still exist in Ticehurst today. They kept in the most part to the drier sandy soils and chose the more fertile sites, and those that were reasonably accessible and fairly level. The poorer ground, the denser forests and the steep gills were left untouched and remained so for a long time afterwards.

Domesday

In 1086 the manor of Haslesse or Hazelerse, which made up most but by no means all of the Parish of Ticehurst, is said to have contained 4½ hides, with land for nine ploughs. These statements are somewhat contradictory because a hide was supposed to be the amount of cultivable land which one man with a team of eight oxen could plough and till in one season. It is a very variable measure but, as stated before, 120 acres of arable is a rough average for this part of the country. There were other manors which held land in the Hundred of Shoyswell, and, therefore, in Ticehurst, but it is impossible to determine from the Domesday entry how much of these lands were in this parish.

At that time the main value of the woods was to feed swine on acorns and other mast, and they must have accounted for a large proportion of the total area. We know from Domesday and from manorial records that the principal beast of burden was the ox, and that swine were used extensively for meat; gradually as grazing land became available, cows were introduced and chickens were kept. The main crop seems to have been barley, with some wheat.

The land was worked on a strict manorial or feudal system with free tenants paying a rent in money, and virgaters, cottars and serfs owing labour or a proportion of their produce as well as a variety of services, such as cartage, fencing and so on, for their lord. The lord owed service to his tenant-in-chief, who in turn owed military or other services to the king. This system continued, with modifications, for about seven hundred years.

Medieval period

During this time parishes, as opposed to manors, became stabilised, more land was cleared for agriculture and houses were built, at first just single-storey hovels with a fire in the centre, constructed of oak framing infilled with wattle and daub, and gradually converted into what we know today as traditional Sussex buildings. Corn production increased and flour mills grew up beside the streams and windmills on the hill-tops. Later a few iron mills were established — all discussed in an earlier chapter. Transport on the farms and to market was by bullock cart, not replaced by the horse until later.

Napoleonic Wars

The latter part of the 18th century and the first quarter of the 19th were marked by a deep recession with serious inflation and the poorer farmers here were affected very badly. In 1820 there were over 800 paupers in this parish with up to 50 complete families out of work, mostly agricultural labourers, the farmers being incapable of paying for their labour, the Poor Rate and other taxes. This culminated in the riots of agricultural labourers which were fairly general all over Sussex in 1830. There is a long account in Mrs. Odell's book of a visit made by the rioters to Ticehurst in the hope of enlisting supporters, but in this they were unsuccessful and the mob was dispersed.

The coming of the Victorian era brought in more stability and there was hardly any change in the farming community here during this period; little or no machinery was available during most of this time, everything being done by hand with large numbers of labourers — some highly skilled — employed on each farm.

Crops

The 'Wadhurst clays' in this area are difficult to work but grow splendid grass and also trees, particularly oaks. Thus through the ages the agriculture of Ticehurst has been mainly stock farming and forestry in various forms. Livestock farming has long been a major enterprise, and to a smaller extent still is, though smaller now due to present-day economics, but sheep are becoming more popular than cattle, and hay has long been a major crop in the parish. The oxen of ancient times are the forebears of our now greatly respected Sussex cattle which have been bred for beef. There was a championship herd at Oakover from 1908-29, and there is no better example of these animals today than on Maplesden farm at Stonegate.

There are, however, pockets of really good farming soils based on the Tunbridge Wells sands and very small areas of brick earth, the latter being comparatively new, derived from erosion in the form of dust storms caused by the very high winds and arid conditions found towards the closing stages of the last Ice Age. Many crops such as fruit and hops can thrive on these soils, mainly due to the comparatively free natural drainage.

On many of the better soils in the parish there is and always has been a diversity of crops: wheat, barley and most particularly oats grow well on our Tunbridge Wells soils. There is of course a limited demand for oats for animal feed and porridge but this area is extremely suited to the crop and it was grown somewhat more extensively for horse feed until the last war.

Through the ages forestry has been and will remain a vital part of the Ticehurst economy with the splendid oaks that grow so well on the Wadhurst clays and the underwood worked on rotation as coppice. Hazel was indigenous, as indicated by the Saxon name Haeselersc, and used to be cut on a seven-year cycle for thatching spars, sheep-hurdles and for the wattle and daub walls of the old 'Wealden' houses. Hornbeam was probably introduced in the middle ages for burning into charcoal for the iron furnaces, and chestnut some time later for fencing-stakes and hop-poles. The oaks, sometimes called the 'Sussex Weed', are as fine as any in the world and are in great demand for building, panelling, veneers and other purposes; in days gone by they were greatly prized for ship-building, the twisted branches especially being used for the curved ribs of the great sailing ships of the king's and merchant fleets, to which they gave great strength.

Hops

The farming world changes continuously and one can easily see by the large number of oast houses — mostly now converted to dwellings — that until fairly recently hops were a very significant crop in the area. Kersteman in his diary, written in about 1796 (see chapter two), refers to 'the increased plantation of hops in this county and Kent'; he says that in 1786 there were 200½ acres of hops in Ticehurst, and in 1835 the *Gazetteer* says there were 504. They were grown on almost all the farms, but the decline was fast and all-embracing due mainly to the brewers' diminishing requirements as they made better and more economic use of hops in their beers. It is sad to see this trend and the older ones amongst us can still remember with a trace of nostalgia the influx of pickers from the East End of London for the annual hop-picking, mixed with the many local pickers who enjoyed their paid holidays in the hop gardens of Ticehurst. There was a spirit never quite recaptured with the coming of the picking machines and the use of oil rather than coal and charcoal for drying the crop. Potatoes could be baked in the embers and tasted like no others!

Mechanical power

Steam engines first started to appear on the land at the end of the last century; enormous machines which gradually took over much of the heavier work such as deep ploughing. The traction engine also provided power for the large threshing machines which went from farm to farm as required. The first tractors, powered by a paraffin engine started on petrol, came in about 1920 and took over from the horse the duties of, for example, ordinary ploughing and pulling the reaper and binder, but the modern diesel tractor with its many hydraulic attachments did not arrive until after the last war.

1914-18 War

The First World War gave a great impetus to the whole of agriculture as it was vital to feed the population as far as possible from our own resources, as the sinking of large numbers of merchant ships by U-boats became ever more serious. Most of the younger and fitter farm workers went off to the war and much of the work was performed by the older generation and women of the village. Much of the hay was requisitioned by the army to feed the cavalry and transport horses, and on the farm the horse was the main powerhouse for all ploughing and cultivation.

1939-45 War

The Second World War saw some great changes in the pattern of local farming. The officers of the War Agricultural Committee were required to advise and occasionally to cajole the local farmers to plough up all the land that was possible to grow vital crops which were in short supply; thus much of the grassland, some rather unsuitable for growing crops such as corn, was utilised. Other than corn there were acreages of flax to make webbing equipment and parachute harnesses, and sugar beet was also grown locally.

Machinery and threshing gangs were provided by the War Agricultural Committee for hire as most farms were not equipped to cope with the changes of cropping involved. Much of the labour was done by the Women's Land Army and very excellent work they did in the absence of men. School children were also used for some tasks such as potato picking and hoeing of sugar beet. Some schools were evacuated from the London suburbs and there was a fairly plentiful supply of perhaps not too willing labour! There was however an assured market for all the produce and at a guaranteed price.

Present Day Trends

In recent years there have been enormous changes in farming systems which have been reflected mainly in the dramatic drop in the requirements for farm labour. Certainly Ticehurst farms are no exception. At Overys Farm, for example, 13 men were employed full time in 1939, whereas now, with treble the acreage, it is run by the owner and his son with one full time worker and two pensioners who help out when required! Of course modern machinery in conjunction with the scientist has made all the difference. The use of fertilizers and proven seeds, together with very specialised equipment and weed control has produced crops of which our forebears never even dreamed.

Sprays for the control of pests and fungal disease and the production of virus-free strains of all forms of crop have combined together with some wonderfully efficient machinery to produce large and consistent yields where it was so problematical before. All this has reduced the labour force to a minimum of specialist workers which has changed the nature of employment within the parish over a very short period.

Due to E.E.C. grain mountains the farmers of the area are looking at more diverse crops that are in demand and can be reasonably profitable. There has been a great increase in the growing of beans and peas for protein, and oil seed rape for the production of margarine; linseed is another oil crop for paints and many other uses. By 1947 flax had died out, but there is thought of reintroducing it for the linen industry to compete with northern France, Belgium and Holland who have the edge on us from a processing and marketing point of view.

Stock in the form of beef cattle, sheep and dairy herds were the main enterprises of Ticehurst farmers between the wars, apart from the limited acreage of hops grown on the suitable soils. Oversupply of milk products in the E.E.C. and quota restrictions have taken their toll but there are still herds at Cottenden, Maplesden and Downash Farm, and long may they continue. The days of hand milking twice a day have gone and machine milking has made all the difference. The old 11-gallon churn has also disappeared and the bulk tank has taken its place, much to the relief of many producers!

The spectacle of charming milkmaids with their churn on a barrow and cries of 'Milko' must have been splendid in the days of yore; however, one doubts that the quality of milk was quite up to the present day standard, but one must assume that this form of distribution took place in the parish!

Fruit growing has to some extent superseded the growing of hops, and there are a number of areas of top fruit, mainly of the culinary variety. Bramley grows well on some of the soils and there are many excellent patches of Cox's Orange and other varieties of eating apples, together with plums and cob-nuts. Top fruit has been grown in the area, particularly on the sandy soils, over many decades, the nature of the trees and their cultivation having changed dramatically in recent times. No longer do we see the huge apple trees planted at 40-ft. intervals, but much lower with bushes almost like hedgerows, planted eight to fourteen feet apart, making pruning, spraying and picking so much easier. Gone are the days of long ladders with all the dangers and hassle of fruit picking. The production of fruit gives seasonal employment to many of the ladies of the parish now that they can reach the fruit! To some extent it is reminiscent of the days of hop picking, being found an enjoyable and somewhat sociable occasion.

Soft fruit in the form of strawberries, raspberries, loganberries and blackcurrants are a feature of the parish as is well demonstrated by the Maynard family at Windmill Farm. They started the system of 'pick your own' which has been so successful from all points of view, where visitors from a wide area come, in season, to pick both soft and top fruit, knowing it to be fresh and available in quantities that only they know are required. They can also enjoy the fresh air and exercise of picking. Blackcurrants are mainly picked by machine these days and are grown both at Windmill Farm and at Rosemary Farm. It is estimated that one machine will harvest a quantity that would require 200 pickers, or about two tons an hour with a crew of five!

Future trends

It is interesting to speculate on farming in the area in the 1990s, and beyond to the next century. It would appear that there are three major factors that could change the use of land in the foreseeable future: the first is the pressure exerted by building developers which only good firm planning will keep in check. The second is the 'green' element which could make the most extraordinary changes in the pattern of modern agriculture and to the viable rural economy, with very small farms, possibly without fertilizers; back it would seem to the days of Saxon farming with oxen as the main motive power! There would certainly be no surplus agricultural products, and starvation might well stare one in the face!

The third suggested change is that a large proportion of the land might be turned over to recreation of all kinds — golf, horse-riding, shooting and a number of other activities, coupled with a large acreage of land planted up with woodlands. The latter is the most probable, where land which is capable of growing good crops will continue to do so in a modern intensive manner. Farmers are not unused to change as has been demonstrated since the First World War and they will no doubt continue to adapt as the needs and pressures of food production rise and fall. And what of the 'Greenhouse' effect? If this is a reality it would seem possible that the weather in this area would be not unlike that in the south of France or Italy. Shall we be growing oranges and lemons?

Chapter Thirteen

Bewl Water[73][23]

It is somewhat ironic that the Bewl Bridge Reservoir, as it was originally called, although affecting deeply the lives of many people in Ticehurst, and making a dramatic impact on the local landscape, was never intended to supply a local need. As long ago as the late 1940s it became clear that the traditional underground sources of water would prove totally inadequate to supply the needs of consumers in north-west Kent by the 1970s. The area, which covers more than 176 square miles, takes in the Medway towns of Rochester, Chatham and Gillingham, through to Gravesend and Northfleet, with Maidstone and its immediate environs to the south. The daily consumption within this area is now running at well over 30 million gallons. Although around two-thirds of the demand comes from domestic consumers, there is a significant call from industry in the area, and the need to guarantee a constant supply to about 400,000 people dependent on the service is vital.

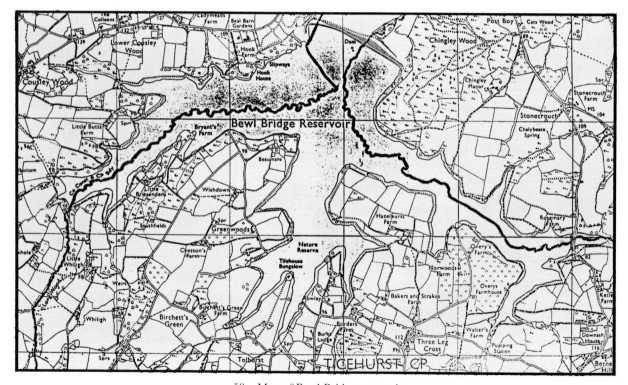

58. Map of Bewl Bridge reservoir.

The answer to achieving this increased supply lay in the River Medway Scheme, which involved drawing surface water from the Medway Catchment Area to provide the additional supplies that the engineers in the 1950s estimated would be needed in the 1970s and beyond. If this demand could be met from catchment water it would relieve the pressure on existing supplies from underground sources. The River Medway Scheme involved creating a reservoir to store water in the Bewl Valley to provide a top-up facility via the River Teise for the River Medway.

The present site of the reservoir was initially identified as a suitable location in 1946, when a survey was carried out to review existing and future water supplies in Kent. It was, however, not until 1962 that the then Medway Water Board decided to go ahead with plans to construct a water storage reservoir in the Bewl Valley. Prior to being dammed, the River Bewl flowed unhindered to the west of Chingley Wood, before running on downstream to meet the Teise. Two small tributaries help to feed the Bewl, one of which is the River Hook; it was this river which originally fed the pond that supplied the iron-works known as Chingley Forge, now submerged.

When looking for a suitable site for a storage reservoir, several practical aspects have to be taken into account. These include the likely disruption to existing property and, more importantly, the actual number of buildings and roads that would be lost. Also to be taken into account is the effect on the environment and whether this will be acceptable to all interested parties. Obviously the site must be able to hold sufficient water to meet the demands that will be made upon it and the ground has to be watertight to ensure it retains the stored water. The Bewl Valley had several distinct advantages over other sites considered by the Water Authority; not least of these was that with the construction of a dam, more water could be stored within this site than anywhere else in the region. Another major factor was that the two basic materials needed for the construction of the dam were available locally, sandstone and clay.

Planning approval was sought for this scheme from the Battle R.D.C. and was given long and careful consideration, as it was obvious that it would have a profound effect on a lot of people and would destroy over 800 acres of farmland, including large areas of hops and fruit. Also a number of farms and houses, some of them 500 years old, would have to be demolished and several lanes and access roads would be cut. Not unnaturally there was an outcry from local farmers and others, some of whom had lived there for generations. A highly organised protest resulted, on the largest possible scale with nationwide publicity. The planning authorities were very uncertain that the undoubted need for this scheme should override the very real local objections; finally the matter was decided by the passing in Parliament of the Medway Water (Bewl Bridge Reservoir) Act of 1968, which received the Royal Assent in July of that year.

The first stage of the project started at a site just to the north of Maidstone, where the scheme's engine room is now based. From here the plan was to draw water from the Medway and pump it via Eccles Lake to a new treatment works at Burham. This stage was completed and fully operational by 1973. The same year saw the start of construction work on the reservoir at Bewl Valley, its treatment works and the intake and pumping station at Smallbridge on the Teise.

Work on the reservoir was completed in 1975. After essential clearance of the Bewl Valley, the construction of the half-mile-long dam embankment got under way; this was made of a central rolled clay core supported on both sides by sandstone shoulders. Two towers were also constructed on the upstream side of the dam; the larger of the two is a draw-off tower to control the flow of water in and out of the reservoir. The smaller tower provides an overflow for excess water. During the building of the dam and the two towers a total of 770 acres of land was cleared and a number of buildings were

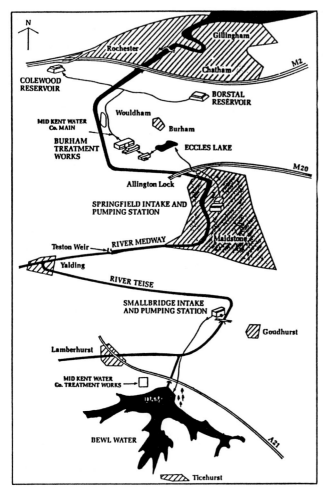

59. River Medway scheme.

demolished so as to leave nothing projecting beneath the surface. Filling began in earnest in September 1975.

So, finally, the reservoir as it exists today came into being, nearly 30 years after the site had been originally earmarked for the project. The total cost, including facilities, was £6.9 million. The capacity when full is 6,900 million gallons, the maximum depth 97 feet, the length of dam 1,000 yards and the perimeter length 15 miles. This mammoth task was not accomplished without a great deal of trauma; two 15th-century houses, Dunsters Mill and Ketley Cottage, were taken down piece by piece and carefully erected above the waterline; Copens, Overys and Lower Hazelhurst farms were demolished in situ, and a large area of agricultural land of all descriptions was lost for ever. The owners were compensated it is true, but to many of them it was home, and had been for generations. In all, 1,200 acres have been taken for this project and are now owned by the Southern Water Authority.

At the insistence of both the Water Authority and the County Council, access was strictly controlled and was finally limited to one road leading off the A21 to the car park and club house; all other roads were sealed off, apart from access to the properties remaining above the water-line, and limited access from the new causeway built to join the two ends of Rosemary Lane, which had been severed.

On the positive side, Ticehurst has now got a very beautiful stretch of water, the largest in south-east England, and quite excellent recreational facilities, imaginatively planned and executed by the Water Authority. The shoreline, both above and below the high-water level, was carefully landscaped by an expert and tree planting carried out with suitable species. This part of the Weald is designated as an Area of Outstanding Natural Beauty; it is largely made up of hills and valleys where fine oaks grow on the seams of Wadhurst clay that lie hidden under top soil. Many of these fine trees, however, have been cut down in the past to build ships and houses and to provide fuel for the furnaces of the iron industry.

Those visitors who stroll along the many miles of nature trails beside the water's edge will appreciate the sheer size of this reservoir. Whether it is angling, walking, studying nature, having a picnic or the more active pastimes of sailing, canoeing, rowing or diving, there is plenty of room within Bewl Water's 1,200 acres to enable everyone to enjoy the extensive facilities. The chief of these are conveniently sited round the Visitor Centre, just below the public car park; from here there are spectacular views across the water. On the wide expanse of grassy banks leading down to the water's edge visitors can sit and relax; this must surely be one of the loveliest and most tranquil settings in the south of England. An adventure playground has been specially created within the trees near the centre to keep the younger visitors amused.

The *S.S. Frances Mary*, which was built in 1922, started life as a passenger ferryboat in Scotland, steaming its way up and down Loch Lomond. It was later converted to diesel and in 1982 it was put up for sale and bought by the present owner who had it transported by road to Bewl, where it makes daily trips round the reservoir in the summer and can carry up to 74 passengers.

The reservoir now lays claim to the title of the premier trout fishery in the south of England and attracts more than 20,000 anglers each year during the fly-fishing season. This runs from April to October, during which period the water is regularly re-stocked with brown and rainbow trout; this normally totals more than 50,000 fish each year. Fishing permits are available from the fishing lodge, which is open each day throughout the season. There are many areas of the reservoir's waterside suitable for bank fishing. For those interested in either learning or improving their fly-fishing skills and techniques, a series of courses is held during the season under expert guidance.

The Bewl Valley Sailing Club now has a membership in excess of 5,000, and is one of the largest in the country. In all, there are some 1,700 boats registered, which include the greatest number of Mirrors and Lasers in any one club. There are also normally about sixty Flying Fifteens on wet moorings in the reservoir. Although the sailing club did not get into the water until the spring of 1977, it was founded 10 years earlier. The club is affiliated to the Royal Yachting Association.

Boardsailing is now the fastest growing water sport in the country and facilities for this are also provided through the sailing club. The Bewl Bridge Rowing Club got under way at the beginning of 1977 and now has more than 50 members. The Bewl Bridge Canoe Club caters for those interested in this sport, and now boasts more than 80 members. The Bewl Bridge Diving Club is a representative body to which other diving clubs wishing to use the facilities at the reservoir can affiliate.

With 770 acres of open water, 15 miles of shoreline and about 450 acres of land around the reservoir, there is a wealth of wildlife to see and enjoy. Although most of this area is open to visitors, a special section has been set aside as a wildlife sanctuary and nature reserve. This covers some 127 acres on the south side of the reservoir and is managed by the Sussex Trust for Nature Conservation. Considerable effort has been put into this reserve to encourage the widest possible use by different species. Nesting rafts and small islands have been made to protect birds from possible predators and 130 nesting boxes have so far been sited to promote breeding. Other work has been carried out to provide shallow areas of water where wading birds can feed and this includes laying a bed of shingle at Barnes Point, within view of the hide.

As well as providing important facilities for divers, ducks, geese and wading birds over-wintering, it is also a useful stopping-off point for migrating birds such as the greenshank, redshank, common and green sandpiper, tern, warbler, wheatear and whinchat. Mini habitats are provided at the waterside and along the streams, with reed, rush and sedges offering valuable shelter for a wide range of insects. In the summer, dragonflies and damselflies abound; plant life here includes water forget-me-nots, water mint and water plantain. Within the woodland areas, some of our larger mammals have found a natural home. Among the regular inhabitants are badgers and foxes, while brown hares use these areas for cover during the day, when they are not out feeding in the fields.

Chapter Fourteen

Ticehurst House and the Newingtons

Ticehurst House is sufficiently important and interesting to have a chapter to itself, but it is so linked up with the Newington family that the two will have to be discussed together. Between the two wars there were about two hundred men and women employed there, and it was by far the largest employer of labour in the parish.

The Newington pedigree begins with Sir Adam de Newington,[31]knt. who was living at Witherenden in 1481, and to date no-one has succeeded in taking the line back any further. The family lived there continuously until about 1880, but whether they were there before 1481, and where they came from, is not known. This Sir Adam of Witherenden in the parish of Ticehurst married Alice, daughter of Sir Alexander Colepeper of Bedgebury in the parish of Goudhurst, by his first wife, Agnes, daughter of Roger Davy of Northfield, Kent. They had a son — Thomas Newington of Salehurst, who married Jone, daughter of John Cheyney of Cralle, Sussex. Esq. Their son was also named Thomas, and he married Jane, daughter of Sir John Dawtrey of Moore Hall, Sussex. They had five sons, the fourth of whom was Joseph Newington of Ticehurst, who probably lived at Witherenden. A map of the manor of Hammerden dated 1614 shows the lands of Jose Newingtonne of Witherenden on the opposite side of the road to the present Mill House; this must refer to him. He married firstly, Dennis, daughter of ... Putland of Kent and widow of John Byne; they were married in Ticehurst church in 1581 and she was buried there in 1586. By her he had two sons, Morgayn born in 1582 and Zabulon, born in 1583, of whom next. Joseph married secondly, Susan, daughter of ... Beale of Kent and by her had a daughter. Joseph died in 1621 and was buried at Ticehurst.

Zabulon Newington of Ticehurst was living at Witherenden in 1619 and married Goodguift, daughter of Goddard Hepdon of Burwash. He died in 1635 and was buried at Ticehurst, having had nine sons and three daughters; their order of seniority is not clear. Joseph (1610-1686) is described as of Ticehurst and Burwash, gent. died without issue and owned Batemans in Burwash; Mr. Benjamin (1630-1689) is described as of Witherenden and he also died without issue. Zabulon (1612-1697) was another son, and he was a physician of Wadhurst.

John Newington of Salehurst, another son of Zabulon, married Elizabeth daughter of William Chele of Old Shoreham, Sussex. She died in 1675 aged 55, having had three sons and two daughters. The eldest son was John Newington of Witherenden, who was born about 1640 and married Mary Luckhurst in 1676; John died in 1706 and Mary in 1714 and both were buried at Burwash. They had three sons and two daughters, and their eldest son was Zebulon Newington of Ticehurst. He was born in 1682 and married Frances Burgess in 1707 in Ticehurst church. He died in 1720 and she in 1768, aged 92 and both are buried in the chancel of Ticehurst church; they had five sons and two daughters. The eldest son was Joseph Newington of Witherenden, who was born in 1707 and married in 1729 Mary Tompsett of Ticehurst. He died in 1790 'aged 82 years 7 months and 7 days'. She died in 1778 and both are buried in the chancel of Ticehurst church, although the inscription on the tombstone would appear to be incorrect. The burial entry in the register describes him as Joseph Newington, gent., of Withernden, aged 82 years and 3 months, which is correct. They had five sons and five daughters, the third son being Samuel Newington of the Vineyard, Ticehurst. He was born in 1739 and married Martha, daughter of Samuel Playsted of Wadhurst. He sowed the seeds of an enterprise which was to prosper in the hands of his descendants. Samuel entered the medical profession and started practice in his native place, residing at the Vineyard, which with its little lawn and spreading trees was the admiration of every passer-by as the ideal English rural retreat. In 1792 he is described in the rate books as an Apothecary, a designation then indicating not only a seller of drugs, but any general medical practitioner, but he had devoted particular study to the treatment of the insane. His uncle, another Samuel, had also been a physician of Ticehurst, and he was buried in the Courthope chapel in 1754. From about 1763 the younger Samuel had been accepting mental patients at the Vineyard, and some time after this date he built Ticehurst House especially for this purpose. An advertisement which appeared in the *Morning Chronicle* for Saturday 26 January 1793 is worth quoting in full:

'INSANITY'

An eligible situation is now offered for the reception of a few Patients under the immediate care and inspection of Samuel Newington, Surgeon and Apothecary of Ticehurst in Sussex.

Mr. Newington, having for thirty years past had patients under his care afflicted with this melancholy disorder, most of whom have been sent home to their friends in a sound state of mind, begs leave to inform the public that he has fitted up and neatly furnished a large and commodious house in Ticehurst aforesaid for the reception of Patients of the above unfortunate description. The situation is remarkably pleasant and healthy, commanding an extensive view over a fine country. The house has an attic story, and contains many neat appartments; is rendered perfectly safe and is so contrived as to admit of every convenience requisite for the reception of patients who do not require strict confinement.

Mr. Newington begs leave to inform his friends that he does not wish to receive into his house any Patients but such as are of a quiet and tractable disposition, as the comfort and convenience of all his Patients are what he means particularly to attend to, and, therefore, if any of a more violent turn, that such will be suitably provided for in his neighbourhood until by his management they become more tractable and proper to be received among those of the above description. Ticehurst is situated ten miles from Tunbridge Wells, twenty from Hastings, Rye and Maidstone, twenty four from Lewes and East-Bourne and forty four from London.

For further particulars respecting the terms and accommodation apply either personally or by letter to Mr. Newington, to Messrs. Slater, Ramrott and Burkitt, No. 7 in the Poultry, Mr. Deighton, Bookseller, Holborn, and at Mr. Pool's No. 24, Whitechapel, London.

The house which had been erected in the grounds of the Vineyard and referred to in the foregoing advertisement soon became well-known, and the good doctor must have needed all the material profit which accrued from his growing reputation, for he had a family of no less than 15 children to provide for — 10 sons and five daughters. Of the sons, four joined their father's profession; Samuel, the eldest, establishing himself in practice in Goudhurst, Zebulon in London, and Charles and Jesse assisting their father at Ticehurst.

The elder Samuel died in 1811 aged 72 and was succeeded in the business by Charles and Jesse. His wife Martha died in 1831 aged 91. They are both buried at Ticehurst and there is a mural tablet to Samuel in the south aisle of the church.

By way of conclusion to this brief account of a noteworthy character, it may be of interest to transcribe a letter (written by George Newington to his daughter Fanny) describing some festivities held to celebrate the birthday of old Mrs. Samuel Newington in 1822. Dating his letter 'Vineyard, July 25th 1822' he writes:

60. Ticehurst House and the Highlands, *c*.1820.

Henry will of course inform you of our grand doings last Wednesday week. I assure you it far surpassed anything I have seen for many years. We pitched your uncle Charles' marquee, which is a very large one, and a large booth a little above the stable, with six willows very handsomely decorated with all sorts of fine flowers, likewise eight willows on the sides of the booth. I assure you they were very elegant, the bottom of the booth lined with hop-bagging and every part so well secured that no-one could catch cold. The tables all mahogany sixty five feet long, seventy six dishes, with roast beef, lamb, chickens, ducks, hams etc., likewise nine tipsy cakes and a profusion of pastry, raspberry creams, etc. etc. Music and cricket in the afternoon. All the boys dressed in white trousers and jackets. Tea in the marquee in the evening, after which we had a most excellent dance, first in the booth and then adjourned to the front of the Vineyard where we kept it up till a late hour.

Your grandmother sat at the head of the table under a canopy of large sunflowers. She never looked better and I assure you she was very highly gratified and delighted. We drank her health with three times three. The tables were fixed rather on a descent therefore she had a most pleasing view of all her children (except one) and grandchildren to the number of sixty four. Altogether it had a most lively and impressive effect. We had ten servants to wait on us. It was conducted altogether in the most orderly and quiet way imaginable.

The next day we dined forty five off two very fine salmon etc. and on Friday we had a very large turbot and soles. The boys and girls kept it up until Saturday when your Aunts etc. finished the day with a lively game of Trap-ball. All cleared off without one cross look or contradiction — very fine weather; children all healthy and well looking. I forgot to say your Aunt Charles was put to bed on Wednesday evening, very sly, as we were dancing, of a seventh son of the seventh son; his name is to be Alexander.

Charles Newington, the seventh son of Samuel and Martha, was baptised at Ticehurst in 1781 and, with his brother Jesse, who was two years older, succeeded his father in the business. In 1802 he became a member of the Royal College of Surgeons; in 1812 he married Eliza, daughter of the Rev. William Hayes, and in the same year built a residence on a piece of land adjoining the Asylum, to which he gave the name of The Highlands. Jesse died in 1819, and, on the death of his mother in 1831, Charles purchased the business and became the sole proprietor. M. A. Lower, in his Worthies of Sussex, devotes an article to him:

> Of powerful frame and energetic disposition, he entered on his undertaking with the most indomitable spirit and determination, and, by gradual additions to the buildings and estate — by ornamenting the grounds in every way that could amuse and cheer the mind — and by great skill and assiduous attention to the patients entrusted to his charge, he succeeded in restoring many to health, and in acquiring for the Asylum at Ticehurst the reputation of being one of the best, if not THE best establishment of its kind in England. His laudable ambition was to render his Asylum a 'model' establishment, and to secure a provision for his own family of six sons and one daughter, by transmitting to them a property enhanced in value through the reputation he had conferred upon it. Simple in his own habits, he was expensive and almost lavish in providing for the benefit of others. He gave his sons a most liberal education: four of them graduated at Oxford and Cambridge, the eldest two embracing the profession of medicine — two others that of divinity — while the remaining two were brought up in the law.
>
> Many a man with such a reputation, and after such a life of successful toil, would have retired with an ample competence, but although the attractiveness of the place, and the character which

61.   The museum at Ticehurst House.

he had established for it, rendered it the resort of those who were able to remunerate him, still the out-goings were enormous; and after they were provided for, and the costs of a large family and a generous hospitality liquidated, other expenses arose. There was always some new conservatory or aviary, some pagoda or flower garden, some evergreen alley or artificial fountain, to construct, in order to make the place more attractive and comfortable. Besides this there were at the Asylum for years, many inmates who had seen better days, who had been admitted on a nominal payment, and who in course of time had become almost friendless; these, however, were fed, clothed and cared for, on a pittance which scarcely remunerated him for their daily bread.

Of a very inventive and ingenious turn of mind, he was ever planning and carrying out arrangements which tended to the safety and comfort of his patients. Amongst his numerous inventions, was that of an instrument for feeding those who were bent on self-destruction by starvation. This in its present modified form, is still used and has never been known to fail. He also lent his aid to the well-known John Read, in perfecting an instrument for removing obstructions; with this, in many instances among his patients, he saved life where all other remedies proved ineffectual. Another very ingenious invention was an accurate 'Tell-Tale' clock, the object of which was to test the punctuality of those appointed to take charge of special cases, and of those who acted as watchmen during the night.

A more responsible and arduous position a man could hardly sustain. Besides conducting, unaided, an establishment containing fifty or sixty patients with an equal number of domestic servants and attendants; the anxiety in guarding against accidents and escapes; the large correspondence which is incident to such a sphere; and the superintendance of the commissariat of a great household, Mr. Newington had the bodily health as well as the mental disease of that household to attend to. He was sustained, however, in his fatigues, and assisted in many of his domestic cares, by his most amiable wife, by his sisters, by his niece, and latterly by his daughter. Once, and only once, did Mr. Newington run a serious risk of his own life from a patient — a thick-set man who was apparently so inoffensive that he was allowed considerable liberty. He had possessed himself of a poker, and finding Mr. Newington in a defenceless position struck him a violent blow on the head. The Doctor recollected his old guard, which in early life he had learnt as a volunteer, and, warding off the second blow with his arm, grappled with his adversary, shouted for help, and so escaped with a severe scalp wound and a slight injury to the hand.

Mr. Newington's features were cast in a severe mould; but his address was singularly mild and prepossessing. Though his frame was stalwart, his temperament was nervous and sensitive. He was modest, and diffident of his own merits, though resolute where action was imperative. Although he had for some years received efficient aid from his two eldest sons, the anxiety resulting from his responsible position allowed him very little repose, and in the last two years of his life he suffered severely from that cruel enemy tic douloureux.

His last illness was a brief one. From over exertion on a treacherous April day, he was seized with a bilious fever, which in a few days terminated fatally. A very remarkable and painful circumstance attended his death: one of the arrangements about which he was most anxious, was that of providing against accident by fire in his large establishment. He had for some months been engaged in procuring every appliance which prudence could suggest to this end; but, by a singular fatality, while he was lying on his death-bed, a fire broke out in the main building of the Asylum, distant about 150 yards from his own house. It originated in the cooking department of the establishment, and in spite of every exertion the greater part of what it had cost him the labour of a life to raise, became a mass of smoking ruins! The room which he occupied was fortunately on the opposite side of the house to that which faced the blazing pile; so that he was never made acquainted with the fearful conflagration that lighted to his grave one of the best, the highest principled, and most estimable of men. He survived this catastrophe five days, and on the 27th April 1852, there ceased to beat as kind a heart as ever throbbed in human breast.

It is satisfactory to add that no loss of life resulted from this calamity, and that by the prudent management of Mr. Newington's two sons, the establishment was restored to its former efficiency. His widow died in 1864 aged 84, and they are both buried in the family vault to the west of the west door of the church.

Samuel Newington, their second son, was born in 1814; he went to Worcester College, Oxford, obtained his M.A. and was a member of The Royal College of Physicians. With his eldest brother, Charles Edmund Hayes Newington B.A. Trinity College, Cambridge, L.R.C.P., he carried on his father's business, and on them devolved the task of repairing the ravages wrought by the fire and of conducting on enlightened and progressive lines an institution which had now a reputation far more than local. The eldest brother Charles lived at the Vineyard and he died in 1863; the house was demolished in about 1952 and there are several cedarwood bungalows now erected on the site inside the high brick wall in the triangle formed by the junction of the main road with Vineyard Lane.

Samuel married in 1841 Georgina Oakeley Malcolm, daughter of Major General Beatson of Knole in Frant, and at one time Governor of St Helena. They lived at The Ridgeway, on the corner of Burnt Lodge Lane; the house was demolished by a direct hit from a flying bomb in 1944 and four cottages were built on the same site after the war. Samuel died in 1882, and his wife, Georgina, in 1898 aged 79. They had seven sons and six daughters, the fourth son, Alexander Samuel Lysaght, M.B. Cantab., M.R.C.S. carrying on the family business in conjunction with his first cousin, Dr. Herbert Francis Hayes Newington, son of Charles Edmund, under the style of 'The Drs. Newington'.

To the great grief of all who knew him, 'Doctor Alec' as he was popularly known in Ticehurst, met his death as a result of a motor accident in January 1914, and shortly afterwards a private company was formed to acquire and carry on the establishment, although 'Doctor Herbert' continued to be Medical Superintendent until his death in 1917. From a contemporary local newspaper carrying an obituary of Alexander Samuel Lysaght Newington:

> Born 12th April 1846 at Knole, Frant, in his younger days he went abroad; returning to England he then took up medicine, studying at Cambridge and at St. Thomas' and graduated M.B. and M.R.C.S. In 1881 he joined his cousin Dr. Hayes Newington in the carrying on of Ticehurst House, a well-known Private Asylum. In 1875 he married Mary Gertrude Fancourt, daughter of the late Dr. Robert Barnes. Doctor Alec was greatly respected in Ticehurst and took a keen and practical interest in all local objects and institutions, and was a liberal subscriber to all parochial objects.
>
> At Cambridge Newington was a noted rifle shot and represented his University in the rifle team at Wimbledon and elsewhere. He was well-known in the hunting field and was an excellent game shot, and was in every sense a popular man. He was an early pioneer of motor cars for which he had a great enthusiasm. He was killed on the 17th January when his car overturned just after noon, when passing a lorry at the junction of Burnt Lodge Lane and the Ticehurst to Wadhurst road. A witness at the inquest said 'he was driving very fast — faster than most people drive motor cars'. He apparently braked, skidded, lost control and the car turned a complete somersault. He was thrown out and received head injuries from which he died an hour later.

Alexander Newington built Woodlands — now Spindlewood Guest House — in 1882, from stone quarried locally, and this was his home. The beautiful carved oak rood screen in Ticehurst church, executed by Frank Rosier of Frant, was erected in his memory by his widow.

Campbell Newington, seventh son of Samuel, was born, probably at Ridgeway, on 19 March 1851. He had a twin brother, Theodore, born a few minutes earlier, who was a graduate of Caius College, Cambridge, and a doctor, who lived at Burnt Lodge and apparently never practised. Campbell was educated at Cheltenham College, and also at Caius; he studied land agency on the estate of Lord Fethersham at Helmsley in Yorkshire, and was always keenly interested in nature and everything connected with the countryside. He lived with his mother at Ridgeway until his marriage, on 21 October

1896 to Margaret Holgate Foster of The Holme, Regents Park and of Oakover, Ticehurst. They had an only daughter, Beatrice, who married Cedric Drewe of Wadhurst Hall and their eldest son, Francis, and his family now live at Oakover.

To return to Ticehurst House, it was, as stated earlier, formed into a private family company in about 1914, but 'Doctor Herbert' was the last member of the family to take an active part. He was the first chairman of the Parish Council, formed in 1894 and held this position until shortly before his death.[66] At this time, and up to 1939, the 'Establishment' as it was known was really a show piece and had a high reputation for the care and treatment of patients. These were mostly well-to-do, and a few would occupy a complete house with their own staff; Woodlands, now Spindlewood, Quarry Villa, now Stone Place, The Vineyard, and one or two smaller houses were all used for this purpose. The much loved and respected Medical Superintendent for many years, from 1917 until 1947, was Dr. Colin McDowall who lived at the Gables, near Hillbury, which was demolished just before he died. He was succeeded by Dr. Green.

The now rare volume *Views of Messrs. Newington's Private Asylum for Insane Persons, Ticehurst, Sussex*, published about 1830, says that the Establishment is on a considerable scale and principally calculated for the reception of Patients of a superior situation in life. In 1827 there were 30 male patients, 20 female patients, 17 male attendants and 19 female attendants. Among the features listed and illustrated are: The Hermitage and Bowling Green, The Summer House in the Pleasure Grounds, the Pagoda, the Moss House, and the Pheasantry, which contained a fine collection of golden pheasants. To these must be added the Chinese Gallery and a spacious well-equipped chapel where regular services were held; the latter has now been stripped and is used for other purposes.

The grounds were immaculately kept with fine flower and vegetable gardens, and there were two farms, Broomden and Brickkiln, and on the latter was constructed a private nine-hole golf course.

After the last war it was clearly impossible to keep the place up in its former lavish style and some drastic changes had to take place. These were carried out in the 1950s by Col. H. A. H. Newington — 'Bertie' as he was always called — son of 'Dr. Herbert' and chairman of the company. The finances were such that he had to be quite ruthless, and he was. On the advice of Dr. Green, who felt that the patients should be concentrated in the main buildings, especially as some of the properties were in a poor state of repair, the two farms and all the land was sold, together with the outlying houses, Woodlands, Quarry Villa, the Vineyard, the Gables, the remains of Ridgeway and many of the cottages. The ground staff, gardeners and maintenance workers were cut right down and the interior of the main house was altered to accommodate many more patients in one building.

When Dr. Green came, he said that he wanted Ticehurst House to be known as a hospital or convalescent home for people with psychological problems and the old titles of 'Asylum' or 'Establishment' to be dropped. In 1973 the family shareholders received an offer to sell their shares to Allied Medical Ltd., and later the ownership passed through the hands of several companies until 1986 when it became part of the group known as Nestor Medical Services Ltd. and became independent after a management buy-out. Finally in 1987 they became a public company with their shares listed on the Stock Exchange.

Dr. Green lived at Broomden from 1947 until 1966, and when he moved out the house was sold and he relinquished his post as Medical Superintendent at his own request, but continued as Consultant Psychiatrist (full-time until 1979). The principle of offering expert medical care in 'hotel-like' surroundings, started by Dr. Green, has been maintained, with separate units for the treatment of acute psychiatric illness and alcoholism as well as accommodation for elderly patients suffering from degenerative mental disease.

After a reorganisation of the local management in 1987, plans are being developed to improve and extend the facilities offered to patients needing psychiatric help. This has been emphasised by the change in name to Ticehurst House Hospital, which maintains its reputation as one of the leading psychiatric institutions in the country.

To end this chapter, the story must be told of the 'Escape of the Mad Prince' which received considerable press publicity at the time. Very briefly, this is what happened.[27]

In about 1898 Egyptian Prince Ahmed Seif-ed-Din, brother in law of Prince Fuad and uncle by marriage of King Farouk, who was 17 at the time, had a quarrel with Fuad and shot and wounded him. There was a sensational trial and he was sentenced to seven years penal servitude; after two years he was certified insane and removed to an Egyptian asylum. In about 1904, still insane, he was brought to England and put under restraint at Ticehurst House;

> that magnificent mental home, with its staff of great mental specialists, and very carefully chosen attendants, its costly furnishings, and its beautiful grounds provides something as near an earthly paradise for the mentally afflicted as one could well imagine. The inmates play tennis, billiards, cards, and any other games they want, and those of them not considered dangerous were allowed to motor about the country with attendants, and have anything that money can buy.

For some time his mother, the once beautiful Princess Nevdjvani, had wanted her son back, but in spite of intrigues in several countries and enormous bribes, the governments concerned were adamant. Eventually she got the aged Ibrahim Feridoun Pasha to help her and in August 1925 he succeeded with the help of William Pilbeam, one of the attendants, who had been promised enormous sums for his part in the operation. Incredibly the Prince was allowed to motor to Hastings on a day's outing, escorted only by Pilbeam, and they had no difficulty in boarding the steamship *Devonia*, making a day-trip to Boulogne, where he was met by friends and journeyed to Turkey in company with Pilbeam to rejoin his mother at her palace on the Bosphorus. After some thrilling adventures and by outwitting the English and French detectives who were following them, they eventually made it via Paris, Marseilles, Leghorn (Livorno), Lausanne, Sofia and Constantinople.

The sequel to the story is more prosaic. Pilbeam received none of the great rewards he had been promised, and returned to this country the following year, a disillusioned man. On his arrival at Dover, he was arrested and taken to Hastings where he was charged under a section of the Lunacy Act 1890, with complicity in the escape, and was fined the maximum of £20.

Chapter Fifteen

Ticehurst in Wartime

As stated in an earlier chapter, Ticehurst seems to have been untouched by the various wars which troubled this country and the continent until in the late 1850s there were general fears of a French invasion, and among the various organisations formed (in 1861) was the 17th Sussex Rifle Volunteer Corps. One Company of this was drawn from Hawkhurst, Ticehurst and Hurst Green, and drills were held at Ticehurst on alternate Tuesdays and Fridays.[1]

Some men from Ticehurst served their country during the Boer War, but the first real impact came with the 1914-18 war. Many men were already Territorials, serving with the 5th (Cinque Ports) Battalion of the Royal Sussex Regiment and were in camp on Salisbury Plain when war was declared. They were immediately sent to their 'War Station' at Dover and the Ticehurst men formed 'C' Company of the Battalion under the command of Capt. (later Lt. Col.) G. L. Courthope M.C. These men were 'in it' from the beginning but many more joined later or were conscripted into various branches of the forces.[37]

On 18 October the Battalion was sent to London to guard the Tower and the Bank of England, the first time this duty had been performed other than by a unit of the Brigade of Guards.[38] On 18 February 1915 the Battalion, after intensive training, went to France, and on 9 May fought the action which stands out in the Battalion's war record as a day always to be remembered with both pride and sorrow. This day was the beginning of the battle of Festubert and the Battalion suffered severely in an attempt to break through the German lines against overwhelming odds, and proved their courage and stead-fastness. The casualties were heavy — about 200 — and 'C' Company was the hardest hit; nearly half the losses from Ticehurst were on that single day.

The Company remained on active service, often in the front line, with short periods of rest, and on 5 July 1917 they were moved to the Ypres sector where, on the first day, they were heavily shelled in the appropriately named Slaughter Wood, where the Battalion lost 40 officers and 300 men, including wounded and gassed. That was their last action, after which they were sent to Italy where they remained until demobilisation in January 1919.[37]

A list of all those men and women from Ticehurst who fought in the war, 331 in all, hangs in the porch of the church, and inside is a memorial to the 62 men who perished, most of them in the two actions described above. In Stonegate and Flimwell churches there are similar memorials to the fallen.

Ticehurst was very much a backwater as far as the war was concerned.[50] Nothing ever happened and the long hot days dragged on with rumours of all sorts as the lengthening lists of casualties began to appear in the papers. There was, of course, no radio, and aeroplanes were rarely seen, but every morning a small airship passed overhead towards the sea, returning again in the evening; there were, in fact, two of them, called the *Silver King* and *Silver Queen*, presumably engaged on reconnaissance work. Then there were a few isolated Zeppelin raids, and one night one dropped some bombs in a wood near Ticehurst Road station in an attempt to hit the tunnel which would have blocked the line to the coast.

The sinister rumble of gunfire from France came strangely in intermittent waves, quite loud in certain places, but not audible a short distance away. The women were engaged in winding bandages and knitting, and all men who were not in 'reserved occupations' were at the front, and even suitable horses were drafted into military service. There was, of course, food and fuel rationing, but in a country village that was not very serious.

By contrast, the 1939-45 war was quite different, and Ticehurst was in the front line.[23] In the late summer of 1940, when Hitler was trying to bomb and destroy all our fighter airfields, he encountered, much to his surprise and fury, intense resistance from the Spitfires and Hurricanes of Fighter Command which decimated his mammoth bomber formations, thus saving the country in what has become known as 'The Battle of Britain'. Then in his anger he switched the bombers to night raids against London, where the risks from fighters were much less, and they had to endure 'The Blitz'. The general strategy was, as with the flying bombs later on, to attack them with fighters over the Channel and southern counties, and with a barrage of anti-aircraft guns in and around London.

Many of the 'dog-fights' between fighters, and between fighters and bombers, took place over Ticehurst and the neighbouring parishes and a lot of planes on both sides were brought down. The German bombers would often jettison their bombs when engaged by our fighters, thus making their get-away easier, and many of these bombs fell on this parish. In fact it has been said, probably correctly, that Ticehurst had more high explosive bombs, and later more flying bombs dropped on it than any other parish in England; in spite of this, there were no civilian losses here during the whole war, but a few people were injured.

The first bombs to fall on Ticehurst, and probably on Britain, were a stick of high explosive bombs which made craters stretching from Dalehill to Wallcrouch, just before 1 a.m. on 17 May 1940, killing a pony at Pickforde and demolishing a chicken house and 40 hens at Landscapes farm. Altogether about 500 H.E. bombs landed on the parish and many incendiaries and small anti-personnel bombs, nearly all of them in open country.[71] Some of them, for one reason or another, failed to explode, and these were dug up and made safe by the Bomb Disposal Units of the Royal Engineers.

An efficient A.R.P. (Air Raid Precaution) service was established to deal with incidents, a Home Guard to help the military to deal with any enemy parachutists or attempts at invasion. There was also a trained and efficient local Observer Corps, formed in 1924, given the title 'Royal' in 1940, with training in identifying aircraft; they had concrete trenches in the recreation ground and in what is now the Flimwell playing field. There were searchlight sites at Sheepwash Farm and at Overy's Farm near Dunster's Mill.

Of course there was a black-out and every window had to be obscured at night; there were no street lamps, and car headlights had to be severely screened, as did hand-torches. The A.R.P. wardens were responsible for enforcing these regulations, and did so very thoroughly indeed, so that not a chink of light was visible anywhere. All signposts and railway station name-boards were removed throughout the country to make it more difficult for any airborne invaders to find their way. These were always expected but never came. There was strict rationing of food, petrol, coal and clothes, and no building could be done except for urgent war-damage repairs. Life was really very difficult!

Church bells were to be rung only on special orders as a warning of imminent invasion, and at no other time. When the risk of this had passed it was announced that they could be rung again, and on the following Sunday every church in the country pealed its bells; a heart-warming sound after over four years of silence.

In 1943 there was a lull in the bombing as we and the Americans sent huge formations of planes over the German cities and industrial zones to smash their war effort. Then in 1944 Hitler loosed his 'secret weapon', the V.1 or Flying Bombs, contemptuously known as Doodle-Bugs. They were launched from sites in the Pas de Calais, concealed in woods, and were aimed at London; they were as fast as a Spitfire, jet-propelled and unmanned and carried a ton of high explosive in the nose. They were extremely difficult to destroy, either from the air or from the ground. The first one passed over here on 4 June 1944 and they lasted for 80 days until our invading armies had overrun their launching sites.

At first the same tactics were used as with the bombers, but then the guns were moved down to the coast. Nineteen of these missiles fell on Ticehurst and 12 on Stonegate and Flimwell; Ridgeway was demolished and Flimwell school and Furze House were so badly damaged they had to be evacuated. The blast from these bombs was terrific, and there was not a house in the parish that did not have its windows broken, ceilings down or tiles ripped from the roof. Many old buildings were very badly shaken, and some had to be pulled down.

In the S.E. Regional report of October 1944 Lord Monsell said: 'Out of 5448 Flying Bombs which came overland, 2341 fell on London ... I cannot sufficiently praise the self-sacrifice, courage and endurance of the people of the Region, who were willing that 100 per cent of the bombs should be brought down on them rather than that they should reach London. It took about 10 bombs to kill one civilian in S.E. England, which had they proceeded to London would have killed 22'.

We have already seen that the local schools were evacuated to the West Country during the worst of this time, but another event must be mentioned which had quite an impact on the parish. In 1940, when the bombs began to fall on London, most of the schools were evacuated to the country. Brockley Park school from S.E. London, came to Ticehurst, and Oakover, which had recently become vacant with the death of Mrs. Campbell Newington, was requisitioned for them, and was used as classrooms, with science laboratories in the stable block; the boys and masters were billeted out in the village and in a hostel at Shovers Green. Their headmaster, Dr. Sinclair, was an outstanding man, liked and respected by everyone, and ruled the boys and looked after the house with an iron hand in a velvet glove. When the flying bombs came the school was re-evacuated to Wales, and then they returned to London and the house was handed back to its owners, in remarkably good condition.[23]

Appendix: Listed Buildings in Ticehurst

High Street, Ticehurst

Nos. 5-8: one 18th-century building; red brick below, tile-hung above.

Nos. 1-4 HAZELWOOD COTTAGES: similar.

FIELD: 17th-century building. North side is a small 19th-century shop front.

CLAYHAMS & COTTAGE.

PLANTATION TEA CO. (Sweet Shop): early 19th-century building. House attached to the east is of the 18th century; painted brick below, weather-boarding above.

THE COTTAGE: 18th-century building faced with weather-boarding.

WESTBOURNE VILLA: early 19th-century building.

Nos. 1 & 2 CERNE COTTAGES: one building of the early 19th century, faced with weather-boarding.

THE LONG HOUSE: early 19th-century building.

CHEQUERS: main part dates from the 19th century; to the west is a wing which was originally two cottages but is now part of the Inn, 18th century.

DUETTE: 19th-century building.

THE YETT: 15th-century timber-framed building re-faced with red brick and grey headers on ground floor and tile-hung above; tiled roof; crown post roof inside.

APSLEY COURT (Steellands): late 17th-century building re-fronted in the 19th century. 19th-century doorway with curved head and semi-circular fan-light.

Nos. 1, 2 & 3 BELL COTTAGES: one 18th-century building; painted brick below, tile-hung above. *THE BELL*: 17th-century (or earlier) timber-framed building re- faced with red brick below and tile-hung above. Modern gable projection in imitation timber-work forming porch with roof over. 18th-century addition projecting at east end with two window bays. NAT WEST BANK & BAKERY: one early 19th-century building, red brick below, tile-hung above.

CROFT VILLA (No. 30 High St.): early 19th-century building.

THE SURGERY (Nos. 31 & 32): one building of the early 19th century, much altered.

36 HIGH STREET: early 19th-century building; formerly Waterhouse, and previously the Poor House.

CROFT COTTAGE: formerly two 18th-century cottages, now one house.

Nos. 2, 3 & 4 HIGH STREET (Butler Cottages): one 18th-century building.

The Square

LLOYDS, FORD: one 17th-century (or earlier) building, timber- framed, re-faced with red brick and tile-hung above. Steeply pitched hip tiled roof; small 19th-century butcher's shop built out at south-east.

CAXTON COTTAGE, OLD MERRIAMS, BEECH HOUSE: one 17th-century (or earlier) building, timber-framed, refaced with red brick and grey headers with rough-cast and imitation timbers above; parrapet at each end of front; steeply pitched hip tiled roof.

BUTTONS & *DUKE OF YORK*: one building, 18th-century painted brick; modern shop front.

Church Street

CHURCH GATE HOUSE and CHURCH GATE COTTAGE: one early 19th-century building.

TICEHURST SCHOOL: described separately.
ST MARY'S CHURCH: described separately.
COOPERS STORES (Warwick House andFuller's Shop): 18th-century front to a 16th-century building.
PHARMACY: early 19th-century building.
HOLGATE HOUSE: *c*.1830.
HURST COTTAGE: 18th-century building with 19th-century gabled porch.
CHURCH HOUSE: early 19th-century building; once a house and workshop. Painted brick with weather-boarding above.
ROMANY COTTAGE: formerly two (probably 17th-century) cottages; painted brick, tiled roof.
CINQUE COTTAGE: formerly two 17th-century (or earlier) cottages. Timber-framed building with plaster infilling.
GABLE END (No. 7): *c*.1830.
Nos. 17-20 CHURCH STREET: one 17th-century (or earlier) building, timber-framed, refaced with weather-boarding below and tile-hung above; 19th-century windows; 18th-century doorways.
Nos. 21-25 CHURCH STREET: one 17th-century (or earlier) building, re-faced with stucco on ground floor and tile-hung above.
NORTHGATE HOUSE (formerly Old Timbers): formerly a house and shop, now one dwelling; dating from 17th century or earlier; timber-framed re-fronted with brick below and tile-hung above.
SHOP (Cheryl, Leslie, Leach): L-shaped building *c*.1830; modern shop fronts.

St Mary's Lane
Nos. 1 & 2: one 18th-century building.
Nos. 3 & 4: one 18th-century building.
WOODBINE VILLA: Early 19th-century building, at one time the post office; faced with weather-boarding, tiled above; small ground floor addition for G.P.O. at the north end.
WATMANS: L-shaped 18th-century house, painted brick, slate roof, modern porch. South-west wing curved to follow the lane; weather-boarded on first floor.
WHITE COTTAGE: 18th-century building, two storeys faced with weather-boarding; hip slate roof; doorway in moulded architrave surround.
FAIRVIEW COTTAGE.

Lower Platts
LITTLE CLAYHAMS: once two 18th-century cottages; red brick with grey headers, tile-hung above.

Upper Platts
LOWER TOLLGATE: L-shaped 18th-century building, once three cottages; painted brick, tile-hung above.
THE INSTITUTE: described separately.
SINGEHURST: 17th-century (or earlier) building; red brick below, tile-hung above.

Vineyard Lane
BROOMDEN: Dates from 18th century; red brick below, tile-hung above, hipped tiled roof.
BARN at BROOMDEN: Dates probably from 17th century, faced with weather-boarding; hipped tile roof with central wagon entrance on east side with pentice to the north and south of this. Tie beams with arched braces inside.

Dale Hill

CHERRY TREE: shown as two cottages on 1839 Tithe map. Dates from 18th century; painted brick below, tile-hung above.

DALE HILL FARMHOUSE: 18th-century (or earlier) building; red brick below, tile-hung above.

Tinkers Lane

WALTERS FARM: L-shaped 18th-century (or earlier) building faced with weather-boarding; south wall tile-hung with a stuccoed chimney breast.

Hurst Green Road

GIBBS REED FARMHOUSE: L-shaped 18th-century building; mostly faced with red brick below and tile-hung above, but some weather- boarding.

BIRCHENWOOD COTTAGE: early 19th-century building faced with weather-boarding. Hipped slate roof and gabled porch. PASHLEY MANOR: early 17th-century timber-framed building, originally half H-shaped. Original front faces north-east and is close-studded with unstained timbers and plaster infilling, restored in about 1947 by the Forsyths. The south-west front dates from the early 18th century when the part between the wings was filled in. Two massive red brick chimney breasts on the south-east wall. 17th-century panelling inside.

LITTLE BOARZELL: double L-shaped building of the 17th century or earlier; ground floor stuccoed, tile-hung above; two small gables over first floor windows; west gable end weather-boarded.

Threeleg Cross

THE BULL: possibly 14th-century timber-framed building of Hall House construction with the timber and plaster infilling exposed in the north wall. Re-fronted with red brick on the ground floor and and tile-hung above.

APRIL, PROSPECT & EBENEEZER COTTAGES: L-shaped range, dating from the early 19th century. Most of the cottages here are the same.

BAKERS & STRAKES FARM: timber-framed house of *c.*1500 with the first floor overhung on brackets, but now tile-hung; steeply pitched hipped tile roof. Crown post roof inside.

UPPER HAZELHURST: 17th-century (or earlier) building. Ground floor faced with weather-boarding, tile-hung above, half hipped tiled roof.

Huntley Mill Road

NORWOODS FARMHOUSE: 17th-century (or earlier) timber-framed building re-faced with red brick below and tile-hung above. Modern L-shaped wing to the north-west.

DUNSTERS MILL HOUSE: has been moved bodily up the hill. 15th- century timber-framed house with plaster infilling.

Burnt Lodge Lane

BURNT LODGE: Early 19th-century building.

ROWLEY: 15th-century timber-framed house restored and re-faced. Red brick below and tile-hung above.

Boarders Lane

BOARDERS FARMHOUSE: Re-faced 17th-century building. Ground floor red brick, tile-hung above.

Birchetts Green
BIRCHETTS GREEN: 17th-century (or earlier) timber-framed building re-faced with weather-boarding.
UPPER TOLHURST.
LOWER TOLHURST.

Claphatch Lane
BEAUMANS: 18th-century building with two parallel ranges; red brick below, tile-hung above.
OLD FARMHOUSE, Beaumans: 15th-century timber-framed building re- faced with red brick and grey headers below and tile-hung above.
BEAUMANS OAST.
CLAPHATCH: said to be an old timber-framed building re-faced in the 19th century.
CLAPHATCH two oast houses and granary.

Ward's Lane
HOLBEAMWOOD: north wing is 18th-century. Red brick and grey headers alternately, stringcourse, eaves cornice of brick cogging, tiled roof. South wing of one window bay added in early 19th century.
CHESSONS FARMHOUSE: Re-faced 18th-century building. Two parallel ranges, red brick below and tile-hung above.
CHESSONS BARN: timber-framed building of c.1700 faced with weather-boarding on a red brick base.
Nos. 1 & 2 CHESSONS COTTAGES: as above.
BRYANTS FARMHOUSE: small 17th-century (or earlier) timber-framed building; red brick below and tile hung above.

Wadhurst Road
TOLLGATE: originally the Toll House c.1762. One storey with two windows, faced with weather-boarding, hipped tiled roof.
GRAVEL PIT: L-shaped house, probably of the 17th century; red brick below, tile-hung above.
TICEHURST HOUSE: described separately.
THE HIGHLANDS.
EAST LYMDEN. THE ROSARY, Wallcrouch.
WALLCROUCH FARMHOUSE: 18th-century red brick building with weather-boarding above.
THE OLD FARMHOUSE, Wallcrouch: 18th-century (or earlier) building, at one time two cottages; red brick and tile-hung above.
WHILIGH: the original part of the building was erected by John Courthope in 1586, but was altered in 1840; additions were also made in the early 19th century. The east front dates from then.
LITTLE WHILIGH: L-shaped 18th-century house of red brick, tile- hung above.
SHOVERS GREEEN HOUSE: L-shaped building. Early 19th-century front to a probably older building; red brick, tile-hung above.

Wardsbrook Road
WYBARNES: see under Vicarage, Chapter V.
OAKOVER.
PARSONAGE FARMHOUSE: 17th-century (or earlier) timber-framed house. Red brick

base now tile-hung; hipped tile roof.

WEDDS FARM.

THE OLD MILL, Wardsbrook: 18th-century red brick with weather-boarding above; tiled roof.

WARDSBROOK FARMHOUSE: L-shaped timber-framed house. North wing dates from 16th century and is close-studded with plaster infilling; the south wing of c.1600 is of lower elevation; the west front is now tile-hung but oversails on a bressummer and brackets; tiled roof in two hips. Two storeys and attic with one dormer. Queen post roof inside.

WARDSBROOK OUTBUILDINGS: 16th-century building considered by some to have been the detached kitchen of the 15th century; this would appear to be a portion built of re-used materials converted into storage for an oast house in 1833.

Cottenden Road, Stonegate

COTTENDEN FARMHOUSE: 18th-century painted brick building.

NEW HOUSE FARM.

Battenhurst Road, Stonegate

EATONDEN MANOR FARMHOUSE: L-shaped house. Original part dates from 17th century (or earlier). Timber-framed, re-faced with painted brick on ground floor and weather-boarded above. 18th- century wing of red brick behind.

OLD BATTENHURST FARMHOUSE: probably dates from 17th century.

CLAYHALL COTTAGE & LITTLE ALE HOUSE.

Limden Lane

LIMDEN FARMHOUSE: L-shaped 17th-century (or earlier) house faced with weather-boarding.

LITTLE CROFT & WAYSIDE.

Bardown Road, Stonegate

COOPER'S FARMHOUSE: L-shaped medieval house much altered in the 16th-18th centuries. Re-faced with red brick on ground floor, tile-hung above. Tiled roof, modern gabled porch, two storeys. BARDOWN. BRICKLEHURST MANOR (School): Early 19th-century red brick building with two storeys.

MAPLESDEN: original portion is a 17th-century timber-framed building. North front re-faced or added in 18th century.

NORMANSWOOD: Of the 18th century or earlier.

Station Road, Stonegate

STONEGATE FARMHOUSE: Of the 18th century or earlier. Two parallel ranges, red brick with grey headers, tile-hung above.

STONEGATE FARM BARN: 18th-century barn faced with weather-boarding; tile roof.

THE OLD VICARAGE.

BARN AT HAMMERDEN: 16th-century timber-framed building faced with weather-boarding on a brick base. Poor condition.

LITTLE HAMMERDEN: now two cottages. 17th-century timber-framed building re-faced with red brick in the 19th century.

WITHERENDEN FARMHOUSE: timber-framed house of c.1620 partly re- faced in the 18th century with stucco on the ground floor in front and red brick behind. The whole of the first floor tile- hung, but the timbering exposed in the east wall. WITHERENDEN

MILL (Originally the Mill House): west end is 17th- century, east end 18th-century; two storeys, four windows, red brick below, tile-hung above.
ROUNDELS, Witherenden: originally two oast houses and a granary.

Union Street, Flimwell
QUEDLEY: Restored 17th-century (or earlier) building; red brick, tile-hung above, half hipped tiled roof.
YEW TREE COTTAGE.

Rosemary Lane
DOWNASH: now flats. Built c.1900 in Tudor style.
KETLEYS: 16th-century building re-faced with white weather-boarding. Two gable dormers.

Hawkhurst Road, Flimwell
ST. AUGUSTINE'S VICARAGE: c.1839. Probably designed by Decimus Burton; similar to houses in Calverley Park, Tunbridge Wells. He also designed the original church.
ST. AUGUSTINE'S CHURCH: described separately.
SEACOX HEATH: Present House built in 1871 to replace an older one; architects were Carpenter & Slater. A tall mansion in the style of a French chateau.
OLD TIMBERS AND HOUSE TO WEST.
MOUNT PLEASANT FARMHOUSE.

Hastings Road, Flimwell
BOUNDARY FARM: 18th-century (or earlier) building; one storey and attic; faced with weather-boarding.
BROOKGATE FARMHOUSE: L-shaped 17th-century (or earlier) house, re-faced in the 19th century. Two storeys and attic; red brick below, tile-hung above. At the south end of the south wing is a massive shouldered red brick chimney breast.
BROOKGATE: two oasthouses and granary.

Notes

1. Hodson & Odell, *History of Ticehurst* (1925).
2. Savidge & Mason, *Wadhurst.*
3. *Sussex Archaeological Collections*, vol. 77, p. 119.
4. Domesday Book, Sussex, edited for S.A.C. (1886).
5. Walker, Thomas, *History of Sussex* vol. I (1834).
6. Lower, M. A., *Worthies of Sussex*, p. 101.
7. Hinde, Thomas (ed.), *The Domesday Book* (1985).
8. *Victoria County History of Sussex*, vol. I, p. 401.
9. 'Perambulation of Kent, 1826', *Sussex Archaeological Collections*, vol. XVI, p. 272.
10. Bevan, G. M., *Portraits of the Archbishops of Canterbury.*
11. *Victoria County History of Sussex*, vol. IX (1937), pp. 251- 57.
12. Ruth Collingridge Collection, E.S.R.O., ref D/982, File 8.
13. Calendars of Charters and Documents relating to the Abbey of Robertsbridge, no.331.
14. Kersteman Diaries, copy in Collingridge Collection, File 1A
15. *ibid.*, File 2(4).
16. Lower, M. A., *Chronicle of Battle Abbey*, pp. 200-1.
17. Furley, *History of the Weald of Kent*, p. 83.
18. Cal. Pat. Rolls 4 Edw III m. 40d. 14 Mar 1330.
19. *ibid.*, 26 Edw III m. 4d. 24 Feb 1352.
20. Wm. Durrant Cooper, *F.S.A.*, S.A.C. XVIII pp. 17-36.
21. Lomas, S. C. (ed.), *The Memoirs of Sir George Courthope 1616- 85*, Royal Historical Society.
22. Kersteman Diaries, *c.*1796.
23. Personal knowledge of the author.
24. Documents in possession of the author.
25. Memorandum in parish register of St Oswald, Durham.
26. Churchwarden's acounts 1685-1736, E.S.R.O.
27. Two press-cuttings in the author's possession, one dated 1937 and the other undated (probably 1926) from which the newspaper's title has been cut.
28. *Gazetteer of England and Wales* (1842).
29. A full pedigree cna be found in Burke's *Landed Gentry.*
30. Cleere, Henry, *The Iron Industry of the Weald.*
31. Estate maps of Hammerden, E.S.C.R.O.
32. Collingridge Collection, File 4(2).
33. *ibid.*, 4(1).
34. *ibid.*, 5(1).
35. *ibid.*, 5(1).
36. *ibid.*, 10 Box 2.
37. Hodson & Odell, *History of Ticehurst*, Appendix written from first-hand experience by Geoffrey H. Hodson, ex-Colour Sergeant. 5th Royal Sussex.
38. The author's father was there and also Ted Field, Croix-de- Guerre, for many years Churchwarden with the author at Ticehurst
39. Letters and Papers Hen. VIII, XIII(2)g 646 (34 & 39) at Sussex University.
40. Tithe map of Ticehurst (1840), E.S.R.O.

41. Land tax records, E.S.R.O.
42. Collingridge Collection.
43. Oakover Deeds and sale catalogue.
44. Oakover rent ledger.
45. See under Witherenden, chapter eleven.
46. *S.A.C.*, vol. VIII, p. 26.
47. Collingridge Collection, File 3A.
48. *ibid.*, File 5(3).
49. *ibid.*, File 18.
50. Memoirs of the author's mother Beatrice Drewe, neé Newington, 1965.
51. *S.A.C.* vol. LXXI, p. 223 *et seq.*
52. Mason, R. T., in *Sussex Notes and Queries*, May 1941.
53. Essay by Mrs. I. M. Baker, ref. F.0156577, dated Sept. 1977 for Mr. and Mrs. Butler, then owners of East Lymden. Copy at Oakover.
54. Mawer & Stenton, *The Place-Names of Sussex*, vol. VIII, part II (1930).
55. Cameron, Kenneth, *English Place-Names*.
56. Recollections of Miss Nancy Gillham and her sister.
57. Hughes, G. M., *Roman Roads in South East Britain* (1936)
58. List at E.S.C.R.O.
59. Letter from Rother District Council.
60. Told to author by Rev. F. J. Law who conducted a short service there with only his two daughters.
61. Recollections of Ted Field transcribed by P. J. Reeves.
62. This chapter is based on Auth: 1, 11, 23.
63. Schedule of Listed Buildings, Rother District Council.
64. Information supplied by Rother District Council.
65. Information supplied by Eastbourne Water Company.
66. Minutes of Annual Meetings of the Parish Council.
67. *V.C.H.* vol. IX, pp. 154-56 & *Arch: Cantiana*, LXXIV (1960), pp. 1-47.
68. *Sussex Genealogist & Local Historian*, vol. 7, no.1.
69. *ibid.*, vol. 4, no.4.
70. Letter from Ticehurst House, 14 Nov. 1988.
71. Scrap book of Ticehurst Women's Institute, 1953.
72. Letter from Sheila, widow of the late Frank Young.
73. *Official Guide to Bewl Water*, Southern Water Authority.
74. D.U.N. papers, E.S.R.O.
75. *S.A.C.*, vol. LIII, p. 193.
76. 1851 Census.
77. Written by F. J. Reeves of Overy's Farm.
78. Supplementary information given by David Martin.
79. Largely based on information given by F. J. Reeves.
80. From an article by Elizabeth O'Kelly in 1989 and information from E.S.R.O. ref. A75 5712/16/2.
81. Berry, *Sussex Genealogies* and parish registers.

Index

Acres Rise, 51, 83
Adam, Stephen, 13
Adam the Priest, 7, 33, 34
Adams: Grace, 44; John, 44, 73
Advowson: 34, 102; of Flimwell, 42; of Stonegate, 40
Ælfgyfu, Queen, 2
Ælfstan, Archbishop, 2, 7, 106
Æthelred the Unready, 3
Æthelric, 5
Æthelwald, King, 19
Agelric, 5
Airships, 131
Akers-Douglas, Ian, 61
Alciston, 5, 7, 101
Alderstrode, Ralph de, 103
Allen, Rev. David, 16
Allied Medical Ltd., 129
Alric, Bishop, 3, 5, 7, 19, 34
Almshouses, 10, 73
Alsfords sawmills, 83
Alvred de St Martin, 8
Alye, Thomas, 17
Ambulance, 59
Aple Dorys, 9
April Cottage, 79
Apsley: family, 25, 108; Anthony and Judith, 69, 97; Henry, 89; John, 89
Apsley Court, 25, 73, 89
Area of parish, 9
Armistead, Rev. G. A., 42
Arnott, Mr., 63
A.R.P., 132
Atkins' Stores, 87
Augustine, Abbot of, 3
Aulus Plautius, 2
Austin, James, 106
Autocar Company, 57
Automatic telephone exchange,56
Aynscombe, Thomas, 97

Baber House, 96
Bagnall, Sister Murial, 59
Bailey, Rev. E. A., 40
Baker, Field Marshall Sir Geoffrey, 65
Baker, John, 17, 29, 97
Baker, Sir John, 35
Baker, Sir John and Elizabeth, 102
Bakers Farm, 79, 89, 98
Bakery, 73
Baldwin, David, 90
Ballards Wood, 83
Bar hyll, 101
Bardens, 77
Bardown, 2, 10, 78, 87, 90, 99
Bardown Road, 78
Barfleur, Battle of, 14
Barfoot family, 61, 63, 85
Barnes, Anthony, 90 Barnes, Mary Gertrude F. and 128; Dr. Robert, 128
Barrow, John, 95
Basing, Sir William and Margaret, 104
Batemans, 123
Battenhurst, 87
Battle, Abbot of, 7, 101
Battle Abbey, 13
Battle of Britain, 132
Battle R.D.C., 49

Bayhall, Kent, 90
Bayham Abbey, 8
Beale, Huburt, 64, 93 Beale, Susan, 123
Bearhurst, 8, 10, 87
Beatson: Georgina O.M., 128; Major General, 128
Beauchamp, Mr., 35
Beaul Barne, 7
Beaumans: 99; Oast, 79; Old Farmhouse, 79
Beckwith, William, 107
Bedgebury Forest, 85
Beech House, 59, 70
Beech House Press, 70
Bell Cottages, 73
Bell Field, 63, 73
Bell Hotel, 73
Bells, 14, 28, 29, 32
Benefaction Boards, 28
Beresford's Charity, 47
Berkeley, Ann, 90
Berkeley, Rev. George, 30, 34
Berners Hill, 83
Bewl Close, 83
Bewl river, 12
Bewl Water, 118
Beyley, Rev. Samuel, 33
Biggs family, 10, 95
Bines, 10
Birchenwood Farm, 81
Birchett Green, 10, 79
Bishop, Mr., 71
Blake, G. H., 103
Blind, National Institute for the, 47
Bloomery, 1
Blundell, Widow, 92
Boarders Farmhouse, 79
Boarzell, 7, 10, 101
Bodiam, 11
Boleyn: family, 104; Queen Anne, 104; Sir John, 12
Booker, Mr., 73
Borders Farm, 10
Boscawen, Rev. John Evelyn, 34
Boundary Farm, 83
Bounds of Ticehurst, 9
Bowers, Mr., 44
Bramall family, 65, 87, 92, 106, 109
Brickkiln Farm, 77
Bricklehurst, 7, 87, 90, 99
Brickyard Cottages, 78
Bridge Inn, Stonegate, 87
Briefs for collections, 18
Brissenden, 111
Broadwater Down, 11, 49
Brockley Park school, 100, 133
Broking, William, 107
Brook: John and Francis, 89; Thomas and Anne, 89
Brookgate Farm, 83
Broomden, 10, 78
Brown, Walter, 66
Browne, Sir Anthony, 8
Bryants Farm, 10, 79
Brykenden, John, William and Sabrina, 107
Budgeon's map of Sussex (1724), 89, 92
Bugseys Farm, 78

Building development, 51
Bull Inn, 79, 90, 93
Burgelstaltone, 5
Burgess, Francis, 123
Burnt Lodge, 10, 12, 77, 78, 83
Burt, Thomas, 99
Burton, Decimus, 40, 85
Burwash, 11
Burwash Weald, 38
Bus: service, 59; shelter, 74
Buss family, 92, 99
Butler, P. J., 94
Buttons, 70
Bygge family, 95

Cabilia, Rev. William de, 33
Cade, Jack, 13
Caesar, Julius, 1
Callow, Roger, 98
Callowe, Rev. John, 16, 33, 89
Calvinist Chapel, 81
Campbell, John Rea and Sarah, 47, 77, 99, 102
Campbell Cottages, 77
Canterbury: Cathedral, 3; Dean and Chapter, 28, 33, 35, 102
Captives in Algiers, 18
Carpenter and Slater, 107
Carr, William, Viscount Beresford, 47
Carter, Edward, 56
Carter, W. D., 99
Cassivellaunus, 1
Catt, William, 90
Cattle breeding centre, 78
Caxton Cottage, 70
Caxton House, 70
C. of E. School, 46
Census returns, 9
Central Stores, 55, 57, 70
Cerne Cottages, 73
Chalkepole, Rev. Richard, 33
Chalvington, 5
Chapels, Wesleyan and Baptist, 67
Charities: 47; for Stonegate, 40
Charity Commissioners, 40, 48
Cheddar, 46
Chele: Elizabeth, 123; William, 123
Chemist, 59
Chequers, 10, 57, 73, 76
Cherry Tree Inn, 83, 92
Cheryl, 70
Chessons Cottages, 79
Cheyney: Joan, 123; John, 123
Chichester, Bishop of, 34, 35
Child, Dr., 59
Chingley Farm, 93
Chingley Forge, 12, 119
Christians River, 34
Church: 19; churchyard wall, 37; clerestory windows, 22, 27: clock, 20; east windows, 24; font, 27; galleries, 32; heating, 30; kneelers, 30; lecturn, 27; piscina, 25, 27; plate, 29; Remembrance Book, 26; reredos, 25; restoration, 30, 32; rood loft, 23
Church Field, 47
Church Gate, 74
Church Gate Cottages, 74

Church House, 76
Church Street, 70, 74, 94
Churchsettle Lane, 87
Churchwardens: 10; accounts, 18
Cinque Cottage, 76
Citchenham, 9
Civil War, 14
Claphatch, 10, 79
Clarke, Canon K., 40 Clarke, Rev. A. D. C., 40
Claudius, 2
Clayhall, 87
Clayhall Cottages, 85
Clayhams, 81
Clayton, Rev. 'Tubby', 66
C.L.B.R., 2
Closed churchyard, 37
Cnut, King, 2, 106
Cock Farm, 15
Cock Inn, 15
Coke supply, 55
Colbourne, Nurse Lilly, 59
Cold Harbour, 10
Colepeper: Agnes, 123; Alice, 123; Sir Alexander, 123
Collingridge, Ruth, 27, 96
Collins, Rev. S. W. A., 42
Collis, Dr., 59
Colonels, The, 25
Colvin, Albert, 66
Combwell Priory, 7, 8, 13, 33, 34, 99
Commonwealth, 14, 16, 35
Commuters, 57
Constable, Rev. John, 102 Constable: Thomas, 90; William, 90
Cooper, Jervase, 17
Coopers Cottage, 74
Coopers Farm, 87
Cooper's Stores, 15, 70
Copens Farm, 79, 120
Corner shop, 73
Coronation Cottages, 52, 83
Cortesley, manor of, 97
Cottage, The, 73
Cottenden, 85, 99, 116
Cottenden Farmhouse, 92
County Police Acts, 14, 29, 32, 35, 37, 38, 40, 44
Courthope: family, 14, 29, 32, 35, 37, 38, 40, 44, 46, 90, 97, 109, 131; Chapel, 22, 25, 59; 'Memoirs', 109
Cowley, Rev. Thomas, 14, 33
Cowling, Josiah S., 89
Crabden, 9
Creed, Mrs., 40
Cricket: 44; clubs, 61
Croft, Mr., 76
Croft Cottage, 71
Croft Villa, 73
Cromwell, Thomas, 16
Crops, 114
Cross Lane Gardens, 79
Cross Lane House, 51, 79
Crotynden, Robert, 92
Crowhurst Bridge, 10, 54, 87
Cruttenden, 92
Cummins, John Blake, 89
Currie, Edward, 27, 106

Dalehill: 10, 51, 83, 101; map of 1630, 83; golf course, 54, 83
Dalehill Farm East, 92 Dalehill Farm West, 93 Dalehill Farmhouse, 83
Dalrymple, John Apsley, 97
Darby, Jonathan, 104
Darby, Mrs., 65

Davy, Roger, 123
Dawe, Robert, 103
Dawson, Rev. J., 39
Dawtrey: Jane, 123; Sir John, 123
'Death corner', 85
Debley, Mr., 81
Decalogue Boards, 28
Dengate, John and Sarah, 102
Denley, William, 70
De Vear, Rev. W., 39
Devil's Brook, 106
Devilsden Wood, 106
Dicul, 19
Diesel trains, 56
District Nurse, 59
'Doctor Alec', 128
Dodson, Rev. C., 102
Domesday, 3, 114
'Doom' window, 25
Downash, 88, 99, 116
Drewe: Adrian and Fiona, 102; Cedric and Beatrice, 100, 129; Francis, 34, 35, 100, 102; Joan, 65
Droweby, Richard, 98
Dry: Cole, 89; Benjamin, 89 Dry, Rev. John, 96
Duckworth, Capt. A. C., 30, 65
Dudley, Rev. B. W., 17
Duette, 73
Duke of York, 70
Dumbreck, Richard, 32, 37
Dungey, Mr., 57
Dungey's Stores, 70
Dunsters Mill, 13, 64, 79, 111, 120
Durell, Rev. David, 29, 34, 102
Dyer, Mr., 111
Dygonson, Rev. John, 33

Eagles, George, 96 Eagles, Rev. Gabriel, 33, 89
Eagleton, Rev. C. J., 42
Earl Haig Fund, 65
East, Dr., 59
Eastbourne Waterworks, 54
East Lymden, 10, 55, 77, 94
East Lymden Mill, 12
Eaton, Col., 95
Eatonden Manor Farm, 87, 95
Ebeneezer Cottage, 79
Ecclesiastical Commissioners, 102
Eckington, 5
Eddystone Lighthouse, 18
Eden: Rev. Arthur, 17, 29, 32, 34, 36, 55; Mrs., 54
Edmund Ironside, 3
Education Acts, 44, 49
Edward III, 13
Edward VII, coronation, 14
Edwards, John, glover, 64
Edwards, Rev. Owen Allen, 34, 36
Eggerton, Rev. John, 33
Electrified railway, 56
Electricity supply, 55
Elliot brothers, 57
English, Jack, 61
Epidemics, 44
Essewelle hundred, 3
Etchingham: 5, 11, 77; family, 19, 22, 25, 101
Ethelric, 5
Eu: Count of, 3, 5; Robert, Earl of, 5
Evacuation to Wales, 46
Evans Rice, Rev., 16
Ewer, Rev. John, 33

Fairview, 74

Farehill, Caleb, 70
Farmer's gallery, 90
Farouk, King, 130
Farquharson, H. C. N., 94
Festubert, Battle of, 131
Fethersham, Lord, 128
Field family, 90 Field, Rev. C. F. T., 40 Field, Jacob, 107 Field, Robert, 66 Field, Ted, 63
Field the butcher, 70
Field's, 73
Filsham, 87
Fire: service, 57; engines, 59; in 1639, 14; in 1938, 59; at Ticehurst House in 1852, 127
Fishing, 121
Fishmongers' Company, 47
Fitton, Sir Edward and Maria, 97
Fitz-Gerald, Mrs. Michael, 94
Fitz Lambert, Walter, 3, 9, 34
Flax, 116
Flimwell: crossroads, 51, 83; parish, 35, 38, 49; St Augustine's church, 40; school, 46; traffic lights, 51; variations in spelling, 7, 13
Floodlighting of church, 30
Flower show, 64
Flying bombs, 46, 132, 133
Footbal club, 61
Footpaths: 64; Society, 64
Ford family, 107
Ford, Mr., 61
Ford, Mrs., 99
Ford the butcher, 70
Forestry, 115
Forge, 74, 77
Forgefield, Stonegate, 52
Forsyth, Capt. Neil, 104
Foster: Margaret Holgate, 25, 77, 99, 129; Maria Isabella, 99
Foull, Christopher, 17
Fowler, W., 90
Franklyn Villa, 70
Frant, 11
French, Amos, 73
Fruit growing, 116
Frythenden, Kent, 102
Faud, Prince, 130
Fuggle family, 79
Fuller, Robert, 29
Furze House, 65, 83
Furzy Field, 40
Fysenden, Symon, 107

Gable End, 76
Gables, The, 55, 57, 77, 129
Garden of Remembrance, 37
Gardener's Association, 64
Gardiner, Rev. J. E., 40
Gardner, Walter and Henry, 103
Gas Company, 54
Gascoyne, John, 8
Gasworks, 83
Gaunt, Rev. Charles, 36
Gawsworth, 97
Gawthrop, Rev. Christopher, 17, 34, 36
Gelards Well, 9
Geology and soils, 113
George V, coronation, 14
George VI, coronation, 14
Gibbs, John, 102
Gibbs Read Farm, 81
Gibbsreed, 10
Gilbert, Mr., 94
Gillham: Mr., 94; George, 47, 49, 55, 70, 77; Henry, 55

Gillham's Stores, 59
Glanville, Mr., 100
Godwin, Earl, 3
Golding, Mr., 61
Good Companions, 64
Goodchild, Rev. Roy John, 34
Gorringe, Rowland, 96
Goschen family, 41, 107
Gould, Susan, 104
Grant, Rev. A. V., 40
Gravel Pit, 66, 77, 96
Gray, Rev. A. A., 40
Gray, Arthur, 107
Gray, Rev. George Holmes, 34
Greaves, Rev. G., 41
Green, Dr., 129
Greenwoods, 10
Gregory, George, 93
Gregory, Rev. William, 34, 55
Greye, Rev. John, 33
Greyhound track, 87
Griffiths, G., 90

Haeselersc Charter (1018), 98, 109
'Hall' houses, 87
Halle, Henry, 7, 90
Hamilton, Dr. P., 40
Hammell, Steward, 11
Hammerden, 7, 10, 69, 87, 89, 90, 96
    Hammerden Cottages, 87 Hammerden
    Farm, 87
Hams, The, 10
Harbotell: George, 97; Guichard and
    Johanne, 97; Ralph, 97; Robert, 97
Hardcastle, John, 34, 35, 40, 109
    Hardcastle, Marjory, 77
Hare and Hounds, 63, 85
Haremare family, 101
Harper, Admiral, 65
Harris, Mr., 102
Harris, Rev. John, 33
Harte, Thomas and Mary, 89
Hartridge, Mr., 102
Hartwell, 9
Haselden, Frank C., 94, 109
Haselerse (Haslesse), 2, 5, 7, 8, 19, 106
Haselholte, 5
Hastings, manor of, 97
Hastings Priory, 19, 33, 34
Hatchet, Thomas, 98
Haughton, Rev. H. P., 41
Hawkesley, Robert and Katherine, 109
Hawkhurst: Gang, 14; smugglers, 107
Hawkwell, Pembury, 90
Haye, Lord John de la, 13
Hayes: Eliza, 126; Rev. William, 126
Hayes-Newington family, 128
Haytoun, Rev. William, 33
Hazeldens, 10
Hazelhurst, Upper and Lower, 3, 5, 7, 8,
    98
Headmaster's Log Book, 44
Heathfield & District Water Co., 54
Heber-Percy, Capt. J., 94
Hemsley, Mrs. Jan, 46
Hendlaye, Lady, 17
Henry VIII, 16
Hepdon: Goddard, 123; Goodguift, 123
Herschel, Sir J. F. W., 40
Hicks, Mr., 111
Highlands, The, 66, 77, 126
Hillbury: 36, 77; council estate, 77;
    Gardens, 52
Hilder: John, 85; Thomas, 85
Hill Tout, Rev. M., 40
Hitchins, Dr., 59

Hoadley: 8, 10, 85; tithing, 7
Hodges, Mrs., 71
Hodges the cobbler, 81
Holbeamwood, 2, 3, 8, 10, 13, 78
Holgate House, 70
Hollist, Dr. G. W. C., 104
Holme, The, 99, 129
Holy Trinity, Hastings, 7
Hook Bridge, 12
Hope, Mr., 99
Hopkins, James Innes, 89
Hopkirk, Rev. F. S., 40
Hops: 10, 115; picking, 44
Horsegrove Avenue, 51, 83
Horsmonden Charities, 99
Hort: Anthony Gilbert, 25; Francis
    Fitzgerald, 25
Hothley, 8
Howard, Robin and Ann, 99
Howlett, Rev. F., 42
Hull, Rev., 33
Humphrey, George, 99
Hunt family, 93
Huntley family, 93
Huntleys Mill, 79
Hurricane, 59
Hurst Cottage, 77
Hurst Green Snooker League, 66
Hussey: family, 99; Edward, 90; Thomas,
    90
Hyde, Jesse, 63
Hyland, David, 29

Illegitimate births, 17, 42
Inkpen, Rev. Bartholomew, 16, 33
'Insanity', 124
Institute, The, 47, 81
Intruders, 33
Irish Protestants, 18
Iron Mills, medieval, 12
Iron works, Roman, 90
Irons, William, 17
Iveymay, Mr., 61

Janaway, Thomas, 28, 29
Jarrett, Nurse, 59
Jarvis, Gilbert, 107
Jarvis, Thomas, 93
Jefferies, Rev. John, 33
Jevington, 5
Johnson, Rev. A. N., 42
Johnstone, Rev. G. D., 39
Jones, Arthur 'Jonah', 63
Jones, Bill, 46
Jubilee of Queen Victoria, 14

Keene, Jarvis, 17
Kelly, Rev. J. A., 40
Kemp-Gee, P. N., 94, 109
Kendrew, Dr., 59
Kersteman, Rev. Andrew, 9, 12, 17, 35
Ketchenour, John and Maud, 104
Ketley Cottage, 120
Ketleys, 83
Kettel, Henry, 40
King Henry, 67
King John, 64
Kingdon, E. C., 89
Kirkby, Ronald, 63
Knole, 128
Knox, Rev. G. G., 62

La Forde, 8
Laing the tailor, 76
Lambarde, 7
Lamberhurst: 11; Early Risers, 61

Lambert, James, 40
Lamerton, 36
Lanfranc, Archbishop, 5
Langford, Philip, 96
Langley, Rev. Edwin, 34
Laughton, 5
Laurel Lodge, 73
Law, Rev. Frank Joseph, 30, 34, 66
Lawrence, Thomas, 70
Le Voirs, 89
Leach, 70
Leaver, Rev. John, 16, 33
Leavers, 89
Lectern, 27
Legas, John, 12
Leslie, 70
Lewes: Battle of, 13; Bishop of, 37; High
    Street, 14
Lewkener, John, 104
Limden Lane, 77, 87, 99
Limden River, 12
Limundcnc, Warinus de, 99
Linkhurst, Stonegate, 61, 87
Listed buildings schedule, 69
Little Ale House, 85
Little Boarzell, 81
Little Clayhams, 81
Little Hammerden, 10, 87
Little Quedley, 10
Little Whiligh, 99
Liverpool Street station, 38
Llanelli, 46
Lloyd's Bank, 70
Local Government Acts, 49
London, Bishop of, 3
London Barn Farm, 81, 102
Long Down, 9
Long House, 73
Long, Nurse, 59
Lord, Rev. Thomas, 16, 33
Lower Hazelhurst, 120
Lower Platts, 51, 57, 83
Lower Tollgate, 81
Loxton, Mrs., 93
Luck family, 39
Luckhurst, Mary, 123
Lulham, Edward, 29
Lunatica, 17
Lunsford, John, 97
Lurker, James, 17
Lutyens, 95
Luxford, J., 97
Lyfing, 3
Lymden, 87, 99

Mabbs Hill Farm, 87
Maclaren, James, 107
Macpherson, Col., 106
'Mad Prince' escapes, 130
Maidstone & District Bus Co., 57
Males, J., 29
Malpass, Mr., 77
Mannser: family, 89; William, 107
Maplesden, 10, 87, 90, 99, 116
Marlpit Dairy, 71
Marlpit Gardens, 67, 81
Marnham, Brig. Geoffrey, 66
Martin, Charles, 111
Martindale, Bartholomew, 17, 43
Martyn, Rev. William, 33
Matthews, Marjorie, 87
Maundrell, Canon D., 40
Mavis, J., 5
Maxwell-Staniforth, Rev. J. H., 42
May: family, 26, 29, 93, 104, 108; Thomas,
    12, 29; Thomas and Mary, 90;

May, Rev. W., 39
McDowell, Dr. Colin, 129
Meals on wheels, 65
Medical service, 59
Medical Superintendant, 77
Medlicott, Rev. Ossory, 16, 33, 92
Medway river scheme, 119
Medway towns, 118
Melford, 87
Mercer, Mr., 70
Merriams, 96
Mill: lands, 10; in Windmill Field, 38
Mills, George, 107
Miner's Arms, 63
Monboucher family, 97
Monmouth's rebellion, 14
Morden Terrace infants' school, 46
Morley, Robert, 97
Morris: Fred, 62; R. C., 62
Mount Farm, 85
Mount Pleasant Farm, 85
Mulleneux, Cdr. Hugh, 22
Mumpumps (Mompumps), 10, 12, 83
Mylls, Rev. John, 33
Myskins, 55, 77, 85

Napoleonic Wars, 14, 114
National School, 44
NatWest Bank, 73
Nestor Medical Services, 129
Nevdjvani, Princess, 130
Newington: family 25, 27, 49, 55, 59, 63,
    99, 106, 110, 123; Dr. Alexander, 24;
    Campbell, 24, 47, 94, 100, 128; Mrs.
    Campbell, 21, 24, 47, 74, 77, 99, 133;
    pedigree, 123
Newington Court, 52, 79
New Barn Farm, 79
New House Farm, 87
New Pond Farm, 78
Newarks Platt, 11
Newman, Tom, 66
No Man's Wood, 10
Noakes family, 29, 76, 89, 96
Noorwoods, 10
Norman, Rev. John, 34
Norman and Beard, 29
Normanswood Farm, 87
North Field Cottage, 73
North Sea Gas, 55
Northgate House, 55, 70
Norwoods Farm, 79, 99

Oakover, 24, 35, 47, 55, 77, 99, 133
Oast Houses, 51
Observer Corps., 132
Odell, Mrs., 32
Odo, Bishop of Bayeux, 5
'Ofrango', 92
Old Battenhurst Farm, 87
Old Boarzell, 81, 101
Old Excelsior, 62
Old Farmhouse, Wallcrouch, 78
Old Forge, The, 76
Old Merryams, 70
Old Pretender, 14
Old Timbers, 70
Old Vicarage, 35, 36, 107
Old Vicarage, Flimwell, 85
Olde Sweet Shoppe, 70
Oliver, Jack, 70
Ollive family, 17, 90, 107
Ore, 5
Ore, William de, 90
Organ, 29
Overy, Henry, 107

Overys Farmhouse, 79, 116, 120
Owls Gardens, Stonegate, 52, 87
Ox-drawn hearse, 18

Packard, Rev. K. G., 42 Packard, Rev.
    Frank, 61
Palliser family, 40, 42, 107
Pankhursts Stores, 67, 68, 83
Parish: Council, 49; Magazine, 18;
    Registers, 16
Parish, W. D., 3
Parfitt, Rv. A. W., 42
Park Garage, 81
Parke, Peter and Margaret, 98
Parochial Church Council, 49, 74
Parr, Lady Julian, 66, 96
Parrish, Mr., 101
Parsonage Farm, 10, 102
Parsonage Farmhouse, 77
Pashley: 7, 8, 10, 12, 43, 103; Chapel, 21,
    26, 103; Manor, 81; Mill, 13; tithing, 7
Passele family, 8, 13, 103, 107, 109
Paton Hunter, Rev. I., 40
Paupers, 10
Pegeford, John de, 100
Penenden Heath, 5
Pensell, Rev. John, 33
Percy, Sir Thomas and Eleanor, 97
Petitt, Joseph, 44, 70
Petitt & Sanders, 70
Pevensey, 5
Pharmacy, 70, 71
Philippa, Queen, 13
Pickforde, 10, 65, 73, 106, 132
Pickforde Lane, 79
Pierce, Albert, 57
Pikeford, Thomas, 106
Pilbeam, William, 63, 130
Pillory Corner, 51
Piper, R., 66
Plantation Tea Company, 71
Playing Field, Stonegate, 87
Playsted family, 99, 109, 124
Police: Constables, 57; House, 83;
    stations, 57
Poor: 10; House, 11; Law Commissioners,
    11
Porch Chamber, 22
Post office, 55, 70, 73
Potter, Joseph F., 90, 99
Powell, Charles, 106
Poyntel, Rev. Robert, 33
Primer, Old, 17
Pump, village, 54, 74
Putland, Dennis, 123
Pyggevorde, Richard de, 106

Quarry Villa, 77, 129
Quedley (Quedlaye), 10, 17, 83, 106

Rabson, Thomas, 92
Railway: 56; tunnels, 56
Ramsbury, Bishop of, 3
Randolph: Barnard, 12, 47, 97, 108;
    Herbert, 106, 108; John, 97; Judith, 97
Ranolph, Bishop of Chichester, 34
Ratton, 5
Rectory House, 102
Red Book, 9
Red Car bus, 57
Red Cross, 63
Red Oast Cottages, Flimwell, 52
Reeves, F. A. R., 61, 96
Reeves, Mr. and Mrs. and Pam, 73
Reid: John L., 99; Michael, 40, 99
Reinbert the sheriff, 7, 101

Reservoir construction, 119
Reservoir, Flimwell, 54
Reynolds, Robert, 17
Richardson, Rev. L., 42
Richmond, Earl of, 97
Ridgeway, The, 47, 77, 100, 128
Ringing Chamber, 28
Ripe, 2
Roads: 12, 50, 51
Roberts family, 24, 93, 99, 101
Robertsbridge Abbey: 8, 103; furnace, 12
Robertsbridge Water Co., 54
Rochester, Bishop of, 3
Rogers, Henry, 89
Roll of Honour (1914-18), 22
Romany Cottage, 76
Rosary, The, 78
Rosehill, 76, 94
Rosemary Lane, 10, 83
Rosier, Frank, woodcarver, 21, 120
Rother District Council, 37, 49
Roughfields, 83
Roundells, The, 106
Rowley, 3, 10, 65, 79, 83, 93, 106
Royal Sussex Regiment, 131
Royce, Bradley, 104
Rushlake Green, 34
Russell, Admiral, 14
Russian Embassy, 107
Rypear, The, 17

St Albans, Abbot of, 3
St Augustine, Abbots of, 3
St Christopher, 25
St Helena, 128
St James, 25
St John, 25
St Mary's Close, 14, 74
St Mary's Fellowship, 65
St Mary's Lane, 56, 73
Sailing club, 121
Salehurst, 11
Salome, 25
Sancto the cobbler, 70
Saunders, William, 107, 109
Saxonbury, 1
S.C.A.T.S., 87
Schools: 11, 77; at Flimwell, 85; in Poor
    House, 43; in St Mary's Close, 43
Schools class locomotives, 56
Scouts and Guides, 65
Scoones, John and Joan, 112
Scotney: Peter de, 7, 8, 34, 90, 97; Walter
    de, 7, 8, 33, 34
Scotney Castle, 5, 90
Scott, Rev. R. E., 42
Scott, Riley, 100
Seacox Heath, 47, 85, 107
Seamen's widows, 18
Searchlights, 132
Sedgemoor, 14
Sedlescombe, 7
Seffrid, Bishop of Chichester, 34
Segar, Mr., 89
Selsey: 19; Bishop of 3
Sewerage, 54, 83
Sheepstreet Lane, 85
Sheepwash Farm, 55, 77
Sheffe, John, 27
Sherborne, Bishop of, 3
Sherrington, 5
Shirley, Anthony, 97
Shovers Green, 78, 87
Shoyswell, 3, 7
Shoyswell family, 109
Siggers, Mr., 71

Silverton, Dr., 64
Simms, Mrs., 66
Sinclair, Dr., 133
Singehurst, 10, 43, 81, 107
Skerrett: Frank, 63; Fred, 63, 73
Slater, William, 32
Smith, Basil, 61
Smith, Francis, 17
Smith, Henry Tilden, 92
Smuggling, 14, 70
Snooker League, 66
Southern Water Authority, 49, 54
Spindlewood, 77, 128
Spinney, Walter, 29
Springett family, 107
Springfields, 52, 54, 79
S.S. Francis Mary, 121
Stanbridge, Andrew, 63
Standen, Stephen, 108
Standen, Thomas, 12
Staplyton-Smith, 89
Startin, Alexander, 47
Startin the builder, 73
Stead, John, 98
Stedman, Mr., 111
Steellands (Steel Land), 10, 83, 89
Stevens, John, 107
Stigand, Archbishop, 5
Stone, John, 97
Stone Place, 77, 129
Stonegate: Eggs, 87; Farmhouse, 87;
    parish, 38, 49; St Peter's church, 38;
    school, 46, station, 56
Stopford, Tom, 96
Storm of 1703, 18
Storrers Farm, 87, 99
Strabo, 2
Strother, Rev., 102
Sturges Bourne's Act, 11
Stykeland, Rev. William, 33
Sunnybank, 85
Sunnyside Cottages, 76
Surgery, 73
Sussex: cattle, 100; East and West, 49;
    Housing Association for the Aged, 93;
    Rifle Volunteer Corps., 131; spaniels,
    100
Sussex Cap, the, 20
Swattynge, Elizabeth, 27
Swayne, Rev. William, 16, 33
Swiftsden: 12, 101; Farm, 81; House, 81
Syde, Rev. John, 33

Tandy, Sarah, 44
Taylor, Rev. F. O., 42
Teagues, 10
Teignmouth, 18
Telegram, first, 55
Telephone and exchange, 55, 74
Terry, Mrs. Margaret, 25
Thampsett, 'Best', 63
Theise (Teise) river, 8, 119
Thomas, Mr., 98
Thomas, Rev., 33
Thomas, Richard, 92
Thompsett, Mr., 63
Thompson, woodcarver, 24, 27
Thorntons, 36
Thorpe, Bartholomew, 17
Three Gates Farm, 81
Threeleg Cross, 10, 51, 54, 77, 79, 83
Thurkil the Viking, 3
Ticehurst: High Street, 70, 74, 77; House,
    54, 55, 59, 77, 78, 123; Motors, 57, 74;
    station, 56; R.D.C., 49; school, 54;
    Union, 16, 49; variant spellings, 7, 8;

Water Co., 54, *see also* church
Ticehurst, George, 107
Tile Cottage, 73
Tindalls Cottage, 79
Tinkers Lane, 52, 54, 83
Tipper, William, 103
Toc H, 66
Tolhurst, Major W. H., 94, 109
Tolhurst, Upper and Lower, 79
Tollgate, 77
Tompsett, Mary, 123
Town Borough, 10
Traffic, 51
Travers: Col., 25, 89; Martin, 25
Tress, William, 56
Tudgay, Dr., 59
Tunbridge Wells Gas Co., 55
Tuppeny family, 17
Turkish captives, 18
Turnpike Acts, 49
Turnpikes, 12
Tutts, 10
Twitten, 87
Tyler, Richard, 111

Underdown, Elizabeth, 43, 47
Unicorn Inn, 15, 70
Union Street, Flimwell, 83
Union Workhouse, 42
Utrecht, Treaty of, 14

Vestry, 10
Vicarage: 35, 55, 77; at Stonegate, 87
Victor, Rev. J., 42
Victoria County History, 69
Victoria, Queen, Diamond Jubilee, 54
Vidler family, 63, 85
Village Club: 47; Stonegate, 87
Vincent, J., 42
Vineyard, 10, 12, 77, 124, 128
Vineyard Lane, 78
Virgin Mary, statue, 22

Wade, Rev. S. M., 40
Wadhurst: 11; Gas Company, 55; modern
    school, 46
Waghorn brothers, 61 Waghorn, Daniel,
    109 Waghorn, Thomas, 32
Walker, Joseph, 29, 83
Wallcrouch, 10, 77 Wallcrouch
    Farmhouse, 78
Wallis, Miss Maud Mary, 26, 96
Wallrigge Gate, 9
Walters Farm, 83
War memorials, 27, 47
Warbleton Priory, 33, 34
Ward, Gordon, 2
Warde: Thomas, 109; William and Agnes,
    107, 109
Wards Brigge, 9
Wardsbrook: 10, 36, 85, 77, 87, 97, 107;
    Old Mill, 13, 109; Road, 77
Wardsdown nurseries, 54
Warren: Derek, 57; Mrs. Derek, 99;
    Philip, 57
Warren's Coaches, 55, 57, 77
Warwick House, 15
Washington, 5
Water supply, 53, 118
Waterhouse's Stores, 11, 71
Waters, Henry F., 47
Waterworks, 87
Watson family, 99
Webb: Sir Aston, 47, 100; Phillip, 101
Wedd family, 109
Wedds Farm, 12, 77, 94, 109

Welches, 10
Welfitt, Rev. William, 34
Welcome Stranger, 83, 85
Wells, Bishop of, 3
Wesleyan Chapel, 79
West, Jack, 61
West, Mr. and Mrs., 48
West Dean, 5
West Firle, 5
West Lymden, 87
Westbourne Villa, 73
Westly, Rev. Thomas, 33
Westminster, Abbot of, 3
Westminster Hall, 10
Wetherell: Lydia Ellen, 104; Nathan, 28,
    107; Rev. Richard, 26, 28, 40, 43, 104
Wharton, Rev. John, 16, 33
Whatmans, 55, 73
Wheatcroft, Edward, 29
Whiligh, 3, 7, 8, 10, 55, 78, 109
Whiligh Oaks, 110
Whitby, Rev., 33
White, John, 97
White Cottage, 74
White Lodge, 36
Whiteman, Alec, 63, 103
Wickeson, E., 66
Wickham, Mr., 93, 111
Wildlife, 121
Wilfrid, Bishop of Selsey, 19
William atte Mulle, 33
William III, accession, 14
William de Ore, 7
Williams: Rev. Benjamin, 34; Mrs., 30
Willingdon, 5
Willoughby, Sir Anthony, 97
Wilson, Anthony, 83
Winch, Edward, 106
Winch, Thomas, 70
Winchester, Bishop of, 3
Windmill at Mount Farm, 85
Windmill Field, 13
Winters Farm, 87
Winton Street, 5
Witherenden (Withernden): 7, 17, 110;
    Bridge, 12, 47; Farm, 87; Mill, 13, 87,
    93, 112; Roundels, 87; station, 56
Wlfstan, Archbishop of York, 3
Women's Institute, 66
Woodbine House, 55, 73
Woodlands, 77, 128
Woodman, Richard, 14
Woodroffe, Dr., 59, 79
Woodroffe Lodge, 52, 79
Woodville, Elizabeth, 104
Woollen, burial in, 16
Workhouse, 11, 71, 83
Wright, Rev. John, 33
Wybarne: family, 90; John, 36, 90, 99
Wybarne brass, 24
Wybarnes, 36
Wydrendene, John and Christina de, 110
Wyke, William, 99
Wynch, Tamison, 107

Yarmouth, 18
Yates, W. N., 61
Yellow Coat Wood, 13
Yett, The, 73, 112
Yew Tree, The, 78, 112
Young, Bill, 63
Young, Canon A., 40
Young, Frank, 26, 77
Youth Centre, 67
Youth Club, 48, 66
Ypres sector, 131